DATE DUE

DEMCO 38-296

Children's
Literature and
Critical Theory

CHILDREN'S LITERATURE AND CRITICAL THEORY

Reading and Writing
for Understanding

Jill P. May

New York   Oxford
OXFORD UNIVERSITY PRESS
1995

ersity Press

Iew York

~~Athens   Auckland~~ Bangkok Bombay
Calcutta Capetown Dar es Salaam Delhi
Florence Hong Kong Istanbul Karachi
Kuala Lumpur Madras Madrid Melbourne
Mexico City Nairobi Paris Singapore
Taipei Tokyo Toronto

and associated companies in
Berlin Ibadan

Copyright © 1995 by Jill P. May

Published by Oxford University Press, Inc.
198 Madison Avenue, New York, New York 10016

Oxford is a registered trademark of Oxford University Press

Library of Congress Cataloging-in-Publication Data
May, Jill P.
Children's literature and critical theory : reading and writing
for understanding / Jill P. May.
p. cm.
Includes bibliographical references and index.
ISBN 0–19–509584–7. — ISBN 0–19–509585–5 (pbk.)
1. Children's literature—History and criticism. 2. Criticism.
I. Title.
PN1009.A1M38 1995
809'.89282—dc20   94–34706 CIP

2 4 6 8 9 7 5 3 1

Printed in the United States of America
on acid-free paper

To my former students
my family
and
my professional friends
who have engaged me in learning

Preface

I have written *Children's Literature and Critical Theory: Reading and Writing for Understanding* to explain what literary criticism works in children's literature, and why it is an important part of studying children's literature, so that scholars from various fields can explore how the prominent schools of literary criticism that are typically used in scholarly discussions fit into children's books and their reading experiences. Throughout, I have attempted to show how critical theory fits within the study of children's literature. As the title suggests, *Children's Literature and Critical Theory: Reading and Writing for Understanding* reinforces theory with concrete examples of students in children's literature classes and teachers in schools who have become practicing critics by "doing it" on their own. In short, I have written *Children's Literature and Critical Theory* to encourage adults to explore criticism, consider why they should be concerned about what happens in a typical elementary school classroom, and how they can view literature and its applications in the world of the child.

In this book, I purposely include the writings of college students who never planned to become professors, who simply wanted to explore children's literature at an introductory level. Some of them intended to be elementary education teachers. Others wanted to re-enter the world of the child by reading and re-reading children's books. I do not use their essays as models of exemplary works: As beginning critics, these students were limited by the amount of reading they had time to do and varied in their writing styles. Like authors of fiction, their styles differ, depending on the critical stance chosen and on their abilities to express themselves. It is this diversity that is important. To see only an exemplary student's paper would suggest that everyone can write at the same level. And that is not true, for fiction writers, professors, or college students. However, these students understood what they wanted to say. And, in the end, they were able to form their critical opinions into validly argued essays. As a result, their writings show a growing understanding of children's literature as a particular group of works that fit into literary studies. Ideally, these students will act as role models and mentors for others who wish to develop a critical stance about the literature they read.

These "novice critics" took the time to read, formulate their own ideas, and decide what sort of critical discussion they wanted to initiate prior to writing. Their writing will show how they viewed children's literature, and what role critical theory took in their ideas about reading. Their conclusions often demand that you react to their readings of children's literature and critical theory. Their papers have been included as "starters" for others who might never have tried to write a critical article before reading this book. I am indebted to all my past students who have given me permission to use their work. These represent a smattering of the papers I have requested.

This book is designed to let the reader come to a decision about the place of children's literature in the world of the child. I hope each reader will begin to consider what school or schools of criticism is personally most appealing. I hope to force readers to consider whether any one way of thinking can be "safely" taught at the exclusion of another. In the end, each reader will have to decide if there is a set group of books everyone needs to read or if individuals need to choose books for themselves. Finally, the arguments presented here will help resolve how children's literature fits into the broad scheme of childhood.

Children's Literature and Critical Theory: Reading and Writing for Understanding is designed to force you to consider that as readers of children's literature you are also conveyers of attitudes, role models for children's reading, censors, and/or proponents for a group of children. I hope you will be convinced that everyone has a stake in early literacy. Since some essays were written by students who did not want to teach in elementary schools, they demonstrate that literature isn't just intended for the classroom.

Authors shape stories for their audiences. Most children's literature authors write primarily for children.—Their publishers hope children will like the books they publish. However, they are adults. They must wait to see how the children react. In the end, children will keep stories alive by recommending them to friends and siblings. They explore their stories seriously, the way adults should explore their literature. All literate readers read for pleasure as well as for information, and they often judge a story by its emotional effectiveness.

Children reading for enjoyment bring their own experiences with them and relate them to the story. They want a positive experience, even when they are reading a textbook. If they are expected to draw conclusions before they finish a book, they are being rushed into the second stage of reading. Pleasure comes first.

Once children have finished their initial reading, they are ready to discuss the book with others. They then can become the implied reader. They can listen to information about the author, they can look carefully at the book's style, they can relate this story to others they have already read. They can look for clues in the book's format, and they can determine what the book means to them. While they are learning about the book, they can be introduced to theories about the story's significance. They can determine for themselves why they are reading it, what benefit it has for them. Their ideas and conclusions are their own. As adults we must learn to listen to children. Children need to have the chance to develop into critical readers, to learn to question, to formulate their personal evaluations based on the literary elements of the author's writing style.

Even though children are the primary audience for children's books, they are not the "authorative" one. The adult who knows about story structure, about genres, about rhetorical style, and who searches for the opinions of others, is often asked to evaluate children's literature. An adult who has studied literary criticism understands why English professors talk one way about the book while elementary school teachers talk another way. Adults who view children's literature as serious writing and make a living out of studying it must ask themselves, "Who can benefit from what I have learned? How can I engage them in a discussion of the book? How can I create an active audience of implied readers for this book? Indeed, is this book worth worrying about?"

By introducing criticism and to its role in shaping response, *Children's Literature and Critical Theory* will encourage adults to first be real readers who enjoy listening to someone else's theories about literature, and later seek answers about the story's meaning. This is the role of critical theory. Critical readers make the best elementary school teachers, parents, citizens, and friends. They agree or disagree with what they read and discuss, but they always want to hear the opinions of others. After they have read something that is engrossing, they feel a need to share it, but they want those involved in their discussions to read the book first and then talk to them. They don't want to just do plot summaries or give book talks. They are intrigued by the author's style, the people who fill the pages of the book, the book's perplexing ideas, and they want to hear how others feel about it too.

Thus, this book is designed to encourage sensitivity to critical theory and to shape real readers into critical readers. Because I advocate readers making choices, I do not believe that there is a best reading approach for this book. In fact, you could read the chapters in a different order and still understand the arguments presented. Each chapter identifies the literary terms used by placing them in italics. They are discussed in a Glossary at the end of the book, but are not defined within the body of the chapter—

that would interrupt those readers who already know the terms and want to hear the arguments out. You may first want to look through the chapters and identify ideas that particularly interest you, locate any terms you are not familiar with, and consider their definitions before you begin reading. If so, you are giving yourself the chance to have a more sophisticated first reader's experience. You may want to read each chapter as you come to it and discover how much you already know. Or, you may want to read up to the italicized terms, examine the definitions, and see how the two parts of the narrative fit together. Your approach will define your own reading strategy.

The arguments presented throughout will be even more accessible if you read the articles that I and the essay writers have referred to and pick up books by the literary critics mentioned in the chapters and cited in the Appendix of Related Readings at the end of the book. They form a backbone for understanding critical theory. Reading the children's books discussed will help you reach your own conclusions both about particular works of children's literature and the arguments presented here. You'll find that you will have reactions to the books that may differ from those presented here. That's good. However, I believe that individual reactions are heightened by considering how others looked at children's literature, that critical sensitivity is enhanced when we read and discuss literature.

The primary rationale for reading this book, then, is to be nudged into new ways of approaching reading and learning. By the end of the discussion, I hope you will find that reading children's literature gives you a more pleasurable and enlightening experience. Almost certainly, you will tie books and children together in new ways.

I must acknowledge that none of this would have even happened if others hadn't taught me how to read and to listen. Every session that I ever attended at the annual conferences of the Children's Literature Association and the Modern Language Association had some effect on my thinking. In the end, however, I have returned most often to re-read the criticism of Lois Kuznets, Rod McGillis, Perry Nodelman, George Shannon, Jon Stott, Chip Sullivan, Malcolm Usrey, Virginia Wolf, and Jack Zipes. As friends and careful writers, they have encouraged my professional reading and inspired me to study critical theory.

My contacts with scholars at the meetings of the National Council of Teachers of English have been equally important. Long conversations with many friends have helped me see how children's literature best fits into schools. Many conference sessions have had an impact on me. However, my close associations with Joanie Glazer, Daniel Hade, Barbara Keifer, Taimi Ranta, Peter Roop, John Stewig, and Richard van Dongen have taught me the most about collaboration and modification.

Equally important are my continual contacts with professionals in the library world who have informed me about historical research and new books. I would be less capable of understanding the writer's craft if I had not known Barbara Elleman, Lee Foerster, Karen Nelson Hoyle, Dee Jones, and Anne Lundin.

I am fortunate to have talented, sympathetic colleagues at Purdue University who have willingly (?) listened to my continual harangues about literature and children. I would be lost without the advice of Mary Ellen Collins, Bev Cox, Charles Elster, Jeff Garrett, Darwin Henderson, Pose Lamb, and Bonnie Nowakowski.

My ability to face reality has come from several contacts with teachers, including my local efforts with TELL (Teachers Encouraging a Love of Literature), the Lafayette Christian School, Klondike Elementary School, Ernie Pyle Elementary School, and with the Burtsfield Elementary School staffs. They have shown me that teachers can do the things I dream of, that they will change if given an opportunity. I must also thank the Growing Child's Dennis and Nancy Dunn for their practical advice and guidance throughout my years at Purdue University.

In many ways, this book is the result of teaching and learning from my students. There are too many who have greatly influenced my life to name them here. They all must know in their hearts who they are. Still, I must acknowledge the group who worked through this manuscript with me, whether they know it or not. Many of the ideas presented here were first parts of our classroom discussions in various graduate classes. During those times, they guided me toward reality. I thank the contingency that hung around in the late 1980s as friends and mentors: Shauna Bigham, Kathy Bonds, Robb Bruce, Susan Bunte, Becky DeWitt, Becky Dick, Al Enlow, Brian Fultz, Beth Halterman, Leslie Murrill, and Cynthy Scruggs Smith.

Finally, I must thank my three Department Heads. Bob Kane supported my work from the embryonic stages, then moved on to become the first Dean of the newly established School of Education at Purdue University. In many ways, Dudley Herron became one of my professional mentors; he always believed in my ideals and supported my work within the public schools. Bill Kyle has listened to my desire to reach a wide audience with my writing and has supported my goals. The atmosphere at Purdue University has given me time to reflect on what I believe and to study literary criticism, even though I reside in a School of Education. *Children's Literature and Critical Theory: Reading and Writing for Understanding* would not have happened without the strong support of all of my colleagues, both those in the field and at Purdue University.

There is, of course, another group of people who have helped make this happen. They are my best critics and friends. Without them I wouldn't do anything. They keep me going when I want to quit. They tell me when I'm off-base. They lead me to new books and ideas. They nurture me to be what I am. My deepest appreciation goes to my parents Floyd and Flo Powell who took time to have me, my husband Bob who decided to marry me and make me into a professor, and my daughters Heather and Beth who have taught me what children's literature, feminist readings, and creativity are all about. Bob has read every word that's in this book; Beth and Heather have read more than they ever wanted. Bob's mother has listened to all of us "talk academic" and has encouraged us. Much of my rewritings have come from Bob, Beth, and Heather. They were this manuscript's first critical audience, and they helped me find ways to express my beliefs.

West Lafayette, Ind.　　　　　　　　　　　　　　　　　　　　J. P. M.
January 1995

Contents

Children's
Literature and
Critical Theory

1

Reading, Discussing, and Interpreting Children's Literature

When I was a child, I was a continual reader and dreamer. I read about Pocahontas and then role played her life, using the tall corn rows in our garden as her forest; I read about Robin Hood and his merry men and I became a part of his merry band, wandering the forest land behind my Wisconsin farm home; I heard of Dorothy's trip in a cyclone to a magical land and imagined I was Dorothy from *The Wizard of Oz,* spreading newspaper across the living-room and dining-room floors to make my yellow brick road.

My parents were understanding people. They never discouraged my reading or my childhood play. Because our farm was isolated from the day-to-day programmed activities of the nearby city, and because my parents were both too busy to be able to drive me to Little League games or the city's swimming pool, I was forced to depend on myself for fun. During the day, I helped with the housework. I did not have time to watch television or walk into town.

Once a week, however, my parents would take me to the public library to get new books. There I found a world of friends. No one bothered me about my literary choices. I was on my own to browse the shelves and pick any books I wanted. My reading habits became an eclectic mix of old and new titles, fiction and nonfiction. By the time I was in the sixth grade, I had lived with Louisa May Alcott's *Little Women*. I was in love with Laurie and was outraged when Jo married her stodgy old professor. I also was enamored with Booker T. Washington's autobiographical account of his life. I'm not sure now what made me so attracted to Washington's retelling of his life, but I do know that the book was important to me since I lived in a town without an African-American population. *Up From Slavery* was a book that I often checked out. Re-reading favorite books was part of my routine. Titles probably drew me to certain books more than anything else. However, I did know the differences between reading fiction and nonfiction, and I chose purposely to read one kind of literature over another at different times.

No one was selecting my books or telling me how to read. I was learning to find materials on my own. I probably enjoyed reading because I wasn't censored by well-meaning adults. If I picked a book out, I could take it home. And my terrible habit of reading long into the night was never discouraged. I was allowed to leave my light on until I "finished the last few pages in the chapter." Since no one came back to remind me that I promised to stop at the end of the chapter, I suspect that my parents knew I would stay awake until I read the last page in the book.

Often, I would run out of books before the week was over. We could not afford to have a large family library, so once the end of the week's library reading came about, I was forced to reread or to wait. I remember once, in frustration, deciding that I would write a book to read. Since I had lots of cats as pets, I thought I could write a cat story. My efforts lasted only a short time, however. Aware of stories with good plots and well-developed characters, my newly created tale seemed lifeless and boring. I wanted others to create reading materials that I could fashion into pretend, could place into my life's experiences.

I have often wondered about the process of becoming a writer, and have concluded that reading and writing go hand-in-hand. Authors are often readers first, creators second. Nineteenth-century author Charles Dickens wrote of his early literary experiences, saying, "Little Red Riding Hood was my first love. I felt that if I could marry Little Red Riding Hood, I should have known perfect bliss." His childhood was full of literary fancies, and as an adult he wrote stories that filled his readers with imaginary adventures and realities. Dickens never suspected that his writing would be used to teach anyone how to read, any more than he might have believed that Little Red Riding Hood taught him how to fall in love. As a writer, Dickens knew the importance of a reader's response in reading, and he sought to create good stories that could evoke an emotional response from his audience.

Today's youngsters seem less able to take time for reading, and they view literature in different ways. Often when you are discussing a particular book with a group of children, they will say, "Oh, yes. I've read that story." What many of them really mean, however, is that they have seen a visual representation of it. For many contemporary children, pleasure comes on a screen. They view reading as part of school work. A recent undergraduate elementary education student at Purdue University is typical of many I have taught during my twenty years there. Her childhood placed reading outside her daily pastimes. She could not name a single favorite children's book that she had read as a child when she entered the children's literature class. She viewed reading as an activity meaningful only if it answered immediate questions. When I asked the class members to describe why children's books were important, this young woman wrote, "Books are designed to teach reading." She went on to explain that "illustrations add to the story, thus giving interest to a book while a child learns to read." Her definition has very little to do with pleasure reading or with formed literary habits.

Unfortunately, unless colleges begin to teach children's literature in different ways, the next generation of elementary students are likely to have teachers who have looked at reading in similar ways. Most of my undergraduate students confess that they themselves were not readers as youths and declare that they want to be teachers because they "love children." Rarely does a student say that she has entered the field of elementary education because she wants to help children learn new ways of thinking or consider new concepts that will help them as adults. Rarer still is the student who declares that he is entering teaching because he loves to read, to spend solitary time exploring the lives of others, or wants to mentor children as they explore their literature and take part in classroom discussions about their reading. Few mention the need to teach children how to find information on their own. Fewer still mention the public library as a favorite haunt. On the whole, my undergraduate students view the elementary school as a place where adults teach children "how to act and live." Because they have never developed reading habits, have never allowed themselves time to reflect on ideas, and have never explored divergent points of view, they lack a philosophy about the role of lifelong learning, and they consider children's literature a teaching tool to use in skills units.

I don't fault the young people who enter my classes. They are the products of their environment. While they attended elementary school, they were not introduced to children's literature in a meaningful way, and they cannot see a purpose for sharing literature in the elementary classroom other than to use it to teach the current curriculum. Unless my class makes an impact on them, they will continue to degrade literature. Their current curriculum portfolio does not encourage them to explore children's literature and the world of the child more than once, and when they return to literature, it is to learn how to use it as a teaching tool in the traditional subject areas of school. So they will probably remember more about using good books to teach other things than the literature itself. Throughout their lives they have been bombarded with visual media and textbook-related tests, and they view learning as something that happens by memorizing, pleasure as something besides reading.

What do experts who determine our children's future learning say about learning to read? How important is the literature we share? How can we begin to learn where stories fit into our lives? A quick glance at several university catalogs establishes one point: children's literature—or for that matter children's culture—is not an area of study. Indirectly, this has a potent effect on our views of childhood and children.

Often the study of children's literature within colleges and universities serves a strange purpose. It takes the place of serious literature study. A children's literature course will usually include both undergraduates in teacher education and other fields. Those students who hope to teach take the course because it is required. They hope to discover how literature can be shared across the curriculum. They want to use "real books" while teaching about things other than pleasure reading. They don't believe that pleasure reading and literary patterns are relevant to their training. Those who are not in education hope to take an enjoyable but easy literature class. The students who come from areas like English, communications, and theater often were readers as children and want to take a trip through some of their past favorites, to see if children's literature can somehow fit into their adult lives. Neither group expects a course that will concentrate on critical thinking, individual analysis, and divergent literary interpretations of one story. One group hopes to learn relevant modes of teaching that most often meet with success, while the other wants time "to read like a child."

Neither group is looking for difficult reading, and neither expects to face much realism in their literature. Future teachers are aware that parents do not always view trade books as acceptable learning tools, that adults tend to censor more trade literature than textbook reading in the schools, and this makes them cautious. Former children who developed into readers and want to take a course that will let them relive their earlier childhood experiences view children's literature as an eclectic field full of pleasurable stories. As children they were allowed to develop their own reading tastes. They remember picking their own books, reading aloud with their families, hearing a teacher read a story to them. They do not view children's books as "serious stuff" or as informational books. And they have little interest in textbooks as children's literature.

Actually, adult readers who are not studying in a classroom are not textbook readers. They read materials that help them function better, that allow them vicarious experiences. Once out of school, they turn to the literature that offers them a pleasurable experience; they read magazines describing conditions in their world; they refer to the local newspaper to see what's happening in their community; they consult product manuals to determine how the product works. Textbooks are only found in the average home when someone is studying a narrow body of knowledge.

A study of Australian five to twelve year olds suggests that students whose teachers rely on teaching them to read through basals recognize the primary purposes of basal instruction as teaching decoding/word recognition skills and practicing fluency in reading. The corresponding worksheets, these children said, were designed to enable teachers to test them (Cairney 421–28). Today, the practice of teaching with textbooks is losing its appeal. Australia's Garth Boomer states that the best elementary teachers in his country "have a sharp apprehension of the political, social, educational structures which contain, shape, and, in many ways, determine the behaviours of their students." Those teachers, he goes on to say, will dare to discuss radical texts with their students so that the students can learn to "question and respond with a purpose" (2–3). Their emphasis is primarily on *using* children's literature in the classroom, but their goal in sharing divergent books is to teach children to determine for themselves what a text means.

New Zealand, on the other hand, has placed its reading and language arts attention on the child's developing attitudes. As one of the most literate countries in the world, New Zealand has stressed student-centered reading instruction. It has encouraged studies that concentrate on individual successes rather than carefully defined statistical studies that prove that children as a whole can acquire testable knowledge. Instead of specifying how to teach, the emphasis is on what to teach. The majority of twentieth-century language arts research in New Zealand has focused on discovering how different children develop ideas and on the teacher's role in helping children devise personal strategies for learning (Hammonds 20–22). But if youngsters are going to develop personal strategies, they need to understand how those strategies work. They need to begin to look at children's literature as *literature*.

Today there are courses at certain universities that look at the literary aspect of children's stories. The professors of these courses maintain that although children's literature has, by the very uniqueness of its intended audience, some stylistic and aesthetic differences from literature as a whole, it has commonalities shared by all literature that affect reader response. Knowledgeable in fields of literary studies as divergent as Marxist, historical, archetypal, feminist, minority, rhetorical, reader response, structuralist, poststructuralist and postmodernist criticism, they wish to focus their attention on the literature itself. In his introduction to the first *Touchstones* volume, Perry Nodelman, one of the acknowledged scholars of children's literature among those teaching in English departments, wrote about literary explorations, explaining that he is most interested in the literature itself. He argues,

> I can think about the books I admire in order to understand why they might be admirable, what they might have in common with each other, why they are indeed excellent children's books. And in doing that, I keep getting closer to an understanding of what is special about children's literature. (6)

Aware that reader response theory suggests that several levels of readers can all be reading the same text at the same time, literary critics hope to show students several ways of approaching stories based on current literary theory. They want their students to discover what is involved in textual interpretation. These scholars demand that students demonstrate the differences between precritical readings and the critical ones that follow study in order to understand their different reactions and contemplations about the stories they read. Often they have their students keep precritical journals that can be referred to as they write critical papers discussing literary theory and arguing for or against points they have read in professional journal articles. They expect their students to concentrate on literary criticism and children's literature. These courses continually ask students to evaluate materials based on literary standards, to compare one text to another, to consider disparate arguments about one book or idea. Ultimately, these professors hope to create an "enlightened imagination" (to coin the words of the noted critic Northrop Frye) within their undergraduates. Their courses explore ideas about language and literature while they expand the typical undergraduate's repertoire of children's literature and understanding of literary criticism.

All professionals involved in English/language arts programs share this goal. In fact, the National Council of Teachers of English's 1986 *Guidelines for the Preparation of Teachers of English Language Arts* declares that language arts education must create an enlightened body of professionals who "respect and nurture students' intellects and imaginations, as well as help them find significant places in society" (6). The guidelines further state,

> teachers must develop strategies which include the use of diverse materials, various types of classroom organization, and activities which allow a variety of responses and behaviors. (11)

The last decade's distress over textbook learning has suggested that something more than decoding and retelling is needed in children's lives. Professional organizations have responded by establishing national study groups. During 1987 the National Council of Teachers of English appointed a new committee to explore the possibilities of changing from a traditional textbook method of language arts instruction to a literature-based curriculum. At their first session, held at NCTE's annual fall meeting, the committee endorsed the formation of a program in language arts that makes literature its focal point. Members stressed that the current language arts programs, with their emphasis on the rudiments of reading, grammar, and identification, were failing to encourage youngsters to maintain a continual interest in literature. They argued that the textbook approach to language arts should be replaced with one that shares literature in an enlightened way, that allows children to discuss, analyze, and critique the materials they read. In 1989 the Children's Literature Assembly formed a similar group, and they too advocated a dynamic approach to sharing children's literature.

Today's children's literature professors in both schools of education and English departments are concerned with the imperative need to stress diversity; they are not content with one textbook. They often seek several approaches. Many now refer to the scholarly articles published in professional journals such as *The Children's Literature Association Quarterly*, the *The Journal of Children's Literature* (formerly *CLA Bulletin*), *The Lion and the Unicorn,* and *Children's Literature in Education* when they are teaching. Their students are encouraged to read one of the leading textbooks in the field so that they can gain a different perspective, and they are expected to read critical theory. Furthermore, students are encouraged to join each other in informal discussions over coffee, to talk about what has happened in the classroom, and to openly disagree with an interpretation when they have a different experience or philosophy from the one proposed by a critic. All these professors role model diverse teaching strategies; many would not advocate a particular teaching stance for sharing a particular book with children. Furthermore, they stress the aesthetic values of reading over the pragmatic implementation of "teaching with literature."

Today's students at all levels must learn to write in several ways if they are going to become literary readers and writers. Whether they are children or college students, they need to keep personal response journals, work together through dialogue journals and group activities, and take formal critical stances about specific children's books or genres. They need to explore schools of literary criticism until they can finally choose an approach they feel meets their needs. Children will find articles that they can read and appreciate in *Cobblestone, Cricket,* and *Horn Book Magazine.* Adults will need to read literary criticism that addresses literary strategies for reading children's literature. At a minimum, both need to use such standard children's literature sources as *Something about the Author,* the *Dictionary of Literary Biography,* and the *Junior Book* volumes. In the end, they should better understand how children's literature and criticism fit together.

If I return to the individual comments of my undergraduate students about books and reading, I can find young people who have come to view children's books as literature worthy of serious attention. For instance, one education student wrote,

A course in children's literature does several things:
1. Exposes you to *good* literature and shows the difference between good and bad literature.
2. Teaches you to read children's literature critically and to use books for a purpose.
3. Exposes you to good authors and illustrators in children's literature and explains what makes them good.
4. Exposes you to children's literature critics and teaches you not to believe everything you read, but to read and form your own opinion.
5. Makes you interested enough in children's books so that every time you go into a bookstore you head straight for the children's section.
6. Teaches you how to teach literature to children and shows how to justify what you are teaching.

The study of children's literature in all college courses, whether the course is designed for undergraduates or graduates, must deal with the content of children's literature and with contemporary literary criticism. That course should meet the needs of a student who wrote,

> I never realized how complicated as well as important children's literature is. I now understand why children enjoy the "baby" books they read. I realize the importance of illustrations in children's books, especially non-fiction. The different scholarly articles contained information that is valuable to an elementary teacher. For example, Nodelman's article "Some Heroes Have Freckles" has really enlightened me about the different types of characters that exist in books and showed me why some fade away, others remain popular. In the past I assumed that any book would seem interesting to a child and would entertain when shared. Now I know that is not so.

All approaches to children's literature are important because they help beginning readers pick out ways to read and explore literature that will work for them. Reading and appreciating children's literature demands that the reader understand generic criticism and be able to identify the typical literary elements found in effective writing, so that she can pick out books that have meaning for her. The reader who does not understand the basic patterns of literature, who cannot evaluate a wide variety of writing styles, and who is not able to determine the difference between reading to learn and reading to relax will not inspire children or encourage them to become literate adults. The adult who has not experienced how criticism works in children's literature will continually look at children's literature as a romanticized picture of reality. Youngsters who are growing up in a visual world of nightly news and horror films will find children's literature less engrossing than other media if they are continually introduced to simplistic stories, and they will not become lifelong readers.

In 1984, The Children's Literature Association held a Symposium on Teaching Literary Criticism K–6. As the Chair of that symposium, I advocated that the divergent fields consider how they might work together. At the end of the symposium, the group submitted a stance on teaching children's literature. That stance was supported by the ChLA Board, and it became the organization's official standpoint. The group maintains that children's literature is the stepping-stone for the child. Literature enables the child to enter junior high with the necessary reading skills for all his classes. If he is taught about literature's various functions, he will understand the difference between the pleasures of reading for personal enjoyment and the process of gaining new understandings through reading. He will be able to determine the differences among literary experiences and seek new information from traditional sources such as encyclopedias and magazines without believing that these experiences are the same as those gained from reading a good book or watching a well-crafted movie. As proponents of literature, elementary school teachers can initiate a K–6 program that fits their school's population. No matter what books are used, they will design a literature program that stresses the following:

- **A wide variety of materials. Teachers should choose to share those stories that develop an understanding and appreciation of literary form, purpose, style.**
  Children need to see how writing style patterns develop and change. They should learn that literature does not need to be relevant to be pleasurable, that everything read will not have great and deep meanings. They need to be given the opportunity to compare and contrast different works, authors, and genres of literature.
- **Reader discernment. Students should develop the ability to evaluate and understand the differences between distinctive literature and mediocre literature.**
  If children are allowed to look carefully at each piece of writing and consider how it is unique from others, they will be able to understand what makes that author's writing style noteworthy. When children learn to evaluate how the author writes and why he or she writes in that way, they will begin to understand how political, religious, and cultural values are placed within a text. If they look closely at the author's ideas, they will see that authors write with a particular point of view and that their ideas shape their text.
- **Teachers should not teach one point of view. Students should be taught to question and analyze. Tests should not force a way of reading onto the student.**
  Literature analysis cannot be passive. Students should be encouraged to actively question the text and the teacher's interpretation of it. Children should be encouraged to discover how their past literature experiences help them interpret a new book or film. Teachers should emphasize that authors use conventional devices to evoke understanding or create a sense of familiarity for the reader.
- **Ideal readers. The goal of the program should be to teach children to be independent readers who can discover the author's meaning for themselves.**
  Although literary terms make discussions easier, they are not the essence of meaning. Learning how to approach a reading or viewing experience, learning the process of finding and evaluating knowledge, learning to share information in conversations and written reports are far better goals.
- **Teachers who are mentors. Teachers must be trained to teach critical analysis. They must be familiar with children's and young adult literature. They must know how critical theory is used to interpret books and films.**
  Teachers should be expected to take courses in children's and young adult literature while they are in college. They should take classes on film and literary criticism. Teachers should be expected to continue to

professionalize their classroom techniques by attending workshops and classes that stress new ideas and approaches to reading and communicating. They must be effective learners and communicators if they are to successfully teach others.

- **School-supported programs of literary criticism. Curriculum models should be developed by teachers within the local school system. There should not be a national canon of books that is solely taught throughout the country.**

  Curriculum plans should not become standardized as new "textbooks" for teaching language arts and reading. Each elementary school faculty should create a program that relies on the concept of building knowledge, and each program should reflect the expertise of the faculty, the needs of the students, and the overall goals of the school's administration and community. There cannot be a universal canon of books because new materials and interpretations need to be shared. Reading lists should be developed that represent the diversity in literature. Programs should be designed to pinpoint student needs. Children should be encouraged to choose the critical approaches they feel are most valuable. Their learning should emphasize growth in understanding as demonstrated in their written and oral communication skills.

- **Literature worth sharing for its own values. The program should emphasize a theory of literature, not one of cultural, political, religious, or social indoctrination.**

  Major issues in the program should concern the structure of literature, the way it causes the reader to think and demands that the reader have knowledge of literary genres and conventions. Books and films should not be used to simply promote other subjects in the curriculum. They need to be shared for their own worth so that children can see the pleasures of reading and viewing in an intelligent way.

When children's literature is studied as a discipline, those involved will see that reading can help to create knowledgeable adults who want to be lifelong learners, and they can propose changes in the way we as a society approach children's reading and children's learning.

Those who specialize in children's literature view the sharing of literature as a very important process. They know that children's literature has been designed by authors who have varying motives for writing but who adhere to certain literary patterns and archetypes. Although scholars in children's literature acknowledge that it is unique, they recognize that it not unlike all other literature in terms of genres, story form, and thematic approaches. They realize that reader response theory expects readers to approach their reading in different ways, and they do not seek consensus of thought. They hope that the study of literature can show children several ways of approaching texts, can suggest that an ideal reader is one who interprets with understanding, and that all readers can understand how precritical readings are different from critical readings. No book worth studying should be relegated to one reading. Important books should be read, discussed, and revisited. Diverse opinions about all literature should be encouraged. Literary critic Perry Nodelman once wrote,

> The willingness to disagree and to enjoy the discussion of what one disagrees about, is the basic assumption. . . . We don't want to proclaim the law: we want to open a dialogue. (11)

In 1988, as editor of *The Children's Literature Association Quarterly*, Professor Roderick McGillis suggested that the question "What makes a reader?" has not yet been answered. He concluded that what is known is that childhood reading, properly pursued, does create questioning adults. Thus, the process of questioning is being stressed by today's scholars, and the ability to communicate about books and about ideas is favored over the ability to score high on achievement tests. Children's literature experts share interests with others in adjoining areas. For instance, philosopher Roger Trigg once advocated individual interpretations of experience, saying, "'Reality' is only reality for a particular society and what is real and hence true for one set of people may not be for another" (ix). McGillis similarly argued that our understanding of reading is tainted by our own experiences, and he concluded, "More often than not, we find what we set out to look for simply because we have a model to start from" (107). We must begin to expand our model for children's literature and its study to include new ways of reading, discussing, and interpreting if we hope to have every reader develop a critical voice.

2

Literary Criticism and Children's Literature

Literary critics assume reading stances and create interpretations of the stories they read that fit with certain ways of reading. Actually, all adults have certain perceptions about how to read and enjoy a good story. Those perceptions are based on past reading experiences and learned knowledge of literary patterns. Most adults are "critical" about what they read, but don't have formal reasons for their decisions. They are "childlike" in their preferences.

Before children go to school, they hear stories that delight them with their events, characters, and resolutions. Yet small children are seldom concerned about the story's dramatic structure. They are absorbing experience, becoming independent book users. When they hear stories that are accompanied by illustrations, they observe the artist's interpretation of the plot and characterization as they listen. Later, when they are looking at the book, they will often be able to retell the action, relying on the book's format. They are exploring the pleasures of stories, and are using the illustrations to entertain themselves, remembering what was earlier read to them as they re-examine the book's illustrations. Once children go to school they learn about stories in very different ways. They are taught to read for knowledge rather than for delight. They become dependent on someone else's interpretation of what is important. By the time they enter high school, many youngsters view critical interpretation as an academic endeavor only done at school.

Adults can determine how much children will learn about their stories, and they can help children communicate about the stories they share.

Those adults who want children to discover how a story works for themselves will collaborate with them to construct new meanings for the literature they share. Since these adults must initiate the discussions, they must know about story structure and critical theory. Unfortunately, since teachers have rarely studied critical theory they often don't emphasize methods of reading that encourage collaborative learning.

When children go to school they learn to read in certain ways. Often they are asked to predict what will happen in the story without being told about literary patterns that define the plot structure. Teachers expect them to respond in certain ways because the textbooks they are using say children will be able to respond in a particular way. Usually those ways have little to do with the child's prior experiences. Instead, textbooks rely on adult interpretations of child development and on the adult meanings found in children's stories.

Sometimes children will be asked to tell who the main character is in a story. Their main character may not be the one adults would choose, and they then will be told that they are wrong. Once they have discovered that adults have a formula for main characters, they try to determine how the adults they are sharing their stories with perceive characterization in the story. Their decisions are being made without relying on their own reader responses to the story.

Many teachers will tell children that all stories that are good literature have a theme, and they will be asked to determine what the story's theme is. However, because children view the story from their more limited experiences, they may choose a theme very different from the adult's. Then they will be told that they have not understood the story correctly.

Sometimes children are asked to sequence a series of events that has come from the story. Unless they have faced similar events in their own lives or unless they know story patterns, they will be at a loss to know what to do. Reading becomes a mystery that they feel can only be discovered by growing older and having more experiences. Instead of learning to rely on their responses, they learn to wait for the teacher's example. This shapes their learning strategies. For example, when they work on the prepared workbook problems, they watch to see how the teacher solves the first problem on a worksheet and then try to find similar answers for the rest of the questions. They are learning to please the teacher by imitating his or her behavior, but they may not be learning to enjoy reading. This can cause problems.

Teachers who expect children to predict the adventure's outcome, to identify a story's theme, to select and define the main characters of the story are assuming that children will understand how to identify, sequence, and describe the stories they read, that they do not need to hear why stories are similar, or how authors write for their audiences. They turn to activities that assume a certain degree of knowledge instead of collaborating with children and helping them become active participants with the story. When teachers share literature without disclosing the common framework of interpretative skills used by all good readers, they ask the children to perform exercises without understanding how stories work. These youngsters are being forced to respond to patterns in texts without understanding that literary appreciation depends on knowing about literary or writerly structures. The patterns most often found in literature contain implied meanings. They elicit responses from readers before these readers understand their meanings. However, literary patterns are not randomly placed into stories. Indeed, they are clues to the author's purpose for writing, his background, and his tone.

Unless the patterns and structures of literature are discussed, children will lose the cultural and social implications of what they are reading. Without some knowledge about tale types, children will not be able to interpret a story. Furthermore, we cannot expect them to see the values of reading stories or of sharing their experiences with others unless we give them a literary framework that applies critical thinking skills to their developing personal analysis skills. When children are not taught literary approaches to reading and discussing literature, they do not attach much importance to how the structures an author chooses create the text's meaning or determine the author's style. Used to writing traditional book reports, to noting their immediate responses to a story in a reader response journal, or to engaging in a classroom activity that is somehow related to the text, these youngsters find junior high with its emphasis on textual analysis confusing. Once in high school, they often feel that literature and its study has little place in their ordinary world. They turn to television or movies for entertainment and seek out news from television broadcasts and newspapers.

Fortunately, many teachers in today's schools have learned something about reader response theory. They allow students to read a book and formulate their own opinions of it. They encourage students to keep response journals about what they read and to tie their reading to their everyday world. However, reader response theory requires more than early responses if the children are going to understand how authors write. And, since children cannot become pleasure readers unless they are encouraged to hear the writer out, to look at the story in relation to its literary form, to use critical processes in order to discover different interpretations for the story they are reading, they must have teachers who will show them that a story can have more than one meaning, encourage them to pursue the meaning in the text for themselves, and convince them that it is not always easy to find a personal interpretation for a piece of writing, but is enlightening and invigorating. Interpretation must be introduced to youngsters because it is an exciting, demanding process that allows readers to define any story's meaning for themselves.

As adults we understand why children become discouraged when they read. We have seen it happen in the adult world also. When college students are asked to read a particular poem and see the same metaphors and analogies as the professor, they often regard the activity as a frustrating one. As readers, they feel they have not been given any responsibility to find personal meanings for the text being shared. Since they are not being encouraged to enter into a dialogue about the text, they feel alienated from the story and suspect that criticism is an unnecessary skill. Furthermore, they become passive learners because they know that their opinions will be devalued in discussion, and they ask the teacher to give them "examples of the best" responses from past classes. They expect that a similar answer will be valued. Sometimes they do not even read the assigned materials because they expect the classroom lecture to give them the needed information. They are not actively involved in the learning process.

Passive readers are not lifelong readers. They see no direct pleasure in reading, and they cannot determine how to argue for or against a text. Forced to take on the role of listeners without a right to respond and interpret, many who attend and graduate from college find reading tedious and uninspiring. They perceive their interactions with texts as being less important than their viewings of media presentations. Their entertainment interests center on visual interpretations of someone else's texts. Today's statistics are showing that the reading public is even turning away from printed news reports and relying on media presentations of events.

Active readers realize that they must read and reread a text before it is theirs. They must hear the author out and respond to his writing before they begin to make sense of the story. They must consider whose perspective the story is told in, why it affects them as it does, if it is designed to inform and instruct or to entertain. Finally, they must determine how that story relates to their interpretation of the world they live in. Active readers are using all the levels of reader response that critics have discussed.

Adults who wish to help children read in more meaningful ways will need to study criticism. They must understand what it is and how it shapes reading practices. In the broadest sense, literary criticism establishes a way of reading. It contains systematic approaches to the texts we read. It sets up methods for studying and evaluating the things we read. In a more narrow sense, it becomes a way of justifying our own readings of the texts we read. Critical theory allows readers to understand how writers depend on the audience's past literary experiences to help them understand what is written in each new story. Literary criticism suggests that readers have a role in the reading process. Just what that role might be often corresponds with the school of interpretation that we adhere to.

Literary studies in the college classroom often depends on the students' ability to discern literary genres and writing styles. Because the professors teaching literature demand that students write more than recall information when they discuss the books they read, college students learn that adult literature has meanings that come from stances, from critical theories. These same critical theories are the backbone for standards in publishing for children.

Professionals in publishing define how children will understand what they read based on what they hope children will see in the text. When adults ascribe to a way of reading, they are choosing a theory about the purposes of literature. In fact, this also happens once the book is available in the classroom. The simple methods that teachers use when teaching children how to read are guided by theories of literary interpretation. For instance, the earliest published books for children were designed to instruct. The authors and publishers wanted children to have *mimetic* experiences as they read. They wanted their readers to learn about the world around them and proper ways to behave. Thus, the literature they shared had implied messages that suggested ways to act. When the first school-related texts were published, children were taught to decode a text for its meaning. Pleasure reading was considered to be acceptable only when the child learned about the acceptable adult code of ethics. Reading became a passive act that did not allow the child a voice. He was taught not to doubt or distrust the text. Later children's literature may seem to be less laden with a certain values framework, but much of children literature that is published is mimetic. And it is shared for its moral implications as often as for its pleasurable experiences.

Education's early theories of reading suggested that the reader need not interact with the text. Instead, she should study the text for its truths. This sort of reading is still often encouraged in elementary schools. In fact, the established patterns for sharing school textbooks with a group of children seem much like the patterns established by the "*New Critics*" when they took hold of academic literary studies in the United States during the 1930s.

In the American Depression, literature began to be viewed differently from the way it had been in the past. As scholars of literature sought to define the literary values of the books they read, they ignored the authors who created their literature. Texts became impersonal. Critics no longer felt author biographical information had a place in literary studies. In fact, university professors in English departments developed ways of approaching reading that concentrated on literature as an entity on it own. No longer considered as historical remnants from another time or as contemporary statements, stories could be isolated and analyzed.

The New Critics also determined that there could only be one true valid reading of a text. They made the reader into a passive recipient of literature. They argued that the story told would remain the same for all readers, but that not all readers were capable of interpreting the story's meaning on their own. Those who read the story could learn ways of understanding the text if they were informed. These critics felt that the values of the text had to be discovered through multiple readings of the same story by experts who then could interpret the text's true meaning. This knowledge, in turn, could be shared with those lay readers incapable of seeing the underlying significance.

It is not surprising that the reading textbooks of the 1940s and 1950s seemed authorless. One need only look at the practices in English departments. There the texts of great literature had been privileged over their authors by New Criticism. They allowed the students to hear about the books without trusting that they could effectively interpret good literature. This practice was mirrored in education. Reading instruction in elementary schools began to focus on teaching decoding skills that led the student to the right answer concerning what was being read.

New Criticism suggested how teachers might teach children to read. Most New Critics felt that the ideal readings of literary texts could only come from a body of knowledgeable scholars who resided inside academia. Thus, the novice's interpretations were not to be trusted. These critics identified a type of text that could be shared with those outside academia: short pieces of writing capable of being scrutinized more carefully. As a result of their theories, they favored using textbooks that contained short, unconnected readings to novels with carefully developed characterization, settings, and plot. Even when the same characters were used throughout the text, the separate entries were, at best, episodic. Furthermore, New Critics did privilege certain writings over others by their practices. Because they were always seeking the "ideal reading" of a text, they were apt to return again and again to the same poems, short essays, plays, or stories. In no time, a list of "the best" evolved. These were the texts taught in college classrooms.

New Critics felt that they could teach their students "how to read" the classics. They did not contend that everyday readers could appreciate the text's true meaning on their own. However, they believed that while ordinary citizens were not capable of notable interpretation, they could be taught to appreciate the true meaning of a piece of literature. Thus, true knowledge of literature was not in the hands of simple readers. It could not be obtained easily, and it stemmed from a more sophisticated practice than learning to read.

The concept of "classical text" eventually sifted down to children's literature. Librarians and teachers often privileged some stories over others, and they usually based their decisions on "literary style." Since none of the New Critics turned to children's literature for study, publishers of reading textbooks were left on their own. They probably designed their school texts around the practices of New Criticism. They began to choose traditional short stories and poems as well as newly written short stories that held a system for reading. The teacher's guide was designed to hold the "right" answer for daily reading. Textbooks emphasized teaching children skills to read the words and recall the story's plot, identify the characters and their actions, and predict how the characters would act. Unison reading strategies were encouraged. Textbooks did not teach children how to explore the story or the poem on their own. Teachers did not control the instruction; it was prepackaged for them. Most of the time, teachers in public schools left the interpretation of the reading selections to someone else (who may have written the teacher's guide or sent out a lesson plan on how to share the day's reading material). They taught the principles of reading without errors and then finding the appropriate replies that "correctly" answered the questions in the workbooks.

In turn, children trained to read with the standard textbooks were ready to respond to literature according to the academic standards of New Criticism. They were used to looking for the right answers in the text, a skill that prioritizes the text over authorial voice and personal interpretation. They knew that every reading segment implied a "correct interpretation," and they readily accepted the insights proclaimed to be valid by the teacher/ scholar.

While New Criticism set up a way to look at the text, *mythic criticism* established a method for understanding how good writing happened. Mythic criticism evolved from the 1930s through the 1980s, but its importance in shaping reading habits was most significant during the 1940s, 1950s, and 1960s.

Mythic critics looked back at the myths, folklore, and legends from ancient cultures and found certain patterns that linked the stories together. Although they might not have expected to prioritize one set of stories over another, they usually studied Greek, Roman, and European stories, and in the end established a way of reading that was largely Anglo-European. The Bible became the most significant myth because it was the one that related most closely to the stories they were studying: European and American literature.

Influenced by the theories of the Swiss psychiatrist Carl Jung, mythic critics argued that all stories contained patterns relating back to primitive rituals, stereotypes, and habits. They maintained that these patterns were unconsciously held in the author's psyche, and in the end these patterns determined story structures and meanings. Cultural or *archetypal patterns* could be isolated in the text and could define a text's meaning. Taken in a general sense, this theory suggested that literature could be examined for its typical structures, and that readers, if they were introduced to typical story structures, could predict what would happen based on archetypal patterns. Thus, they could automatically understand how stories worked based on cultural implications. Although mythic critics certainly believed in archetypes, they would not have advocated teaching them in isolation. All the mythic critics believed that total stories had to be shared if readers were to understand their meanings.

Northrop Frye, in his book *Anatomy of Criticism*, established a "scientific way" of reading that allowed the reader to determine the story's genre and place in literary studies. Frye traced all stories back to Biblical patterns, and defined story types that could be seen in later writing. Seeking to establish a rational way of looking at stories, he introduced the idea that all stories could be separated into five categories. These were myth, romance, high mimetic, low mimetic, and irony. In turn, they formed the patterns of *irony, romance, comedy,* and *tragedy*. Each had identifiable traits that could be used to categorize stories into genre studies.

In 1964 Frye published *The Educated Imagination,* a compilation of a series of radio lectures that included an essay that discussed mythic criticism's role in society. One chapter specifically examined how to begin the literary process with children. Frye advocated starting with the biblical tales and continuing with Greek and Roman mythology. Frye commented, "If we don't know the Bible and the central stories of Greek and Roman literature, we can still read books and see plays, but our knowledge of literature can't grow, just as our knowledge of mathematics can't grow if we don't learn the multiplication table" (70). Probably Northrop Frye's ideas would have caught on more if the American public had been less concerned about separating church from state. However, since the Bible has not been considered acceptable fare for twentieth century public school textbooks in the United States, his ideas have not been embraced in public schools. Still, Frye had a major effect on teaching literature in the colleges, and he indirectly affected children's literature.

In children's literature, stories were sought that held the beginning/middle/end composition found in traditional narrative. Characters who were stereotypic were identified and their outcomes predicted. Picture books were published that presented romantic adventures with a happily-ever-after ending. Most of these simple stories reflected Anglo-American standards of behavior. Older children's literature written for U.S. youngsters centered on American experiences. Often authors placed their events in the times of the American Revolutionary War or the Civil War. Because they were telling contemporary audiences about continual struggles that youths have had with societal values, their stories' resolutions often contained irony. In addition, since they reflected a sense of acceptance in the world's values over the hero's, they were often tragic tales for adolescent readers. Stereotypic characters reacted in predictable ways that fit contemporary cultural values. Female protagonists in girls' fiction usually dismissed their earlier tomboy activities and attitudes to become "young women." Boys in fiction sought adventure; often they were pitted against society only to learn to accept the values of their culture. Few minority children were portrayed as main characters in their own adventures; when they did appear, they learned to "fit in" to the American mainstream by the end of the story.

A quick glance at the *Caldecott* and *Newbery* winners in the 1950s and 1960s reveals an American bias toward European and American legendary/folkloric traditions. Even those books that seem to protest American values reaffirm those cultural beliefs in the end. For instance, John Krumgold's two Newbery winners, *And Now Miguel* (1954) and *Onion John* (1960), depict young protagonists who are struggling against traditional values. Miguel is a minority youth living an isolated shepherd's life away from the influences of the American majority culture. However, he does not break free of American society's standards. In the end, he realizes that his new maturity results from his brother's induction into the U.S. military, and he must accept his life as defined by Anglo-American cultural demands. Most adolescent heroes are ironic heroes because they must learn to accept an unfriendly society's patterns and beliefs. While they are not tragic heroes, there is something tragic in the reshaping of their ideals. These stories contain a good deal of realism.

Mythic criticism engendered a positive atmosphere that could support the later development of minority criticism. Many mythic critics believed that all peoples had rituals that caused stories to evolve, and they sought to study the sociological structures of all societies. They welcomed the work of anthropologists, and compared various myths and folktales for "universal" images and values. However, most were more familiar with the stories of Europe and America, and so they emphasized these legends in their studies. Mythic criticism did not study minority literature and it did not advocate variety. The archetypes most often discussed and studied were patterns and tale types found in "classic literature."

One early mythic critic was different because she went beyond the patterns of literature and culture. Maud Bodkin linked mythic criticism to reader response theory. She advocated Jung's theory while calling for the development of a receptionist theory in literary studies. When she published *Archetypal Patterns in Poetry* in 1934, Bodkin looked at female roles in literature and set up a base for feminist theory. Yet Bodkin's work had less immediate effect on the teaching of literature than Northrop Frye's, possibly because she was working against the mainstream of critical thought.

Reader response theory did become an important strand of criticism later on. It has greatly affected the study of children's literature since the 1970s. Some of the earlier arguments of literary critics were pivotal in shaping its use in classrooms today. In educational circles, Louise Rosenblatt's arguments for studying literature based on reader reactions was central to response theory. She shifted the educator's concentration in teaching literature from the text to the reader. Later, the work of David Bleich, Norman Holland, and Alan Purves suggested ways to interpret readers reading that went beyond New Criticism and mythic criticism and changed attitudes about the act of reading.

Norman Holland succinctly argued for a method of reading that did not rely on an authoritative reading of a story. in "Reading Readers Readings," he suggested the personal response diary, stating, "We need to begin, not with a set of impersonal procedures designed to make our inquiry 'scientific,' but with immediate, personal data about (and, I would claim, a more telling model for) the dynamics of literary response" (8). Alan Purves conducted an extensive comparison of the reading preferences and analysis skills of adolescents in several cultures. He suggested that reading is shaped by culture, and he argued that "one cannot examine response to literature without considering the effects of school. There are few 'untrained' responses, if any. Through school, children are taught to read and, in school, literature has traditionally played a large part in the process of leading people to literacy" ("That Sunny Dome" 65).

Although scholars have had less direct effect upon the elementary schools than on the thinking of those who teach about literature, they have changed contemporary attitudes about how literature works. And their innovations in literary studies have established different schools of theory. Feminist critics, Marxist scholars, minority critics, and even those who adhere to the practices in deconstruction and semiotics have played roles in shaping how adult scholars look at literature. In turn, they have indirectly changed education's attitudes about children's literature. And these attitudes have indirectly defined what books are published for children since schools are the biggest market for children's reading materials.

Today's literature found in the schools has evolved from many current literary theories concerning reader reception. For instance, the feminist movement in the 1970s suggested that female readers needed new kinds of texts, and stories were printed that contained female protagonists who followed the traditional *bildungsroman* pattern, who refused to become "little women," who defied cultural attitudes to establish a new concept of feminism. Because cultural diversity has been stressed in the public press, attitudes about canons have changed. Publishers are more aware now than in the past that they must include stories from various ethnic backgrounds, and are actively seeking minority writings. Scholars like Jack Zipes and Perry Nodelman alerted the general public to the values of exploring children's literature through Marxist or semiotic practices, and new books with revolutionary plot structures and unusual perspectives have begun to be published. Critical theory establishes trends that are gradually absorbed into teaching materials and lesson plans.

Even when literary scholars and educators were not talking with one another, theory did effect teaching. However, theory is no longer separated from the study of children's literature. Today many university scholars actively engage in discussions with public school educators about children and their literature. Professors in departments of English, philosophy, anthropology, foreign languages, ethnography, and communications gather with those from schools of education and library science to talk about literary patterns and school practices. Although children's literature, much like reader response theory, always had a theoretical base for study, reading stances that concentrate on the literary aspects of children's literature did not evolve until the 1970s.

The change in interpreting and valuing children's literature all started with a small body of scholars situated in English departments who hoped to pursue literary analysis skills in their teaching. As professionals, they had studied literary criticism. Now they were teaching children's literature in English departments. Their first loyalty was to the rigors of literary theory, but they were not antagonistic toward children's stories. Most were not teaching children's literature because they had to. Instead, they were pursuing a body of literature that, for one reason or another, strongly appealed to them. Because they were used to pursuing the textual aspects of stories, they sought critical discussions that fit into the already established schools of critical theory. Immediately they noted a lack of literary scholarship in the field of children's literature and they felt disgruntled. In the end, they formed a professional organization dedicating itself to the research and scholarship of children's literature. One of the founders of the Children's Literature Association, Anne Devereaux Jordan, writes,

> While teaching Children's Literature in 1972, I found I had a number of complaints about the field. There was no consistently excellent body of criticism being published; to find out what was happening in the field one had to belong to quite a number of organizations; and the children's literature courses on the college level were usually derided or dismissed in favor of other, "more scholarly," courses. What was needed was an organization to remedy these complaints. . . . [I]n June of 1973 . . . I met with Francelia Butler, Founder and Senior Editor, and Bennett Brockman, then Managing Editor, of the annual *Children's Literature*. . . . At that meeting . . . we proposed the members of the first Executive Board . . . John Graham, University of Virginia; Jon Stott, at that time at Western Michigan University; Glenn Sadler, then at Point Loma College, San Diego; and Rodney Morrisset (now deceased) of the University of London, England. ("Early Days and Sweet Dreams" 14)

Ann Jordan's dream of creating an organization that would include members from various fields who were determined to improve the climate for the serious study of children's literature slowly became a reality. The original board planned an annual conference and supported *Children's Literature* as their annual literary journal. In addition, they established a newsletter edited by Margaret Esmonde, a member of the English Department at Villanova.

In 1978, when the group met at Cambridge, the Board included Marilyn Apseloff, Ben Brockman, Francelia Butler, Margaret P. Esmonde, Dorell Thomas Hanks, Jr., Alethea Helbig, Rebecca Lukens, Ruth MacDonald, Francis Molson, Taimi Ranta, Stephen Roxburgh, Jon C. Stott, and Jane Yolen. There were active members who presented their research at the conference from a variety of fields, including library science, English, and education. Ethel Heins, editor of *The Horn Book Magazine,* gave one of the keynote talks. Papers were read by Jack Zipes, a scholar in German literature whose writings adhered to Marxist scholarship; Carole Henderson Carpenter, a folklorist who taught at York University in Toronto; and Perry Nodelman, a Canadian who would become the Association's leading critic during the late 1970s.

The organization held a large block of Canadian members. Since Northrop Frye was also Canadian, ChLA began with his theories. Scholars who used mythic criticism as a stance gained the group's respect; they came to the conference to deliver exemplary papers that discussed children's literature in light of literary patterns. In their personal discussions, they stressed that children's literature was a serious field for literary studies. One of the Canadians, Jon Stott, had helped to found the organization. In 1978, he was serving as the organization's first president, and in his presidential address he asked, "What is children's literature?" Then, he went on to say, "We all have ideas—and in the end, there may be thirteen different ways of looking at this particular blackbird. But, in the end, by making an attempt or attempts we will clarify our own views" (*Festschrift* 60).

Those involved in children's literature who attended these early conferences brought ideas from different schools of criticism. Unlike critics of adult literature, they were less concerned that one theory of literary study gain priority over another. Instead, they were determined to ensure that children's literature would be discussed as serious literature. Since discussion suggested publication, they sought and supported journals that addressed the literary elements of children's literature. These journals subsequently changed attitudes about how to read children's literature and share it with youngsters.

New journals that studied children's literature for its literary elements evolved during the seventies. A quick look at *Children's Literature* and the *ChLA Newsletter* attests to the change in critical theory concerning children's literature. These two journals sought to publish scholarly articles that adhered to the publication standards set in English departments. They sought authors who would address children's literature as a serious group of texts.

By 1975, *Children's Literature* had established itself as a scholarly journal. That edition's subtitle, "Annual of The Modern Language Association Seminar on Children's Literature and The Children's Literature Association," alluded to the growing agitation for a children's literature division in the Modern Language Association. The issue contained a special section on children and literature in the Middle Ages, a topic of interest to literary scholars. The articles looked at medieval literature to see how it shaped childhood. Because the articles concentrated on a period within history, the authors were less concerned with the literary values of the texts than how they influenced the child and what that implied for future writers of children's literature.

The journal also featured another group of articles about contemporary children's books that had established literary trends in the field. All these discussions looked at the books as pieces of literature that hold literary patterns worthy of attention. Their literary analyses paved the way for work on the Children's Literature Association Touchstones list.

Virginia Wolf discussed *Harriet the Spy* by Louise Fitzhugh. She looked at the book as contemporary fiction, then argued that it was more than a realistic novel. Wolf focused on Fitzhugh's careful use of journal entries in a story that was otherwise related in a third-person narrative. She argued that the journal entries' first-person narrative causes the reader to respond to Harriet's evolving concept of self and creates a psychological novel that explores a child's attitudes about her environment. Wolf concluded that *Harriet the Spy* might become a children's classic, saying, "*Harriet the Spy* is not a message book. It is first a foremost an experience. . . . Louise

Fitzhugh has proven that contemporary, realistic fiction of psychological and philosophical depth is a viable possibility for children" (125).

Rosa Ann Moore considered Laura Ingalls Wilder's orange notebooks found in the Gifts and Rare Books Division of the Detroit Public Library. Those that she studied contained skeletons of the episodes Wilder had placed in her children's books. She argued that the children's books are more appealing in their retelling of actual events earlier recorded in the orange notebooks. She showed how the author restructured ordinary scenes, combining creative conversations, carefully drawn character studies, and detailed descriptions. She discussed how the notebooks contained events purposefully left out, and suggested that they have been shaped into stories the author felt were appropriate for children. Moore talked about Wilder's manipulation of events into a timeline that fit her retelling. Finally, she argued that "the finished work [is] both less literal and more true and beautiful" (118).

Geraldine D. Poss analyzed *The Wind in the Willows* as a pastoral novel. She argued that the book is nostalgic and romantic and that it holds a dreamlike Arcadia free of death and women. Poss discussed how these traits make *The Wind in the Willows* a perfect children's book for the young reader who innocently travels on the animal adventures and enjoys the pastoral pleasures of idyllic adventures.

There were also review articles that looked at the literary aspects of regional children's literature and book review articles that discussed a group of children's books containing similar patterns. Finally, the journal included a listing of dissertations and suggested topics for future research. *Children's Literature*'s format and emphasis have remained largely the same since the 1975 issue. Currently, because the *ChLA Newsletter* has gradually evolved into a quarterly, *Children's Literature* has become one of two major journals supported by the Children's Literature Association.

The *ChLA Newsletter* changed from a newsy discussion of Board decisions and upcoming annual conferences to a quarterly containing book reviews of professional books, critical discussions of children's literature from a variety of approaches, and regular columns that address topics of literature from a worldwide perspective. By 1976, the newsletter held short book review articles of critical books that examined critical issues in children's literature. During its early years, the newsletter published several special sections on particular topics that pinpointed the possible connections between adult contemporary literary criticism and children's literature.

In 1982 the Children's Literature Association formed a publications committee to produce book-length publications dealing with children's literature as a field for literary studies. One of the first publications to be released was *The First Steps: Best of the Early Children's Literature Association Quarterly*. It was compiled by the journal's second editor, Patricia Dooley. Dooley included what she deemed the best from the early newsletter and journal, and commented, "one can see the range and depth of the essays grow as ChLA itself expanded and defined itself." She added, "The collection might also serve to introduce a number of scholars whose names will—or should—be familiar to serious students of children's literature" (*The First Steps* 5). The volume held materials from 1977–1981 publications. It contained special sections on Canadian children's literature, reader response criticism and the child reader, *realism* in children's literature, *science fiction*, literary theory, *folklore*, the Newbery and Caldecott awards, and children's book illustration. The special sections on reader response and critical theory suggested new directions for scholars to follow in the field. They opened the door for critical inquiry in children's literature and changed the way scholars in children's literature look at readers and criticism. Not surprisingly, ChLA's 1983–1984 President Alethea Helbig called it a milestone, adding, "it completes the history of ChLA early publication by bringing together in a single volume the early criticism for all scholars in the field to use and enjoy" (*The First Steps* 4).

Peggy Whalen-Levitt edited "Literature and Child Readers" for the Winter 1980 edition of the *Children's Literature Association Quarterly*. Placed in the center of the journal and set off in a contrasting color, this section addressed issues of the child as reader that were being discussed in several theoretical camps of academe. In her article, "Pursuing 'The Reader in the Book,'" Whalen-Levitt discussed the lack of work concerning children's reading interests, interpretative patterns, and acculturation through literature. She commented that response theory has a direct tie to John Dewey's discussion of experiential learning, and she explored works of Wolfgang Iser and Louise Rosenblatt to show how they interpreted the reader's role in response theory. Finally, she commented,

> It is ironic that the children's literature field should be so out of step with recent developments in literary theory during the very period of literary history when respected theorists have paved the way for a consideration of the reader . . . Following Iser's directives, we might expect a study entitled "The Implied Reader: Patterns of Communication in American Prose Fiction for Children from Goodrich to Goffstein." (*The First Steps* 18–20)

The issue also included an interview with Alan C. Purves, an annotated bibliography of theory and research on children's literary experiences by Marilyn Cochran-Smith, an article that discussed diary keeping of children's responses by Peggy Whalen-Levitt, and an article by Wendy Saul describing how children's responses to literature fit into the children's literature courses taught in colleges. Critics who turned their attention to reader response criticism began to consider how children and their literature fit together.

The next issue of the *Children's Literature Association Quarterly* (Spring 1981) contained an article by Jon C. Stott lauding the publication of professional articles addressing the literary elements of children's literature. Stott commented that many articles might be more theoretical than practical, but he argued that the ideas could be applied to library and classroom situations. He also suggested that children should have a particular group of books to explore while they are young. Stott concluded that school teachers need to know both children's literature and critical theory, and added,

> Within the space of four hours, I taught two classes dealing with structural patterns in fiction. In the first, I discussed Gerald McDermott's *Arrow to the Sun* with second graders; in the second I considered *The Scarlet Letter* with a group of graduate students. . . . After the classes were over, I realized I'd been doing much the same thing with both groups. However, there was a difference—the responses of the second graders, though less precise in their articulation, were more perceptive. (40)

Stott's comments are not atypical of the thinking of literary scholars who have worked in both college and elementary school classrooms. They reflect Northrop Frye's earlier writings. Although Stott's approach to sharing literature fits into Frye's description of mythic criticism, his own explorations with children are also centered in reader response theory. He allows the children he works with to express their opinions about literature, and listens carefully to their responses. Stott has continued to advocate teaching children about literary patterns and then allowing them to explore their literature for their own meanings.

"Children's Literature & Literary Criticism" was released in the Spring 1981 *Children's Literature Association Quarterly*. Again, the section was placed in the middle of the journal in a separate color with articles that reviewed current trends in literary studies, and suggested how children's literature fit into the larger arena of literary criticism. It openly embraced several different modes of critical theory, including structuralism, linguistic methods, and textual analysis. But it was not without criticism of the strategies used in the various camps of literary analysis. The section's editor Perry Nodelman wrote that adult literary criticism contained too much jargon for the common reader of children's literature. Still, he argued that knowledge of literary criticism was essential to those in the field because it allowed adults to continue to discuss "the particular kind of literature we are most interested in" (*The First Steps* 73).

Despite these advances, academics involved in children's literature who gathered together at MLA and ChLA continued to express dissatisfaction about critical standards in the field. Lois R. Kuznets rephrased the often heard arguments in her article "Essays on 'The Theory of the Novel.'" She complained that very little that had been written about children's literature was actually criticism, and stated that criticism's role in children's literature was poorly defined. Arguing from a New Critic's stance, Kuznets maintained that critics in children's literature should not concern themselves with reader reception until they had dealt with studies of formalism or textuality. While Kuznets acknowledged that good criticism could take into account a reader's responses to a text, she argued that reader response criticism on its own did not create "good analytical readers and observers of the response of others" (*The First Steps* 77). Kuznets was not anti-reader response criticism as much as she was anti-real reader response as an ultimate method for exploring children's literature.

Part of the frustration that members of ChLA expressed derived from the diversity within the field that inhibited agreement on common methods or terminology to be shared in discussions. While literary critics wanted to talk about children's books with educators and librarians, they sought a familiar framework for their discussions. The group was advocating that those involved in the field needed to read certain key books in order to understand what they wished to talk about and how they wished to talk about it. Susan Gannon argued that all students of children's literature had to pay attention to rhetorical and narrative authority. She looked at the work of Wayne Booth and Frank Kermode, and concluded that their classic works would be worthwhile studies for those who turned their attention to children's literature. Of Booth's books, she wrote, "*The Rhetoric of Fiction* remains, after twenty years, an engaging as well as an impressive book. . . . [It] still has much to say to critics of children's literature" (*The First Steps* 78). From Kermode's writings she chose *The Sense of an Ending,* and observed "certainly one of its important features was the critical interest it initiated in problems of narrative sequence, an interest which is still very much alive" (*The First Steps* 79). Anita Moss reviewed the recent works of Jonathan Culler, Gerald Graff, and Eugene Goodheart, and suggested that critics in children's literature needed to consider how the structures of a text create meaning for the reader. She ended by saying that Culler, Graff, and Goodheart are not easily read and understood, but they "invite us to think critically; they provoke us to question, and in that way are valuable studies" (*The First Steps* 86).

The 1981 special section pinpointed critics and books that could fix the boundaries for critical explorations in children's literature. While it did not include all the fields used in today's criticism of children's literature, it suggested that literary analysis in children's literature need not follow one pattern. It also set up perimeters for entering into literary discussion. Certain works had to be studied prior to beginning analysis, and certain methods had to be acknowledged. These, in turn, could help critics define what was good about children's literature.

In Jon C. Stott's 1978 presidential address, he called for the formation of a children's literature canon. A dialogue that divided the field soon followed. The proposed canon emerged as one of the most controversial areas in early critical discussion. Librarians and school teachers already had lists of "best books" that they adhered to when discussing literature. Many members of the Children's Literature Association wondered why they needed to discuss what a canon of children's literature would look like. In response, D. Thomas Hanks, Jr., a member of the first ChLA Canon Committee, suggested that the canon would help determine what was being taught in college classes of children's literature. He wrote that the canon should come from the practices of those in the field and added, "it would be both fruitful and helpful for ChLA members to examine the courses they teach or the library programs they administer, and begin to determine the specific works" that might fit into the ChLA canon (*The First Steps* 11). In 1980 another member of the Canon Committee, Perry Nodelman, wrote that the organization was not interested in creating a binding list of teachable titles. What was needed, he argued, was "a list of admirable books, if only so that we can define what is admirable in children's literature" (*The First Steps* 39). Such a list emerged during the early eighties, but not without attracting considerable criticism. In fact, the tension concerning the legitimacy of a list of "the best" became so strong that the list was renamed "Touchstones." In an effort to explain the choices, the Publications Committee asked Perry Nodelman to edit a series of articles that would discuss why each book was considered an important landmark in children's literature. Three books featuring a critical article devoted to each title were published by ChLA in 1985–1989.

The *ChLA Quarterly*'s format has continued to encourage diversity in critical approaches to literature. More recently, it contained articles concerning teacher planning for literary studies in the elementary schools, African American literature, religious literature as a literary endeavor, and postmodernism in contemporary children's literature.

Meanwhile, other journals appeared that looked at children's literature from a literary standpoint. Some began with editorial boards and contributors who were active members of ChLA, and they continue to have close links to ChLA's leadership. One of these journals, *Children's Literature in Education*, was first released prior to the formation of the Children's Literature Association. Currently, its United States Editor is Anita Moss, a formative leader in ChLA during the late 1970s and early 1980s. It has an American Editorial Board largely composed of ChLA leaders. The articles in this journal concentrate on the literary aspects of children's books and look at children's literature using the stances outlined in the 1981 special section on criticism. Several articles are important philosophical pieces that help to restructure critical thinking in the field. For me, one of those articles was Samuel Pickering, Jr.'s "The Function of Criticism in Children's Literature."

Pickering, a former editor of *Children's Literature*, had reviewed several articles dealing with children's literature. He argued that much of what was being written from a critical stance was "unintelligible to the common reader" (13), and that some methods, such as close readings of a text, did not fit well into the world of children's literature. But, he maintained, criticism did belong in the field. And he advocated that teachers should be doing more of the writing. He continued,

> Writing criticism forces a teacher to think, and although the gap between
> what is written and what is taught is often great, the effort to produce

critical writing improves classroom performance . . . reading criticism can invigorate teaching. But reading criticism is far inferior, I think, to the attempt to write it. (16)

Most of us would argue that we cannot write critical articles until we understand how literature works. One way to understand the ways critics look at literature is to study the stylistic patterns found in all literature. A book that discusses the familiar literary elements that are also found in children's literature was published in 1976. Rebecca Lukens, a professor in English who taught children's literature, released *A Critical Handbook of Children's Literature,* a book that was to become a standard critical study in the field. Lukens is a strong advocate for a structural approach that would give students in all fields a basic understanding of the literary elements found in all texts, whoever their intended audience might be. Now in its fourth edition, the book succinctly discusses genres, characterization, plot, theme, setting, point of view, style, tone, and nonfiction. In addition, Lukens spends a good deal of time looking at the picture book as a unique format and poetry as a unique form. Most of us can learn much about the traditional approaches to writing essays by reading Lukens. To the teacher or student who has no other background in children's literature, this book seems to hold all the answers needed to write criticism. However, it is important to note that Lukens is basically a New Critic, and that much has evolved since we began viewing texts through close readings of the elements recognized to make a text "literary."

In an attempt to make the undergraduate student in children's literature aware of the diverse approaches available, ChLA Publications released a readings book in 1983 that contained critical articles discussing children's literature in a variety of ways. Ruth MacDonald, the ChLA President for 1982–83, explained that the book was "aimed at the new scholar or teacher whose interest is children's literature." She called it a "versatile collection" and pointed out that the volume was proposed to "present a variety of approaches for a wide range of literary forms available in the best recent essays in the field" (5).

The book was arranged to showcase literature and literary studies in a challenging way. Whenever possible, controversy was included. For instance, the section on classical tales presented Jack Zipes's critical review of Bruno Bettelheim. Zipes's strong Marxist piece suggested that all readers, and all critics, need not agree about the values of sharing folklore with children. Virginia L. Wolf's article "The Symbolic Center: *Little House in the Big Woods*" is found in the section on literary forms. In it, Wolf alluded to the earlier work of Rosa Anne Moore, but looked at a particular book in Wilder's series and analyzed it in terms of *bipolarism,* an important theory when studying the textual constraints of children's literature created for young readers. She wrote, "Setting, in other words, functions as Northrop Frye says it does in romance, creating mood, generating symbols, and embodying theme" (68). Wolf concluded that the book "often slips out of the realm of fiction to become lyric—a celebration of a way of life embodied in the image of a little house in the big woods" (69).

Since the 1980s, the field of critical inquiry in children's literature has grown at a rapid pace. New journals continue to approach literature in a variety of ways. Critical reference materials, such as the special editions of the *Dictionary of Literary Biography* that address children's authors and *Writers for Children,* edited by Jane Bingham, have been published. Monographs that approach children's literature with a variety of stances are being systematically published by university and commercial presses.

If these writings are not for us, then who can they be aimed at? Let me answer that question with a personal anecdote. When I first joined ChLA in the late 1970s, I was busy teaching children's literature in a way that fit with the theories of New Criticism. I was using a standard textbook of children's literature that discussed a vast number of children's books within genres and told the inexperienced adult reader of children's literature what was particularly good about the books. Because neither my students nor I had the time to read all of the books listed, we assumed that what was said was true. We were all passive learners in one sense or another. Once I joined ChLA and listened to those who were studying children's literature and pursuing the theories of criticism that were being talked about in English departments, I realized that criticism should have more of a role in deciding what I thought about children's literature and its place in the world of the child. I began to read as much as I could about ideas and attitudes concerning literature, children, and the ways the two interacted. That reading is reflected in this book's bibliographies.

In the end, I realized that Pickering was right. I might read and read, but unless I was forced to sort out my ideas and take a stance, I would not truly understand the role that children's literature might have in schools, in the home, in society as a whole. By 1980 I was a firm believer that children needed to be taught to read all their books—both those designed for educational purposes and those designed to entertain—in new ways. But I also realized that they could not be taught unless the adults they shared their literature with knew something about criticism and sorted it out for themselves. As a community of readers, we needed to read, to discuss, to write, and to learn how to share literature.

In 1990, Lawrence Lipking wrote that he had once received a letter from the National Endowment for the Humanities asking him to "list ten works that every American schoolkid ought to know" (8). He gave it a good deal of thought and finally made up a list and sent it in, but not until he resolved that he couldn't list ten texts that everyone should read. Instead, he listed ten theoretical pieces that contained arguments for diversity in criticism. Lipking concluded, "one can have worse effects on one's students than to teach them a scholarly skepticism toward flimsy evidence and glib generalizations. . . . If English teachers could do that, and cultivate a lifelong habit of reading, then the lights would go on all over America and the tubes would click off" (10).

In 1983, armed with Rebecca Lukens' book, ChLA's *Children and Their Literature,* and a reference listing of journals and books that would help the new scholar find a voice in the critical community, I began to teach college students that children's literature had not yet reached closure, that determining how to share it was still a hot topic among educators and librarians and psychologists and sociologists and countless others, and that they had a right to be heard. I found that the students became active learners and that I was learning as much from them as they were from me.

I have continued to share criticism as we discuss children's literature. Within our classes we explore various approaches to any one book we read, and we discuss why one book might be privileged over another. When the *Touchstones* volumes were released, we found a way of looking at literature that involved research, self-reflection, and personal interpretation.

My students have learned that they have a right to argue with the opinions of the experts in the field. But they have also learned that the privilege of arguing does not come easily. It involves researching ideas, reflecting on their meanings, and carefully shaping personal interpretations. However, as Debbie Padgett Boocher's paper shows, criticism gives the student of children's literature an active role. And it allows for the reader's voice in her or his final interpretation.

Debbie was one of several young women who compared the benefits of reading a Touchstones girls novel—in this case *Harriet the Spy*—with a popular book she had seen many girls reading when visiting the public schools. She kept a reader's response journal as she read both books, and I periodically read her comments and wrote marginal notes. I suggested that when she finished reading the books she might want to look at the article on Harriet in the *Touchstones* volumes. With these guidelines, Debbie started out on a quest of her own.

When we read Debbie Padgett's paper, we see how criticism shapes the reader's thinking, and how, if allowed to challenge what is read, the reader's attitudes will be more precise about how she reads and why she wants to share certain types of literature with children.

To be a Touchstone or Not to be a Touchstone:
A Comparison of *Beezus and Ramona*
and *Harriet the Spy*

BY DEBBIE PADGETT BOOCHER

Harriet the Spy by Louise Fitzhugh and *Beezus and Ramona* by Beverly Cleary are both popular books among children, but they have very different writing styles. Because the authors were writing for different children at different age levels, language usage and character development are dissimilar. *Harriet the Spy* has been acknowledged as a noteworthy book by the Children's Literature Association, while none of Cleary's books have had the same success. Yet, I believe that *Beezus and Ramona* is just as good as *Harriet the Spy*. Both authors remember their audiences and write in an appropriate style. Should one be favored over another?

"Who decides what children need to learn? . . . And who says what children like to read?" Perry Nodelman asks (4). The Touchstones Committee created a list of books that everyone on the committee agreed were significant. *Only* those books everyone agreed upon were accepted. This list represents, according to Nodelman, "the agreement of a highly diverse group of librarians, educators, and English teachers about which children's books have both merit and significance" (8). He asserts that the books are in harmony with the tastes and interests of "those who already have power: educated, relatively wealthy, male or male-dominated members of the establishment" (9). I would argue that the list attempts to "manipulate" what children will read. Nodelman agrees with this, stating, "Children's books which are always written by adults for children, always claim adult values; while adults can hardly be faulted for wanting to teach children what it cost them much pain to find out for themselves, the adult message to children is always conservative. This [list] . . . will serve an important purpose if it does nothing more than make that obvious . . ." (10).

Both of the books are family stories. *Beezus and Ramona* depicts the typical middle class family living in the suburbs. They spend time together as a family and do not really encounter any serious problems. Although the Quimby family may not be "picture perfect," the members are all sympathetically portrayed. Cleary gives her reader a humorous view of a typical family and the events that take place in their day-to-day lives. Fitzhugh, on the other hand, portrays the life of a lonely girl who is left in the care of her nurse, Ole Golly. Harriet's parents are never around to console her, and they do not spend much time with her. Her mother is busy attending all of the social functions of the elite, while her father is busy handling his business. Ole Golly is Harriet's family. The child sees a very different kind of family when she reads Fitzhugh's book. The fact that both books concern family relationships is the only similarity between the two books.

Beverly Cleary wrote *Beezus and Ramona* primarily for children in grades two through four. She really understands the language that children this age will comprehend. According to Margaret Novinger,

> Simplicity of style and manner is almost deceptive in Beverly Cleary's stories. She seems to be a natural story teller with an ear for the language of the contemporary child and an intuitive understanding of the unique personality of the child and his world. (81)

The language in *Beezus and Ramona* is, for the majority of children, very easy to comprehend and enjoyable to read.

Cleary has added a great deal of humor to her story. The humorous adventures of Beezus and her pesky little sister Ramona reflect events which could happen to anyone. Part of Cleary's success comes from using her own childhood as a source. "Ideas for individual stories are found in my experience, the experience of others, or the world around me," says Beverly Cleary (*Something About the Author* 63). This makes the story more enjoyable for the children who read it. They can identify with the "ordinary" children in the stories. They have seen children who were "sometimes naughty and only sometimes well behaved" (Novinger 71).

Children enjoy reading stories they believe could really happen. Cleary once said,

As I wrote I discovered I had a collaborator, the child within myself—a rather odd, serious little girl, prone to colds, who sat in a child's rocking chair with her feet over the hot air outlet of the furnace, reading for hours, seeking laughter in the pages of books while her mother warned her she would ruin her eyes. That little girl, who has remained with me, prevents me from writing down to children, from poking fun at my characters, and from writing an adult reminiscence about children instead of a book to be enjoyed by children. ("The Laughter of Children" 132).

Cleary achieves her goals in this book. The dialogue is natural and suitable for the characters involved in the action. The book is written for the child in the primary grades, yet it honestly portrays a family's experiences. Children can visualize all of the neighborhood children arriving at the Quimby's front doorstep on a rainy day to attend an unexpected party which Ramona had arranged without her parents' permission. It is easy to picture the children marching around the house playing parade with a few instruments and flags made from Mr. Quimby's handkerchiefs attached to rulers. Readers can imagine the children as they march in a straight line. They can watch Ramona unhappily participate in the events of *her* party.

Although everything is typical, there is never a dull moment in *Beezus and Ramona*. Critics have noted this about Cleary's writing style. When discussing Cleary, Mary Lickteig commented, "The stories are well-written and easy to read and reflect many real situations of being a child and growing up with insight and humor" (259).

What child reader would not enjoy the books about Beezus and Ramona? Beezus is a very mild mannered nine-year-old who sometimes is envious of her little sister because of her fabulous imagination and because of the attention she gets. Beezus does an incredible job, for a person her age, of putting up with Ramona and her antics. Ramona is four years old, and she exasperates Beezus. She is always up to something and is always getting into trouble. In addition, she is constantly around. Ramona will never permit Beezus to do anything or go anywhere without her, and she always manages to get all of the attention when they are together. She even intrudes on Beezus's one private project, her weekly art lessons at the park, and keeps the art teacher's attention through most of the lesson. The child reading can see why Beezus gets angry at Ramona.

The characters in *Beezus and Ramona* are life-like and natural. Children will see people like Beezus and Ramona in their lives, no matter where they live. They have typical nine-year-old and four-year-old sibling problems. This was Beverly Cleary's intent.

Writing for young readers was my childhood ambition. I was an avid reader, but I had had enough books about wealthy English children who had nannies and pony carts or books about poor children whose problems were solved by a long-lost rich relative turning up in the last chapter. I wanted to read funny stories about the sort of children I knew and I decided that someday when I grew up I would write them. (*Something About the Author* 63)

Cleary has achieved her goal and captivated the minds of the children who read her books.

Louise Fitzhugh created her book, *Harriet the Spy,* for older children. I believe that children in grades four through seven would be interested in her story. The language and format of the book suggest an older audience. In fact, the language may be too difficult for many children, even those in the seventh grade. Ruth Hill Viguers agrees, writing, ". . . many adult readers appreciating the sophistication of the book will find it funny and penetrating. Children, however, do not enjoy cynicism. I doubt its appeal to many of them" (443). Yet, this book is very popular with adult critics who can understand the deep, underlying meaning being conveyed through the words of Louise Fitzhugh. When discussing the book's significance, Hamida Bosmjian mentions the use of satire, and she notes, "Much of the humor comes from the distance the intelligent mind puts between itself and what it perceives" (74).

The characters in *Harriet the Spy* are complex. The main character, Harriet M. Welsch, is a very confused and lonely eleven-year-old girl. Harriet is not a romantic heroine. She is an outcast, first in her own family and later with her friends and classmates. Harriet keeps a journal and writes harsh perceptions about those she cares about. In the end, the other children find her journal and are hurt by her remarks. Ole Golly answers Harriet's questions with quotes from past read literature which will go unperceived by most youngsters. Usually, Harriet does not see their significance either. Harriet has two special friends. Simon Rocque, better known as Sport, is a motherless boy with an irresponsible father. Unlike Harriet, Sport is not allowed to spend his time on his own diversions. He is responsible for all household affairs; he cooks, cleans, does all of the laundry, and is in charge of the financial matters of the house. He is a boy who virtually has no time to enjoy being a kid. Janie Gibbs, Harriet's other friend, wants to be a chemist so that she can blow up the world some day in the future. She is continually rebelling against her parents. Harriet sees their problems accurately, but she cannot see her own. In the end, she changes her behavior patterns so that she will fit in better, but she is left still trying to understand herself.

I first read *Harriet the Spy* when I was in the fifth grade, and I certainly did not see the book as the adult critics do. I thought it was a great book because Harriet was different from any other character I had read about. I certainly did not learn lessons throughout the book. Even after reading it for a second time ten years later, I still did not see hidden, underlying meanings in the events. For example, I did not see Harriet's role as an onion in the school's Christmas play as having symbolic meaning, but according to the critics it does. Wolf writes that "she has learned to be an onion" (123), and Bosmjian calls the act "a symbol that becomes crucial in Harriet's growth." In fact, Bosmjian claims,

> Fitzhugh's choice of an onion is not accidental. An onion is a bulb beneath the ground; it is nourishing potential, not a fruit. As a symbol for the self it suggests something quite different from another symbol of the self: the kernel in the nut (the fruit of a tree). Both are compact, round, self-contained, but the latter signifies centered essence while the former projects the self as many-faceted, very much in keeping with the existential implications of becoming. (80)

In my opinion, no child would read this into Harriet's becoming an onion. Indeed, as Nodelman asks, "Who decides what children need to learn?"

I believe that *Harriet the Spy* is a very good children's book, but not because it holds hidden layers of meaning. What it holds for the child is unique characterization and unusual events. I believe that children will like it if they are allowed to read it for enjoyment. It will not really matter if the child understands the possible symbolism in the story. It will matter that the reader is enjoying Fitzhugh's characterization and plot. As a past child reader, I wonder, "Who says what (and why) children like to read?"

Two families, the Quimbys and the Welsches, contain interesting characters in intriguing situations. For the younger child, *Beezus and Ramona* is better than *Harriet the Spy,* and it deserves to be considered a Touchstones book for a less mature audience who will enjoy the humorous events, the sympathetically portrayed characters, and the easy-to-read narrative. Beverly Cleary sparks an interest in reading for young children. Her family stories cause children to want to read and introduce them to basic elements of family stories which they will look for long after they outgrow *Beezus and Ramona.*

References

Hamida Bosmjian. "Harriet the Spy: Nonsense and Sense," in *Touchstones,* Vol. I. West Lafayette, IN: ChLA Publications, 1985.

"Beverly Cleary," in *Something About the Author,* Vol. 43.

Beverly Cleary. *Beezus and Ramona.* New York: William Morrow and Company, 1955.

Ibid. "The Laughter of Children," in *Horn Book Magazine,* October 1982.

Louise Fitzhugh. *Harriet the Spy.* New York: Harper and Row, 1964.

Mary J. Lickteig. *An Introduction to Children's Literature* Columbus, OH: Merrill, 1975.

3

Looking at the Basic Elements of Literature

Reading is essential in America, even if it means only reading labels on food containers, logos of companies, or street and highway signs. This rudimentary decoding allows us to control our day-to-day activities and decisions. If we cannot read the label on a can in the grocery market, we cannot understand how many additives or preservatives have been used and we cannot determine what product is best for us. When we cannot follow a road map, we are afraid that we will get lost in a strange city and are less apt to travel. Not understanding written job memos means loss of power. Reading is a basic skill for living in today's modern world. Being able to decode the messages printed on can labels or read the road maps of a city or state allows for personal independence. As adults read and decide what they want to buy, where they want to go, they are taking respon- sibility for their lives. Since everyone wants to make decisions about how they live, they need to read more information than the listings found on cans or maps. And so, scholars have tried to determine the levels of reading proficiency for being a functionally literate adult. That information has helped establish what knowledge is needed for a person to be able to live successfully within society.

All societies use narrative to create traditions. Stories become a vital part of a group's daily world. As individuals tell each other about day-to-day happenings, they suggest what they believe should happen and their stories become allegorical narratives. Stories hold a structure that reflects heroic journeys, traditional holidays, and acceptable cultural practices. This struc- ture helps a group understand their interpretation of the world and their place in it. It is the structure that each culture places in its stories for children.

Most of us, when we begin to share literature with preschool children, automatically model certain literary patterns of literacy behavior. We help children pick out books by their covers, looking for attractive book jackets, clever or enticing titles, trying to pinpoint who the main character is, what the plot is all about, before we begin reading out loud. Sometimes, after we have shared the book, we ask, "Did you like that story?" or "I guess Peter Rabbit learned his lesson about running away, didn't he?" Then, we listen to see if the child liked and understood the story or watch to see if she wants it read to her again. If the book is a hit, we soon learn that one reading isn't enough. A child will pull a favorite book off the library shelf again. Once the rhythm of the story's text and the plot have been mastered, the child will readily "read the book" on her own. She already has discovered that reading is a pleasurable act, that it allows her to experience new adventures in the safety of her home or her day-care center.

Many of us remember our early trips to the public library where, if we were lucky, the children's librarian told us stories, taught us finger plays, shared puppet shows. Although the librarian did not always ask us if we liked the story, he invited us to follow him back into the children's room where we could select new books to take home.

Even if we weren't lucky enough to go to the library, we watched our parents read the newspaper, look at the ads that came in the mail, wait for bills and letters to arrive and be opened. Many of us anxiously awaited the first time we could go to school and learn to read. It is a highly anticipated act. I remember my older brother leaving school for his first day in kindergarten and telling me, "Tonight I'll read you the funnies." And, although I should have remembered that he didn't come home reading sentences after one day, I looked forward to my first day in kindergarten for the same reason: soon I would be a reader.

Even before children read, they hear stories. In fact, as a preschooler my interest in books had been instilled when my mother read stories to me and my brother began to read books on his own. Prior to school, I had already met characters who appealed to me and knew that picture books could take me to lands beyond my own back yard. I liked the children found on the pages of books. I hope adults will continue to share stories that have traditional plot structures and archetypal patterns found in children's literature.

Although many authors of children's books will say that they are not aware of their audience's age as they write, they may be more aware than they are willing to admit. They use realistic characters to draw their young readers into their stories. They try to create main characters that readers will like or sympathize with as they read. Although all authors try to create realistic characters, the characters found in picture books are different from those found in books for older children.

Psychologists have said that child's play is a work paradigm. Through play, the preschool child enjoys relating his imaginary world to the adult world of rules and structure. While playing, he can work out some of his social problems. He can discover answers to his questions about the world around him by imposing situations similar to those he meets in his day-to-day activities in his play. This is reflected in the heroes of preschool literature. Often they are involved in fantastic adventures, and impose rules on their imaginary playmates. Thus, the books become training grounds for everyday experiences.

The preschool child best identifies with a character about his own age. He wants that character to react in ways that seem familiar. He is looking for a vicarious experience in his stories, and he appreciates characters who act and talk like he would. Even when that character is involved in new experiences, he will feel most comfortable if the character behaves in predictable or logical ways.

Adult readers of children's preschool books sometimes forget that at this stage the child is ego centered enough to create a world of his own while playing in the real world. They misread preschool stories, making them cautionary tales. To the child, the stories hold solutions for dealing with adult rules. The child looks at the adventures as possible answers for some of his common frustrations. He cares less about the adult message of caution than about the hero's ability to solve his own dilemma. He is trying to make sense out of the "illogical order" of the adult world.

Like small children who play on their own, main characters in preschool literature act alone. They may interact with others, but they make their decisions based on their need to discover how the world works for them. Although they may begin their adventures at home, they usually venture away from the watchful eyes of parents. Once alone, they determine how to act for themselves—rarely are they influenced by siblings or adults. Almost always, their adventures lead to discoveries about themselves and the world they live in.

Ezra Jack Keats's hero Peter has a typical preschool hero's adventure in *The Snowy Day*. Peter wakes up to find that snow has fallen, and he goes out alone to play in the snow. Although he sees some older children playing together, he realizes that he cannot join their activities. And so, he entertains himself by drawing a straight line in the snow with a stick as he walks along, making snow angels, and packing some snow into a snowball to take into the house.

Children who know that snow melts will find Peter's attempt to bring the cold into his warm house humorous. They know that it won't work. The snow will melt. However, they will listen to see what happens, and will admire Peter for discovering on his own that snow melts. Even those preschoolers who have never experienced a day in the snow can identify with Peter and his winter play. He is adventuresome because he leaves home, yet he is content to investigate the area near his home. He explores nature, using a stick to draw in the snow, walking along and making snow prints. He is not disturbed to find that he will spend his day alone because he likes discovering how the snow works by himself. When his day is through, he tries to extend his pleasure by bringing in the snow.

Peter does not ask his mother or father what happened. When he finds that his snowball has melted, he simply concludes that snow cannot be brought into the house, and he hopes that new snow will fall so that he can play in it again. Children are apt to try to find answers to their questions also, and will admire and identify with Peter when they hear this story.

Traditional *bildungsroman* heroes fit a home-away-home pattern. The plot structure centers on the hero's journey away from home to prove himself, his success and triumphant return, and his receiving the hero's acclaim from his society. *The Snowy Day* seems to have the *bildungsroman* pattern. Peter leaves home in the morning to journey through the snow and returns home with new knowledge about the snow. His mother seems to be happy with him. After all, she lets him go out again the following day. But his understanding of the snow's melting is not part of this pattern. He does not discuss the snow's disappearance with his parents, and so he is not acknowledged with praise. Peter's journey cannot be successfully explained within the traditional journey.

The Snowy Day starts with the story's hero awakening. He sees snow and travels outside. This is the story's beginning. During the day the hero plays in the snow. At day's end he returns home with a snowball in his pocket. This is the story's middle. It contains the natural action that evolves from the story's beginning. At the end of the story, the boy awakens to see new snow and goes outside to play. This is the story's end. However, when we consider the story's entire plot, we feel that something is missing in this retelling of *The Snowy Day*. Couched within this simple story about a boy's adventures outside is a subplot about his discovery inside his house at the end of his day. If we define plot as simply having a beginning, middle, and end, we will be hard put to explain Peter's discovery that his snowball melts.

Perhaps *The Snowy Day* is best defined as having an adventurous plot with a happily-ever-after ending. It does contain a story that holds much action and very few psychological underpinnings. However, it is hard to argue that the plot is more important than Peter is. Keats is purposefully creating a believable and likable personality for his primary audience, the preschool child. Peter is a solitary hero whose adventures take him away from the security of his home. He returns home in the story, but at the end he is adventuring out once again, this time with a friend. His home-away-home pattern is continuous, and the last scene implies that he is encircling more territory with each venture away from his parents' supervision. As the author of a preschool adventure, Keats has realized the importance of a satisfactory ending. His book ends with new beginnings. The plot and main character successfully draw the preschooler into a realistic setting.

Picture-book writers carefully develop their settings. Some of these author/illustrators create books, such as *Goodnight Moon,* which have very little plot structure. All storytellers try to involve their audience in the story, using characterization, plot, and setting in believable ways. They mix the familiar with the unfamiliar to create plausible stories for their audience. When creating for young children, the successful author will describe the setting with some element of detail, being careful not to lose the reader's interest with long passages of description. The use of regional language or place names can pinpoint the story's setting.

Sometimes the child is drawn into the story through a quick scene. In Niki Daly's *Not So Fast Songologo,* the story begins with a lively family scene.

> What a lot of noise!
> "Weh, weh, weh!" Uzuti, the baby was crying.
> Adelaide was shouting, "Mongi, give me back my ballpoint pen."
> Mama was calling, "Malusi, hurry up! Come on Malusi."
> Next door, Mr. Motiki's dog was barking at someone coming up the road.

For the American child, this South African setting has both familiar and unfamiliar elements. Everyone has been in a situation of chaos at some time or another, and the family activity makes the scene seem realistic for all children living in a large family. But the children's names separate these children from many American children. They will be apt to consider where this story is taking place.

The second paragraph sets up the hero and introduces his problem. Daly's hero is Malusi, the youngster who "liked doing things slowly." Since many children don't like to feel rushed, they can identify with Malusi. He has, the listener is told, "very old tackies" that he inherited from Mongo. The listener knows by the word tackies that this story has a particular setting, and if he lives in a North America city, he knows it is not his area. Thus, Daly's text stretches the American audience's experiences while reinforcing familiar scenes of twentieth-century city life. Picture-book authors usually will establish regional settings with very few words.

As the child hears the story and looks at the illustrations, he becomes the main character in the story. Because the typical preschool child cannot read the words, he depends on the illustrations to retell the hero's adventures. A wise picture-book author/illustrator knows that the child will become the hero if the hero's adventures are plausible to the child, and if they are imaginative enough to capture his attention. Since the adventures are seen from the preschooler's perspective, the story need not contain adult supervisors. Clues in the illustrations are often related to ideas not found in the text. A close observer can grasp an idea not revealed in the written plot.

Uri Shulevitz's first-person text in *One Monday Morning* draws the listener into an imaginative adventure that would appeal to many preschoolers. Shulevitz begins his story with the illustration on the title page. A small peephole shows the tops of three building during a rainstorm. This peephole illustration is enlarged on three succeeding pages. On the next double-page spread, the perspective is changed. Now the buildings are seen through a window. Again, the peephole effect is used, but with a different perspective. A lumpy toy is first seen leaning against the sill; the second half of this double-page spread has a slightly larger peephole with a child standing beside the toy, peering out the window. The child and toy are linked before the story begins. Although the toy is a key to the "pretend" story in this text, it is never mentioned. The illustrations carefully detail the child's imaginary play and reference it to the text.

Shulevitz first depicts the rainy day as viewed by the story's youthful hero and later places a key symbol—the toy—in his scene. By the time the child is depicted, the viewer has been enticed into Shulevitz's tale. He accepts the child and his toy as main characters. Shulevitz has shown the viewer that the child is inside his apartment, looking out at the rain. His child audience is allowed to guess what will happen before the adult begins to read. Because children have seen rainy days, whether they live in the city or the country, they may have had experiences like the young hero. Probably they have spent some time looking outside, wondering when the rain will quit, when they can go outside again, imagining where they might be instead of inside. Preschoolers, then, can relate to the hero's feelings. They also escape from their mundane world by pretending that their toys come alive. Shulevitz's opening text, "One Monday morning the king, the queen, and the prince came to visit me" does not seem incongruous to children who use imaginary play in their everyday world.

There actually are two young heroes in this tale. One is the narrator who lives in his everyday world, and the other is the prince who leads a royal party to the boy's apartment and, finding no one home, declares that they will return on the next day. Shulevitz's use of the first-person narrative draws the preschool listener into the story. As he listens, he becomes the hero. As the adult reads the simple text stating that the hero is gone, the child "reads" the illustrations. He notices that the royalty's trips to the apartment are complemented by a visual drama concerning the child who is the first-person narrator. He is shown outside his apartment, doing things that young children do in the city: waiting for the bus, riding the subway, waiting for clothes to be cleaned in the laundry, bringing home groceries from the corner market, looking at toys in the stationery store, trying to fly a kite. As the visual reader, the child hearing the story knows that the book's hero is remembering what it's like to be outside doing things he can do on his own. Thus, as the child vicariously explores the hero's independence, he watches fancy visitors arrive at the boy's home. The listener sees that the narrator is an ordinary child who does not spend all his time at home, and is probably not upset when the narrator misses the royal prince and his entourage. Both characters are independently making decisions, and they are involved in parallel journeys. Both heroes are successfully carrying out daily adventures and dealing with minor disappointments. As a child in the real world, he probably identifies with the boy who lives in the apartment, but he also admires the prince. At the end of the text the young prince arrives when the narrator is home, declaring, "We just dropped in to say hello."

The written story has reached a satisfactory conclusion for a preschooler used to make-believe adventures, but the story's visual resolution continues. Three peephole illustrations follow. In the first, the boy is holding a Jack from a deck of cards, and other cards are shown laying face up on the table. They look like the boy's visitors from the earlier scenes. The second clearly shows the lumpy toy resting in a now sunny window. He has been the Royal Barber in the prince's entourage. The preschool child understands that the boy in the story used his imagination to escape a dreary day, much as he uses fantasy for the same purpose. The book ends with a small peephole showing that the sun is now shining over the three buildings. It brings a doubly happily-ever-after story for the preschooler. The hero first escaped from the rain by using the objects around him in imaginative play. Now that a change in the weather has occurred, the young child can go outside and play. The need for imaginative play is gone both for the listener and Shulevitz's youngster.

Two heroes in the same story are not uncommon in children's picture books. It is also not uncommon for one of the heroes to be a real child, the other a personified toy or object. For instance, in Raymond Briggs's *The Snowman* a boy awakens and finds that his snowman is alive. First, the boy guides his newfound friend through his house, introducing him to what seems to the snowman to be fantastic adventures. Once outside, the role is reversed, and the snowman leads the boy through uncanny adventures on a journey to the North Pole. When they return home, the boy goes to bed and the snowman to his place in the yard.

Unlike *The Snowy Day,* this story does not have a traditional happy ending. In the morning, the boy finds that his snowman has melted. This story has the home-away-home adventure pattern for the hero to follow, but does not end with an optimistic scene. The child hero's journey fits the traditional pattern, but his reactions once home are unique to this story, and he does not share them with his parents.

Picture-book authors seem to know that the youthful hero's journey is his alone. His new knowledge will help him cope in his day-to-day world, but it will not bring adult approval. Wandering out alone on a snowy night is not acceptable childhood behavior in adult terms, even if the independent journey does help the young hero better understand the natural world. Furthermore, adults will tell the young adventurer that snowmen can't come alive, so the adventure will not be believed even if it is shared. If Briggs's hero were to share his adventure with his parents, they probably would not believe him. Instead, they would explain it away as "a dream," and tell him that his snowman has melted, but that another one can be built on another day. If the author were to have adult sensibilities intervene, the story would not be a hero story. Consequently, the heroes in early children's literature rarely share their experiences with the adults around them.

Many heroes in children's literature set out on a circular journey. They leave their homes and families, travel on their own, return with new experiences, and settle into their daily routines. In fact, characters in books for children are largely solitary heroes. They rely on their wits and those friends whom they meet and trust during their journeys. Usually they are busy trying to understand how to fit into the society they live in, and they often defy cultural rules in order to be successful.

As children grow older, they read books that show them how other children solve their own "mysteries of life." Books that are popular with school-aged children contain youthful heroes who are finding out for themselves how to solve their problems. Although there may be kind and sympathetic adults in the stories, children rarely depend entirely on them for answers to their questions. Instead, they form associations with adults who help without explaining how or why they should do something.

One of the longtime favorite books of children has been Gertrude Warner's *The Boxcar Children*. First published in 1942, *The Boxcar Children* contains a simple vocabulary that can be read by children who are bridging the gap between early readers and lengthier chapter books. Because the story revolves around four youthful characters of varying ages and their attempts to survive on their own, older children with reading difficulties can enjoy reading the story. The children are orphans, and they are struggling for their independence. They strike out on their own and settle in an abandoned railroad car. In the end, they are discovered and reunited with their wealthy grandfather. These children are typical children's heroes. They are orphans, they search for a new home, and they learn to exist within new surroundings.

Children have enjoyed many of the classical heroes and heroines in children's books because they are gutsy children who independently seek solutions to their problems. Orphans are not uncommon in children's literature. *Anne of Green Gables, The Little Princess, The Book of Three, Johnny Tremain, Tom Sawyer,* and *Heidi* are exemplary tales whose main characters are orphaned. Nor is it uncommon for young heroes or heroines to be sent to live with elderly relatives or family friends. *Little Women, The Lion, the Witch and the Wardrobe,* and *Tom's Midnight Garden* all contain characters who have been relocated by their families for their own good. And it is not unheard of to isolate the child hero from all friendly adults or from society as a whole. *Alice in Wonderland, The Adventures of Pinocchio, A Wrinkle in Time,* and *Treasure Island* contain children who must survive in alien, strange worlds.

Memorable characters in children's books succeed because they dare to journey alone, to question their situations, and strive to understand why things happen as they do. When they are threatened, they react with trepidation, just as real children would, but they bolster their courage and continue to search for a positive ending to their story.

Characters in children's literature don't always have happy endings to their stories, and youthful audiences understand that. The child in Briggs's

The Snowman is left without his snowman. When one two year old understood the story's final scene, he looked up at his mother and cried, "Mama! Snowman gone!" Youthful readers quickly see that the sisters in *Little Women* must face their sister Beth's early death. Beth is nursed by Jo during her long illness before her death, and she tells her sister, "You must take my place, Jo, and be everything to Father and Mother when I'm gone. They will turn to you, don't fail them; and if it's hard work alone, remember that I don't forget you, and that you'll be happier in doing that than writing splendid books or seeing all the world; for love is the only thing we carry with us when we go, and it makes the end so easy." Girls have wept for Beth for generations. Most children's stories, however, allow their readers to experience tragedy while showing them main characters who survive and learn how to cope in serious situations. The characters change and gain a newly developed understanding about the events leading to the tragedy.

Children also read many stories that contain animals, toys, or other objects as main characters. Some, such as those in the series of picture books about Frances and her understanding family by Russell Hoban, are animals who live and act like people. They eat their food at tables, ride in cars and buses, and wear clothes. They talk to one another just as any group of humans in similar situations would. These *personified* animals, toys, and objects are replacements for humans. Generally, their stories are family stories in fantasy format. They remain true to human nature, and they can be allegorical. Some, such as Wilbur and his friends in *Charlotte's Web*, eat animal food or (if they're objects or natural elements) eat nothing, live as their species would, and shun clothing. However, they have the power of speech and use reason to solve dilemmas. These *anthropomorphic* personalities are found in more fanciful tales, usually written for a more mature audience than those in personified tales. Often they are involved in moralistic tales about human failings. As children grow older, they will discover that authors have written stories about animals depicted in accurate terms, true to their natural habitat and species. These *realistic* animals do not converse with humans, but they can show unusual loyalty to their human owners or cunning in the wild. The authors who have written these stories usually consider their audiences to be nearing or at adolescence. And, although the animal is essential to the plot, the humans who own them are the stories' main characters.

As readers grow older, they are faced with main characters who act in less than heroic ways. Characters are most believable when they face an unusual situation, learn how to cope, and develop an understanding about why things happened as they did. Then the plot's drama evolves around the author's main character, and becomes most effective when the story's audience identifies with the main character. If the plot's final resolutions to the character's conflicts seem plausible, the characterization will seem realistic to their audience. In the end, though realistically depicted children are less heroic, youthful readers feel strong alliances to protagonists who deal with complex situations and act in admirable ways.

All this suggests that the author's choice of characterization is very important. Characters usually reflect the author's implied audience. If we look at the hero's size and relationship to the adults in the story, we can predict who the author thought he was writing his story for. The author's choice of plot structure also helps us identify his intended audience. Children's books are not randomly written. They do have plots and characters that fit the needs of a particular audience.

Stories must have carefully structured plots if they are going to work. Authors who construct believable stories do not try to trick their reader. They create a series of events whose actions seem to follow a logical order, and they place characters in their stories who will capture the audience's imagination. These characters follow a plausible series of adventures. The child may feel the hero's adventure is like something he has encountered, or it may resemble something he has imagined. If so, the plot is predictable. It fulfills the reader's expectations based on prior knowledge or expectations. Reading and listening experiences that are pleasurable are often directly related to the child's earlier experiences. Once children understand how stories work, they enjoy the unusual. Often, they read a new genre without realizing that it strays from the patterns earlier shared.

Sometimes adults will not immediately recognize that the plot of a children's book is innovative, but will sense that its story is unusual. Sometimes the book will be praised for its characterization and discussed as a masterpiece in characterization, but it may be that an innovative plot has allowed the reader to enjoy the characterization. One example of an unusual book that seems to hold a typical fantasy plot is E. B. White's *Charlotte's Web*. Yet White begins his book with a realistic scene. The farmhouse where the child hero lives is alive with action when the girl learns that her father intends to kill the runt of the pig litter. When she leaves the house and runs through the wet spring grass, White creates a realistic picture of Fern's urgency, writing, "Fern's sneakers were sopping by the time she caught up with her father." Fern is a childhood heroine; she is defying the adults' rules of sensibility by demanding that her father let her keep and raise the pig. Once saved, the pig is brought into the kitchen. He is the center of attention, but his reactions to this attention are never discussed. Instead, White concentrates on the family scene. Sibling rivalry is introduced when Fern's father tells her brother Avery that he can't have a pig. Fern got the pig, he says, because she was "up at daylight, trying to rid the world of injustice. It just shows what can happen if a person gets out of bed promptly." During the first two chapters of the book, White concentrates on Fern and her reactions to her pet pig. The reader's attention is on Fern and the animal as a pet. Then, White abruptly changes his tactic. Fern is told that the pig has to be sold, and a sale is arranged. White ends his second chapter, telling his audience, "Next day Wilbur was taken from his home under the apple tree and went to live in a manure pile in the cellar of Zuckerman's barn."

The reader is forced to take on a new scene and a new narrative direction. A second series of adventures, loosely tied to the people first introduced, is established. The story's perspective is changed from a little girl's to a pig's. And, since this barnyard will contain anthropomorphic animals, the audience is reintroduced to the setting. This time, White draws the audience into the barn until it seems too realistic not to exist. He writes,

> The barn was very large. It was very old. It smelled of hay and it smelled of manure. It smelled of the perspiration of tired horses and the wonderful breath of patient cows. It often had a sort of peaceful smell—as though nothing bad could happen ever again in the world. It smelled of grain and of harness dressing and of axle grease and of rubber boots and of new rope. And whenever the cat was given a fish-head to eat, the barn would smell of fish. But mostly it smelled of hay, for there was always hay in the great loft overhead. And there was always hay being pitched down to the cows and the horses and sheep.

E. B. White has placed two very different plots in one story. One is credible in the everyday world; the other is an imaginary fable featuring anthropomorphic animals. Both depict Wilbur's plight as a farm animal: if he is not useful, he cannot be allowed to live. Wilbur's first brush with death ends in very realistic terms. Fern is allowed to raise the pig until he can be sold. His second escape is more miraculous. Charlotte, who is portrayed as a vampirish spider, spins words in her death trap to save Wilbur. Thus, a most unlikely heroine ultimately wins the heart of the reader and a most unusual plot seems plausible. Like many authors, E. B. White devised a compelling set of scenes to draw the reader into his story.

It is the author's ability to tie scenes together through characterization and setting that causes the reader to accept the unfolding drama. The characters hold the plot together. Almost all plots are somewhat episodic; however, since most stories contain the same set of characters throughout, the action seems to be tied together. The reader is familiar with the characters, and if the episodes reinforce the characters' previous thoughts and actions, the story makes sense. The same characters are involved in the central episodes, and their actions cause the story's resolution. In *Charlotte's Web,* White makes the actions of all the story's characters seem realistic because they are tied together in a particular locale and participate in a series of conflicts that seem appropriate to the book's various settings and end in the familiar barnyard.

Even though E. B. White's *Charlotte's Web* appears different from other modern children's literature, it is not unusual in its use of setting. *Charlotte's Web* resembles the earlier oral fairy tales that usually had two very different settings placed side-by-side within the plot. In addition, although these older stories often began in the house, the major confrontation almost always took place in a more dangerous environment. The two settings often foreshadowed something about the story's action and outcome. Often, both settings were explicitly identified in the beginning of the story.

In the traditional tale of "Hansel and Gretel," the sister and brother are first placed within their father's cottage, situated on the edge of a forest. Lucy Crane's 1886 English translation begins, "Near a great forest there lived a poor woodcutter and his wife, and his two children; the boy's name was Hansel and the girl's Grethel." Their survival adventures, which pit their intelligence against that of a cunning woman, begin when they are taken into the forest and abandoned. Lucy Crane starts her version of "Little Red Riding Hood" with a description of the little girl, and then continues, "Now the grandmother lived away in the wood, half-an-hour's walk from the village; and when Little Red Cap reached the wood, she met the wolf; but as she did not know what a bad sort of animal he was, she did not feel frightened." After reading a few folklore adventures that end up in the forest, including *Hansel and Grethel* and *Little Red Riding Hood,* the youthful reader instinctively begins to anticipate unusual adventures and realizes that in the forest "anything can happen." E. B. White's barn has a similar isolation. It is far away from Wilbur's first home, and is a dangerous place for a young pig.

Like many books of children's fantasy, *Charlotte's Web* contains the traditional folkloric structures of two settings: secure home and unpredictable nature. Fantasy often begins with the mundane life of the protagonist in a very ordinary, civilized world. *Alice in Wonderland* starts off in an English garden; the children in *The Lion, the Witch and the Wardrobe* have just arrived at the country house of a professor; Dorothy in *The Wizard of Oz* is living in Kansas with her aunt and uncle. Characters step over societal thresholds to begin their fantastic adventures, whether they fall down a rabbit hole, walk into a closet, or are spirited away in a cyclone. Once in their new lands, things begin to happen. Much of the early children's fantasy stories contained the distinct separation of the real and the unreal. The introduction of a second setting tips readers off to the fact that something fantastic is likely to happen in the story's plot. However, there is another traditional fantasy pattern found within children's literature.

Twentieth-century fantasy authors will sometimes rely on the Arthurian *bildungsroman* pattern. Based on earlier Celtic mythology, these stories are set in the fantasy world, an established and completely plausible place. Usually this land has a strong link to our perceptions of what Europe and England would have looked like during medieval times. Often, these well-known literary patterns linked to fantasy and legend are used. Sometimes the tales present new twists to old plot patterns. Always, the fantasy world is the real one.

For this to work, the imagined world must be linked to the reader's world. Typically, plausible countryside scenes draw the reader into the adventure before the fantastic elements are introduced. For instance, the twentieth-century American author Lloyd Alexander begins *The Wizard in the Tree* with a forest setting and a mystery, writing,

> Mallory's oak was down. It lay where the woodcutters felled it. The villagers hired to clear that stretch of woods had already moved on, leaving a wake of toppled trees and raw stumps. Once, Mallory had pretended the old oak was her enchanted tower that would stand forever; now it was sprawled with limbs tangled in the underbrush. She would have turned bitterly away, but then she saw it: a gray wisp curling from the trunk. Falling, the tree had split along much of its length and something was caught there; likely a squirrel or weasel. She hurried through brambles that plucked at her skirt, knelt, and peered into the crack.

Alexander expects his reader to have read fairy tales and other books of fantasy. Though his book will work for the inexperienced fantasy reader, it will be best enjoyed by a child already aware of the traditional elements of setting. That child will remember that wizards since Merlin have been doomed to exist in trees until they are freed by quirks of nature or, in this case, by man's disruption of nature. She will recognize that Mallory is alone in a forest setting and will realize that anything could happen. Alexander's next sentence—"What she had taken for the tail of some small animal was, instead, the tip of a straggling beard"—will not surprise the reader who has enjoyed fantasy and folklore. However, even the novice will expect a wizard in the story. After all, she picked the book up because it promised a wizard in a tree.

Science fiction authors use similar devices to get the reader into their newly established countries. Usually, they give the reader clues about their setting in their titles. Often they include prefaces, dedications, or introductions that offer some background to story's setting. Sometimes they format the book to hold clues about the story's outcome.

William Sleator's classic adolescent science-fiction book *House of Stairs* immediately tells the reader that the story will happen in a strange place. Step by step, Sleator sets up his book's format and, by implication, alerts his reader that the book is science fiction. The title tells the reader where the action will take place. The dedication, "to all the rats and pigeons who have already been there," warns the reader that this house will be a scientific experimentation station. The book is divided into two parts with an epilogue. Epilogues are attached to books with inconclusive or unfinished plot structures. They "tidy-up" the story's conclusions for the reader. Sleator begins his book with a description of the setting and the main character's alienation. He writes,

> The whirring around them had been going on for quite a long time. It sounded as though they were in an elevator, but the movement was so smooth that he could not tell whether they were being carried up or down or even to the side. Once again, as they had done several times in the past hour, his hands moved involuntarily to reach up and push the blindfold away from his eyes; and once again they were stopped by the cord that

bound his wrists. But he did not struggle against the cord. Peter never struggled.

Sleator and many other science-fiction authors write for an adolescent audience. Like fantasy authors, they expect their audience to anticipate events based on clues. They create plausible settings, but also ask their readers to suspend reality and imagine the reality of the impossible as they read.

Children's books can be created by teams of people. Then the illustrators and authors combine their efforts in picture-book presentations to create a scene and a mood for their story. Throughout their texts and illustrations, they work to help the child imagine what it would be like to step into the adventure. An author who wishes to write a realistic story about a commonly faced dilemma will sometimes give specific details that seem to pinpoint the setting but also cause the audience to believe that the story could have taken place in their locality. For instance, Barbara Cohen employs first-person narrative in her book *Molly's Pilgrim* to draw the reader in to the story. She begins, "I didn't like the school in Winter Hill. In Winter Hill they laughed at me." The artist Michael J. Deraney has complimented Cohen's text and help established a mood with his illustrations. He has embellished the simple introductory text with two full-page drawings. They establish the place and time the narrator is remembering. On the left, the viewer sees a young girl in turn-of-the-century clothes. She appears to be looking directly into the right-side scene, and is obviously unhappy. The right side depicts a two-story brick school in front of a muddy road. Children are walking into the school. They appear to be rushing. The setting is firmly established before the plot begins. And, when the words and illustrations are combined, a childlike feeling evolves. This little girl who will narrate her own story is recalling a difficult time at a particular school. The second double-page spread draws the reader into the drama. Cohen writes,

> Elizabeth laughed most of all. I never raised my hand to answer a question, but when Miss Stickley called on me, I had to say something. My English wasn't perfect yet, so Elizabeth always giggled at whatever I said. Miss Stickley would stare at her, and then she'd shut up. But later, in the schoolyard, she'd say, "You talk funny, Molly. You look funny."

The corresponding illustration shows Molly in the center of the schoolyard activity. She is sitting on a swing, but she is not enjoying herself. Her face scowls at the laughing girls who surround her. Both setting and mood have been created. Together, the author and illustrator have established a believable character who is facing a traumatic time in her life. And they have portrayed a realistic scene where their plot will occur. Furthermore, by placing the story in the past, they have suggested a story that seems less moralistic.

Settings are often clues to the story's final outcome. And they are clues to the story's genre. Fantasy, for instance, usually takes place in an unsettled land where civilization is forming; science fiction often evolves out of a scientific society that has placed technology above humanity; realistic fiction is traditionally depicted in a contemporary setting, whether rural or urban. Indirectly, the story's setting and time period establish the narrator's perspective for the audience.

Every story has a time period, even if it is not directly stated. Fantasy is often placed in the past, science fiction in the future. Realistic fiction happens in the past or the present, and it accurately reflects events and cultural attitudes. Authors choose a time period to fit the type of story they plan to write.

Many authors write contemporary fiction when they write books for children. When an author chooses to write about the society she lives in, she is writing for an audience who will see commonalities in the characterization, situations, and story's outcome. The story will tell its readers something about societal stereotypes, help them face everyday problems, and give some insights on current attitudes concerning childhood and its place in society. Two early children's novels written for female audiences demonstrate how authors write contemporary tales to help young people cope with similar situations. Both Louisa May Alcott and Lucy Maud Montgomery wrote girls' stories for a particular contemporary audience. Neither thought they were writing a children's classic.

Louisa May Alcott's *Little Women* contained episodes that evolved out of her life in New England during the Civil War. Set during that war, the story holds situations similar to those Alcott and her family faced. The book was first published in two parts between 1868 and 1869. Since the Civil War ended in 1865, Alcott knew that her contemporary readers had recently faced its rigors, were often "genteely poor" like the sisters in the story, and knew men who had returned home from the war with health problems. Furthermore, since the United States was experiencing its first wave of feminism during this time, the girls' attitudes are not uncommon to those expressed by young women who still held on to the American dream of a family and security while aspiring to a life beyond the parlor.

Lucy Montgomery's book was the second important contemporary girls' novel to be published in North America. Montgomery was living on Prince Edward Island while she was writing *Anne of Green Gables*. Published in 1908, the book reflected the youthful attitudes of her contemporary society, and the story centered on the trials of an orphaned young girl who longed to be accepted by those in her new home. Indeed, orphanages were common at the time, and children were often adopted more for their assets as farm workers than for their own needs. Montgomery was the wife of a minister, and she too was struggling to make sense out of the traditional standard of female success. Montgomery's writings allowed her to explore how she might combine marriage with her desire to have an intellectual career of her own. Both authors affiliated their heroines' happiness with the ideal of a happily-ever-after marriage while they depicted them as women who continued to maintain independent goals outside their marriages.

Often these two books are regarded as historical fiction. Readers point out that the books have identifiable settings and that the stories can be placed in a specific time period. The stories contain realistic elements and have become good representations of another time. Yet they were not written by authors looking backward. Instead, they were written by authors who suggested changes for their contemporary society.

Today's feminist critics who turn to Alcott's and Montgomery's books sometimes consider them weak representations of female attitudes and lifestyles. Those who view *Little Women* and *Anne of Green Gables* by our contemporary standards fail to remember when and why the books were written. It is important to recognize when the authors wrote their stories, why they chose their particular timeline, and how this timeline would affect their stories when viewed by their immediate audience. In the case of both Alcott and Montgomery, these female authors were writing contemporary fiction for a youthful female audience who had been encouraged to read *The Pilgrim's Progress* as pleasure reading. Many incidents included in the stories showed young women breaking the then-established traditions of society. Jo cuts her hair, an unheard of act in the 1800s; Anne dyes hers, an equally brazen act for the early 1900s. Both authors created high-spirited heroines who venture away from their home towns to attend school or seek further enlightenment, yet few girls were leaving their households to gain diplomas in higher education or to travel abroad with maiden aunts. The books showed a new sense of womanhood to young girls, one that would continue to entertain generations.

As time passed, some readers began to view the March sisters as staid and prissy in their behavior, and they saw Anne as an all too typical version of the happy orphan. The books began to be enjoyed as romantic fiction, and they were seen by many of their readers as nostalgic remembrances of the past. Yet the books were considered pleasurable reading because the setting seemed realistic, the characters had definite personalities, and they faced challenging situations in realistic ways. It is important to realize that these books have survived despite modern criticism, probably because the characters are perceived as naturally overcoming the obstacles they face to live happily ever after in their era. Thus, the characterization becomes authentic because of the timeline.

Some authors place their stories in the past. They have determined to write about past conditions and be accurate in their reflections of attitudes and events from other eras. It is important to remember that they are telling their stories about the past to their contemporary audience. Usually that means the story has some current significance. Often the author will try to alert her audience to the story's realism and its tie with the past.

One story that illustrates this is *Molly's Pilgrim*. Cohen starts her story with a narrative flashback, and the illustrations by Michael Deraney reflect a turn-of-the-century setting. The author and illustrator have set the story in the American past and have carefully distanced it from the reader's contemporary scene. Cohen's narrator tells her own story, becoming a storyteller and recalling a real situation from her childhood. To show the reader that the story is historically based, Cohen alludes to the story's history in her dedication, writing, "In honor of all the family stories that I heard during my childhood, and in memory of all the tellers, heroes, and villains of those tales—my grandfather, Henry Marshall, and my great aunt Molly Marshall Hyman." Cohen's dedication suggests that the story she is going to retell is a family story about becoming an American that was first told to the author either by the real Molly or by her brother. Because Molly is Jewish, she faces prejudice. Her problem is one not unique to the past. Contemporary children who have recently moved to the United States or whose families retain cultural traditions that are not mainstream continually face prejudice on school playgrounds. The story deals with a situation that could happen today. However, Cohen's narrator is a young girl who is shown overcoming these attitudes with the help of an understanding teacher; her reflections indirectly show children how to deal with prejudice without being too didactic.

The author's allusion to a time in the past helps distance the story, and it allows the reader to emphasize with Molly without feeling that the story is directed at her. Cohen's choice of perspective is equally important and is directly related to the story's significance as a true experience. By using the first-person narrative, Cohen forces the reader to identify with the heroine, whether or not she is from a minority culture. Cohen's narrator tells her own story, and the reader must consider the problems of prejudice from the child's point of view. However, because Molly's story begins with a flashback, the reader should realize that the storyteller is not a child. This is the grown Molly retelling an event from her past. And the reader should indirectly sense that this was an important event in Molly's childhood. After all, she has remembered and retold it when she was grown. Thus, Molly's story becomes a parable about prejudice. It contains events that were significant to the teller. Those events hold an experience for both the teller and the listener. Because Cohen has dedicated this book to the storytellers in her family, we know that the lesson Molly learned is one that Barbara Cohen learned by listening to her great aunt. Her vicarious experience as a listener has caused her to retell the story in a first person narrative, hoping that the story will affect her listener in the same way it affected her when she heard it.

As readers, we infer what the author's message might be. Our inferences are based on our experiences and our identification with characters in the story. If stories are placed in another time period, they force the reader to experience new situations based on different cultural values and expectations without feeling threatened by a contemporary scene. The stories distance readers from events while suggesting that the problems addressed by the characters still lurk in society today. The retelling of past values and expectations should cause the reader to reconsider his own society, to determine its strengths and weaknesses.

Authors create meanings for their stories through characterization, plot, and imagery. They suggest how the story should be interpreted by establishing a narrative style, using traditional literary devices of a particular genre, and setting up a narrative point of view. The meanings are implied; good authors will indirectly state their meanings. They strive not to preach. Since they hope to predict how the reader might react to their stories, they rely on images that have cultural significance, characters who fit certain stereotypes, language that suggests or predicts future outcomes in the plot. Most authors, however, do not purposely tell their audience how to respond. And they don't label their stories as ones written for a particular audience. It is to their benefit not to direct their text at one group of people. After all, children's books are read by adults and children, so the books do not have one audience. As texts with dual (or multiple) audiences, children's stories hold more than one meaning. The theme, or central idea, may be perceived in different ways.

The child hearing *The Snowy Day* may see the story as one that centers on a boy's independent adventures on his own. To him, the story may show how a child can discover answers to environmental questions through self-exploration and analysis. *The Snowy Day* holds meanings about independence and scientific exploration for children. To the adult, who already knows that snow melts and who often goes out alone, the story has less significance. It may remind him of activities that children enjoy in the winter. It may allow him to explore the idea of nature and the elements with the child. Or, it could show him that children of all cultures enjoy similar adventures in the snow. However, the adult will not see a direct application of the story's meaning to his world because he is not involved in childlike play.

The child viewing *The Snowman* will unconsciously see that there are two adventures in the story, and that in one the boy leads while in the other the snowman leads. He may be able to separate the real from the imaginary adventure, especially if he is old enough to know that snowmen do not come alive at night and that Santa Claus is a legendary figure. However, he may suspend reality and accept the entire plot as possible. If so, the story will have a different reality for him. Perhaps the youngster's plaintive, "Mama! Snowman gone!" is an apt explanation of the story's meaning for many preschoolers. The adult who views *The Snowman* sees several cultural and literary images that signal the story's outcome. For instance, the child awakens near midnight, a traditional time for inanimate objects and animals to become like humans in fantasy literature. And the adult reader knows that since the child is in bed, the adventure may be perceived as a dream sequence. Therefore, the story's outcome is more predictable. He knows that when the adventuring hero returns from his fantastic journey he will face a realistic world. The melted snow will not jolt him in the same way. The central question may be: "Can I place a melting snowman some-where else in my child's fantasy world?" Briggs seems to suggest that all snowmen flee warm weather and journey to Santa's neighborhood. If the adult reader wishes, he can suggest that the hero's snowman has just returned to the North Pole. Once done, however, he is creating a myth for the child. But Briggs's text implies that cultural myths are al-ready shaping children's fantasies. To the adult who is uncomfortable with these myths and their relationship to the real world, the story is a dis-turbing one without a central childlike theme for him to share with the child.

Many of the problems that arise from sharing children's literature in any setting stem from the dual textuality of stories written for children. Since the authors are adults, they can never fully comprehend how their stories will be received by their primary audience. They must write a story that works for them, hoping to remember childhood experiences and attitudes. Children's authors are also aware that just as they are not children, neither are the professionals who will publish and evaluate the worth of their stories. Books written for children face more direct censorship by pub-lishers and critics than books written for any other audience. Most chil-dren's authors understand this and carefully place meanings that are not necessarily supportive of the mainstream culture within the text. Their messages must be constructed around the child's perceptions, but they must be couched in a familiar structure that will appeal to adults. And so, children's literature texts hold traditional patterns and seem to address acceptable societal concerns about childhood and growing up, even when they are subversive.

Most adults don't know much about literary structures or interpretation. They judge a book on personal taste, saying something like, "I enjoyed that book because the characterization seemed realistic" or "The setting was accurate and the plot fit the genre." In turn, they share books with children in uncritical ways. Instead of looking at the book as a piece of literature, they regard it as a representation of cultural values. The meanings they see are usually adult ones. Because picture books seem to deal with situations that are not applicable to their day-to-day experiences, they assume that they have "outgrown" the author's texts. They do not relive their child-hood as the authors have. They pick up books that help them socialize the child to the adult world.

What if preschool children explored literature for its patterns? How might a teacher share ideas with a group of children to prepare them to become enlightened readers? These very questions were addressed in 1989 by Dana Hershey, a graduate student in my children's literature class who was also a preschool teacher. After reading articles written by Mary Ake, Sonia Landes, Anita Moss, Kimie Nix, and Jon Stott, Mrs. Hershey con-structed a preschool program. Throughout the semester, she kept a jour-nal, recording student responses and lesson plans. Once finished, she wrote about her experiences. Her paper shows what might be accomplished if literature was shared collaboratively, allowing for "child talk" as well as establishing an early introduction of critical theory.

Dana Hershey read critical theory prior to planning her lesson plans and created her own program designed around theories she felt were applicable to children's experiences. She determined to concentrate on settings, characterization, and the *bildungsroman* pattern in her classroom. These were all concepts she understood. Her efforts show that adults with knowledge about critical theory and children's literature can apply them in daily classroom activities.

Mrs. Hershey's activities were innovative. She was pioneering critical practices within an untested environment. Her study suggests that adults who understand how literature works and who plan their literature-sharing sessions will more effectively prepare children to be lifelong listeners, readers, and learners.

A Children's Literature Curriculum for Preschool Children

BY DANA HERSHEY

Teacher: Did Little Red Riding Hood learn anything on her journey?
Elise: No.
Nik: Never go in the woods alone.
Ryan: Don't talk to strangers.
Teacher: Did Hansel and Gretel learn anything?
Alex: Don't go in the woods alone.
Nik: No, that wasn't the question. They got left in the woods.
Teacher: So, they didn't learn anything?
Alex: Don't go into any houses.

Journal Entry

The four- and five-year-old children involved in this conversation are at the beginning of a journey of their own—the lifelong journey of literature appreciation. What makes this group of children different from other preschool classes is that they are being encouraged to think about, question, compare, and scrutinize the stories that are being read to them. Together, we took a journey through ten of the Children's Literature Association's Touchstones books.

I had always carefully chosen my books to share. After reading literature about children's responses to stories, I felt that these books might be shared in more critical ways. Stott's belief that "the individual who has a fuller understanding of a story can enjoy it more" (165) became my motto for our explorations. Mary Ake had asked, "Why not begin . . . with the kindergarten children?" (302), and I thought, "Why not begin with nursery school children?"

I developed a five-week program to share with a group of nine preschoolers. I was interested in two areas: Could pre-kindergarten children talk about stories and illustrations with a critical view? Could I develop a curriculum which would be developmentally appropriate and educationally sound? With this in mind, I selected criterion set up by Anita Moss and Jon Stott when they were working with older children. I wanted the children to recognize certain character types, specifically heroes, protagonists, antagonists, disobedient characters, and animal characters. I hoped they would be able to recognize how the journey worked in literature and distinguish between realism and fantasy by looking at the garden and forest as settings, discussing the conflict/resolution in stories shared. I wanted them to use color, design, details and size when they discussed the story elements emphasized in illustrations. I hoped they would begin to recognize the work of certain artists and see each story's uniqueness. Finally, I wanted them to learn that authors write their stories from a specific point of view.

During the first week of the project, we explored different versions of *Little Red Riding Hood* and *Hansel and Gretel*. Before I began, I asked the children, "What is a hero?" They replied, "Somebody that saves somebody" and "He gets the bad guys and takes 'em down." Immediately, some of the children named certain superheroes, including Robin Hood and *The Wizard of Oz*'s Tin Man and Dorothy ("because she melted the witch"). I asked them to listen closely while I read Bernadette's *Little Red Riding Hood* based on the Brothers Grimm version of the tale.

Throughout this reading, as through all the following readings, these non-readers paid close attention to the details in the illustrations. They were an active audience, talking about the stories during the presentations. I did not discourage all the talking because I interpreted it as a sign of involvement, but I did keep reading in order to maintain the flow of the story.

After reading the first story I asked, "Is that the same story as the one you've heard before?" A few children said "no," pointing out the differences in illustrations—Elise: "The wolf pulls the covers up"—and characterization—Jessica: "Mine's a woodcutter—has an axe." Grant and Stephen wanted more changes; they wanted a trap set for the wolf. I returned to the term hero to see if the children could relate it to the story.

Teacher: Who's the hero in this story?
Ryan: The hunter!
Teacher: Is the hunter who the story's mostly about?
Jessica: No—Little Red Riding Hood.
Nik: But, Little Red Riding Hood's not the hero.
Elise: Hunter.

During our discussion, I discovered that the children's definition fit with their interpretation of what a hero does, and we continued to use their definition.

Next we looked at Perrault's version of the tale. The children immediately began comparing illustrations. There were different opinions on the "best" and "meanest" wolf and which Red Riding Hood was preferred. Perrault's version ends with Little Red Riding Hood's demise. I read the story to the children, and they quickly pointed out differences of language—Grandmama instead of Grandmother—and story—Shayla: She never got saved! There was a lengthy discussion about which ending was preferred (three boys held out for the Perrault version) and which version was more likely to happen ("You can't cut 'em open." You could, too." "There aren't really wolves." "Uh-huh—only in the woods.")

Hansel and Gretel, illustrated by Susan Jeffers, took about twenty minutes to read. The entire class was fascinated with the plot as well as the illustrations; the book held their complete attention. Shayla, particularly, became engrossed with the idea that the witch and the stepmother were the same person. She was first alerted to the idea when the witch used the stepmother's very words, "Get up, you lazybones," and expressed confirmation when she learned that the father's wife had died, exclaiming, "See, she was the witch!" This book became a favorite at free time with the most popular event of Gretel pushing the witch into the oven continually re-enacted.

I introduced the literary term "journey" once both stories had been shared, and we reviewed the journeys of Little Red Riding Hood and Hansel and Gretel. As a group we drew murals of both journeys. I drew the basic elements which the children dictated, and they added the details. Each student added embellishments to the Little Red Riding Hood mural, including a self-portrait by Shayla and a very elaborate grandmother's cottage by Jessica. The children spent most of their energy on the first mural.

Nik: When we draw Hansel and Gretel's, will you draw a house like that for the witch's house?

Jessica: I don't think I can.

Jessica did not draw a second house.

We returned to Little Red Riding Hood once more, this time sharing Trina Hyman's version. The children were intrigued by seeing yet another view of the same story. Most of them agreed that they liked "all of The Little Red Riding Hood books." Finally, our week ended with the beginning discussion of the journey.

Week two centered on *Goldilocks and the Three Bears* and *The Tale of Peter Rabbit.* The former story had already been claimed by these children; they enjoyed arranging the entire classroom for its dramatic presentation. This time I read Leslie Brooke's version to them. The children thought that "Goldenlocks" was funny— and wrong. They didn't believe the girl in the illustrations looked like "Goldilocks." They did like the bear motifs which decorated much of the house, and they closely scrutinized Middle Bear's quilt. I showed them the versions by Jan Brett and Armand Eisen, and they said they preferred these illustrations. During our discussion, the children couldn't decide who the story was really about. Some felt it was Goldilocks's story, while others said it was more about the bears than the girl. However, they all agreed that the bears took a journey, and they noted that all three of the stories shared so far took place in a forest.

A few children were familiar with Peter Rabbit. Again, they all were interested in listening to the story and exploring the illustrations. Nik, a child who came to school with a wide literature experience, became very involved in the project from the start. He was quick to point out connections between stories and to draw conclusions. When I asked how *The Three Bears* and *The Tale of Peter Rabbit* were alike, he quickly responded, "They went on journeys."

During our small group time, my aide and I wrote down the children's dictated versions of the two stories. One group retold *The Three Bears* from Goldilocks's point of view; the other group retold their story in the first person, using Peter Rabbit as the narrator. These children found retelling the stories in the first person difficult, but they could easily retell the plot structure of both stories.

Week three began with *Millions of Cats,* a new book for all of the children. The children immediately picked up the repetitive chant, and a few joined in each time it was read. Jeff and Alex had earlier been discussing what the biggest number was "in the world," and so they literally lit up when they heard, "Hundreds of cats, Thousands of cats, Millions and billions and trillions of cats."

When we finished reading *Millions of Cats,* we made a chart of the animals from the stories read. The children identified and described the animals as:

wolf	mean
	hungry
three bears	curious
	nice
	angry
Peter Rabbit	naughty
	fast
	into the garden
	under the fence
	lost his clothes
cats	millions and trillions
	fighting
	one didn't fight
	they thought they were pretty

The question, "Which of these animals is most like real animals?" initiated a very interesting discussion. At first, all the animals received votes. Then Alex, who had shown very little interest in academics throughout the year, said, "No, they all acted like people." The children debated how the animals acted like people, and narrowed it down to their ability to talk and their wearing clothes. All the children except Alex eliminated the animals who wore clothes and chose the wolf and the cats. Alex, in an uncharacteristic display of independence, refused to vote for the two, maintaining that real animals did not talk.

Finally, we took a popularity vote to see which animals were liked best. Six children voted for the cats, one voted for Peter Rabbit, and one voted for the wolf. The remaining child was absent. Perhaps the children voted for the cats since that was the last heard story. However, they did list a part of the rhyme in their discussion, so perhaps the story appealed most to them.

We had read *The 500 Hats of Bartholomew Cubbins* two months earlier, so I tried a framing activity with the class. I explained that when we hear a story we form pictures in our heads, and these pictures are what we remember about the story. The discussion continued:

Teacher (holding up book):   Do you remember this book and what it was about?
Students: The 500 hats!
Teacher: That's right! Who was the boy?
Stephen (very distinctly):   Bar-tho-lo-mew.
Teacher: Great! Do you remember his last name?
Stephen and Nik: Cubbins!

Teacher: Wonderful! Now, I want you to tell me what pictures you remember in your heads about *The 500 Hats of Bartholomew Cubbins*.

They came up with the following list. (Parentheses indicate information that was added after teacher probes.)

The little boy (King's nephew) tried to shoot off his hat with a bow and arrow.

A big guy tried with a great big bow and arrow.

That one guy couldn't chop off his head if his hat was on.

(The last hat—number 500) was big and had a whole bunch of feathers and a golden thing on it.

The King liked it so much he gave Bartholomew gold for it and he took the gold home to his family.

(First the King was mad because Bartholomew didn't take off his hat, but he really did.)

(Bartholomew lived in a little cottage.)

After this, I mentioned that many stories have a problem and asked what the problem was in this story. The children responded, "He couldn't take off his hat."

We wrapped up the third week with an old favorite of mine, *The Story of Ferdinand* by Munro Leaf. The children told me they had seen the story on the Disney channel, which explained why they occasionally cut in to tell the story themselves. No one could identify the hero in the story, so I told them we were going to learn two long words: protagonist and antagonist. The protagonist, I explained, is the main character in the story, and the antagonist is the person who makes the protagonist act. Although the children did not readily add the words to their vocabulary, they remembered the concepts and continued to use them throughout the year. During this conversation they showed that they understood the terms:

Teacher: Who is the protagonist?
Children: Ferdinand.
Teacher: Who is the antagonist?
Children: The bee!

After some discussion, they allowed that my choice of the five men from Madrid as the antagonists could be included, and they discovered that a story can have more than one antagonist. Next we discussed the idea of the journey. That evening I wrote in my journal:

"How about a journey? Is there a journey in this story?"
Everyone agreed there was one; Ferdinand went to the bull fight. I asked if he went anywhere else, and they answered, "home." I told them as I drew a circle in the air that this was the circular journey of stories. He left home and came home again. "Did Ferdinand want this journey?" Someone said, "No, he wanted to stay and smell flowers." In the middle of our discussion, the children reached an Aha! moment of exploration. Nik said, "Hey, I know something about Peter Rabbit!" I asked what. "He went on a circle journey!" I asked him to describe the journey and he said, "home-garden-home." I drew in the air and asked the others what they thought. They all agreed. Then Jeff, who had lost interest in the recent sessions, said, "The cats' story!" I asked him

what he meant, and he replied, "There's a circle in there too!" I probed some more and he explained that the man had gone on a circular journey to get the cats. He added that the cats had only gone one way and had been eaten up. Then Nik said, "The three bears went on a circle journey." We all talked about that and agreed that they did, but we didn't know about Goldilocks since we don't know where she went at the end of the story. I brought out *The 500 Hats of Bartholomew Cubbins* to see if a protagonist, antagonist, and circular journey could be identified. (Bartholomew Cubbins; the King; yes). The children also noted that Bartholomew didn't want to go on his journey either. He set out to do something else.

I felt very pleased with our progress. The children displayed real enthusiasm and application of the literary concepts found across the stories. The discussions that had evolved provided a strong case for Nix's assertion that "Reading a book of fiction trains long-range thinking skills like no other facet of education. Readers . . . must remember an extensive and cumulative amount of material, and they must respond emotionally as well as intellectually to the material" (132). Three weeks of questioning and critical discussion had revealed the capabilities of preschool-aged children to employ thinking skills as well as their enjoyment of the process. I believe the project has implications for these children as future learners. The skills of attribution, categorization, comparison, and retrieval from long-term memory will continue to be important throughout their educational careers.

The fourth week was dedicated to the chapter "In Which Christopher Robin Leads an Expotition to the North Pole" from Milne's classic book *Winnie-the-Pooh*. Although the children were familiar with the characters of the story, they did not like this format. They disliked the illustrations, saying things like, "He doesn't have any clothes on!" and "He doesn't look like the *real* Winnie-the-Pooh." We talked about the difference between this story and Disney's version.

As we read, much of the humor had to be explained to the children. They did, however, get the joke about the North Pole. In the end, the children were equally divided in their preference of Pooh over Ferdinand. Most of the children decided that Pooh was the hero, but Nik argued, "It's Christopher Robin's story too." We concluded our week by bringing teddy bears and going on a rainy day expotition which Nik said turned out to be a "round journey."

During the final week we looked at the Caldecott Award-winning books *The Snowy Day* and *Make Way for Ducklings*. I brought in other books by Ezra Jack Keats and Robert McCloskey, and the children spent a great deal of time exploring the illustrations together. We had done collages, and they were excited to see a photograph of that art style in one of their books. Since they had already made collages, I decided to have them try to draw something to look "real" like McCloskey had.

By the fifth week I could see a definite difference in this group of children as listeners. In the past, when I had shared *Make Way for Ducklings*, the children had lost interest in the monotone illustrations. This group sat attentively. They not only followed the plot, they enjoyed the humor and were impressed with the illustrations.

At the end of the fifth week I asked them which book they had liked best. Although each child could name a favorite, Alex's response—"I just like all of 'em"— best sums up their feelings. Looking back at my journal, I realize that children can develop critical responses and I believe that we do them a disservice by just reading stories to them. Furthermore, I believe that children need to continually experience literature and to be allowed to question, compare, and form their own evaluations of the books they read.

References

Mary Ake. "The Touchstones in the Classroom," in *Touchstones: Reflections on the Best in Children's Literature,* Vol. I. Perry Nodelman, ed. West Lafayette, IN: ChLA Publications, 1987.

Jan Brett. *Goldilocks and the Three Bears.* New York: Dodd, Mead, 1987.

Leslie Brooke. *The Story of the Three Bears.* London: Frederick Warne and Co. Ltd., n.d.

Armand Eisen. *Goldilocks and the Three Bears.* New York: Alfred A Knopf, 1987.

Wanda Gag. *Millions of Cats.* New York: Coward-McCann, 1928.

Jacob and Wilhelm Grimm. *Little Red Riding Hood.* Illustrated by Bernadette. New York: Scholastic Book Services, 1971.

Trina Schart Hyman. *Little Red Riding Hood.* New York: Holiday House, 1983.

Susan Jeffers. *The Brothers Grimm Hansel and Gretel.* New York: Dial, 1980.

Ezra Jack Keats. *The Snowy Day.* New York: Viking, 1962.

Munro Leaf. *The Story of Ferdinand.* Illustrated by Robert Lawson. New York: Viking, 1936.

Robert McCloskey. *Make Way for Ducklings.* New York: Viking, 1941.

A. A. Milne. *Winnie-the-Pooh.* New York: Dell, 1926.

Kimie Nix. "On Producing Brand New Book Lovers," in *Children's Literature Association Quarterly,* Vol. 12:3.

Charles Perrault. *Little Red Riding Hood.* New York: Henry Z. Walck, Inc., 1972.

Beatrix Potter. *The Tale of Peter Rabbit.* New York: Dover, 1903.

Dr. Seuss. *The 500 Hats of Bartholomew Cubbins.* New York: The Vanguard Press, 1938.

Jon C. Stott, ed. "Teaching Literary Criticism in the Elementary Grades: A Symposium," in *Children and Their Literature,* Jill P. May, ed. ChLA Publications, 1983.

4

Rhetorical Style
in Children's Literature

If you look back on the past two chapters, you will determine that there is a conversational tone to this book. I use first-person pronouns when I discuss my experiences and my reactions to literature. Sometimes I use the plural pronouns we or us, suggesting that we are having a dialogue and that I am thinking about you as I write my remarks. At other times I focus my conversation directly at you, using the personal pronoun "you" as I write. When I do this, I am suggesting that I am aware of who you are, of how you will respond to what I write.

You are not experiencing a random choice of voice. All authors consider the sort of impact they hope to have on their audiences and pick the appropriate voice. The tone the author chooses is related to his attitude toward the subject he is writing about. The author's writing style suggests his mood.

Most school textbooks are written in the third person. The reader is not drawn into a conversation because the writer does not want to appear to be relating "fictions." The author's tone implies that the information presented is valid, that it should be considered valuable and noteworthy. Although most textbooks do contain real information, they are not infallible. Facts and events are chosen by an author when he is presenting his interpretation of a factual account. Ways of presenting science and math are shaped by authors who have convictions and believe in certain pedagogical standards. Textbook authors tell their readers what they wish them to know often less because they wish to censor than because they cannot begin to tell their readers everything. Since textbooks provide broadly based information about subject areas, they relate generalized stories or principles. And, because they omit details, they are inaccurate in their coverage.

Critics who are interested in discovering the author's voice in his writing are often called *rhetorical critics*. They carefully examine how the author uses writing as a means to communicate with a specific audience, and they discuss the author's efforts to instill a particular idea, attitude, or belief in his reader. Rhetorical critics look at writing as persuasive argumentation that presents a point of view and assumes the reader can be persuaded to agree with their conclusions.

Some critics have argued that authentic *nonfiction* can never exist because all authors are bound by their own perspective of reality. They tend to drift toward certain subject matter and include it in their explanations of a subject. Today, many schools of criticism are skeptical of absolute realism in texts. People who work as *Marxist or social critics, feminist critics,* and *minority critics* often will *deconstruct* a text in order to reconstruct or reinterpret the author's implied messages. They argue that writers cannot form a neutral text, that they are influenced by their experiences, their ideologies, and their audiences when they shape their writing. These critics believe that no text can be entirely neutral or objective.

Many critics in children's literature suggest that children's attitudes are manipulated by the seemingly authentic approach in their nonfiction, *historical fiction,* and *realistic fiction* literature. Yet critics in children's literature seldom primarily judge children's literature for its authenticity. And authors of children's literature are rarely considered subject experts in a particular field. Many of the texts we share with children are not masterpieces of research. Instead, they are reflections of what one author and publishing house agree is appropriate for a child to read. Authors of children's nonfiction books are not evaluated for their research. They are usually judged by the same standards used to discuss the works of children's fiction.

In 1981, Paul Heins discussed historical treatments in children's literature and commented,

> One thing ought to be clear to us from the start. We are not dealing with history per se, for most of us are not concerned with the subject matter of history but rather with the presentation of historical material in literary form. . . . It would take factual inquiry—research, as we call it—to determine, or rather to weigh, the reliability of the facts reported. In dealing with children's literature, we obviously want to have assurance about facts . . . but we expect that liveliness, I would rather say the life-like quality of the presentation, is what concerns the teacher and the librarian as well as the critic. (1)

One of the most respected authors of children's nonfiction, Milton Meltzer, has written several pieces explaining how a "story" is created out of reality. On one occasion, he explained that the author of biography must read anything he can to piece together a life and "create character" (18). He claimed that the biographer need not tell a chronological story, that he could use his information in an imaginative way. And he argued that nonfiction books should be regarded as stylistic retellings, concluding, "In reading history and biography, then, one listens to a writer's voice. In that voice he tells his story . . . [and] must meet the task of any writer: being read" (19).

Critics in children's literature have continually argued that the same events in history can take on different meanings, depending on the author's notion of reality. One of the most prolific and respected Marxist/feminist critics, Jack Zipes, argued in 1981 that children's literature has often been used to "socialize children." Zipes wrote,

> Literature for children acts as sociopsychological agent, legitimizing and subverting. . . . It uses many disguises, masks tricks, and illusions. Literature seduces and challenges children to take sides, see, grasp, tolerate, hate, dream, escape, and hope. Words in print form a context, a frame, in which possibilities for work and play are pictured, as projections of a better life. . . . Literature for children is script coded by adults for the information and internalization of children which must meet the approbation of adults. (19)

Critics like Zipes look at literature as a force within society that is used to manipulate attitudes. They suggest that the author's rhetorical style controls the reader's response, and that the author shapes his writing to fit his adult attitudes about what is "best" for the child's life within the culture surrounding him. Indirectly, these critics suggest that if children's literature is carefully analyzed as language used to form cultural values, it will not reveal "truths reprinted" but will instead show adult interpretations of reality. Rhetoric can create an illusion of truth by the perspective used within the author's retelling of known facts.

If we take history as an example, we can see how this works. Children's literature can use rhetoric to create a purposefully developed image of history that favors a particular view about the past. Often, this image offers a reflection of cultural attitudes. Textbooks seem to present the one "true" vision. Teachers sharing these textbooks often teach from guides written to reconfirm what has been stated in the text. One point of view is stressed. The children who are taught to view reality in this way begin to assume that events happened in a particular way.

Simplistic textbooks have several unfortunate consequences. They cause one generation to view certain attitudes or ideas from a particular point of view. In the end, the children who learn from textbooks become adults who hold certain prejudices as truths. They observe peoples in other cultures from one point of view—usually a point of view valued by someone who is not a member of that culture.

The vision derived from textbooks is similar to the visions we get of wild animals at the zoo. Though we see their exterior features and hear their ways of communication, we cannot perceive how they respond to us or how they feel when we disrupt their natural behaviors. Those people and animals who are reflected in stereotypical ways become victimized because we think we know how they exist and feel, but we fail to consult them. Often, during times of stress, these same groups become contemporary scapegoats.

The early treatment of Native Americans in our U.S. history presentations shows how this can happen. Early textbooks for elementary schools and representations in children's literature stressed the peaceful settlement of Europeans among Native American peoples, and concentrated on events in a way that implied that controversies evolved from the Native Americans' "primitive warlike ways." These works not only oversimplified Indian lifestyles, they also contrasted Native American life with the lives of the European settlers to suggest that the European onslaught on Native American property was unavoidable.

Although there were some earlier attempts to discuss European attitudes about Native Americans, Roy Harvey Pearce's *The Savages of America,* first published in 1953, presented an in-depth description of American history's stereotypes of Native Americans and their place in history. As a literary scholar with an interest in how cultural images cause people to view history, Pearce researched early Native American images in narratives and discovered that the Indian became a "symbol" in literature. Because the European settlers wished to place their invasion in a positive light, they represented the Native American as a primitive subgroup of heathens. Thus, the idea of savagism was introduced in their narratives. Writers played down the idea that Indians fought to survive the invasion of foreign peoples. And they continually linked Native American attitudes to a more primitive time, thus stripping Indians of their own cultural history. As a result, "American history" in literature began with the settlement of the Europeans. The earlier societies were "written out" of literature, and the only role given the Indian was precultural. Even when writers tried to view the Indian in a favorable light, he was shown as a person devoid of the "cultural mannerisms" held in common by the invading Europeans. In the end, the "noble savage" in literature became a stereotype of a man who refused to be civilized and who could not survive within white man's higher, more sophisticated and "civilized" culture.

When any subject is controversial enough to evoke varying interpretations, it can be presented in conflicting ways by various children's authors who wish to recreate historical events for young audiences. In 1920, Olive Beaupre Miller's third book in the "My Book House" series contained Annette Wynne's traditional rhyme "Indian Children." Wynne's careful use of the word native to reflect the European children suggests that the land always belonged to the settlers. In addition, her implication that religion did not exist in Indian cultures and that the land was full of wild and dangerous beasts gives the feeling that these people were primitives without an understanding of their spiritual essence or desire to live in civilized ways. The author uses a personal voice, contrasting "us" with them." Her comparison between the civilized European and native cultures is clearly seen.

Indian Children

Where we walk to school each day,
Indian children used to play—
All about our native land,
Where the shops and houses stand.

And the trees were very tall,
And there were no streets at all,
Not a church and not a steeple—
Only woods and Indian people.

Only wigwams on the ground,
And at night bears prowling round—
What a different place to-day
Where we live and work and play! (93)

Early award-winning children's literature contained similar images of Native American cultures. These were a reflection of contemporary cultural attitudes. At the beginning of the 1940s Newbery Award committees picked historical presentations that contained vengeful images of Indian peoples more savage than the ones found in Wynne's poem.

In 1940 the Newbery Award committee selected James H. Daugherty's biography *Daniel Boone* to win the Newbery medal. Daugherty paid homage to a man he described as belonging "to the Indians and the buffalo" (6). Yet, by the end of the book it is obvious that the Indians Daugherty portrays are bellicose and full of revenge, and that Boone was noble to stand up for them.

Daugherty deceptively begins his descriptions of Native Americans by saying that the Indians in North Carolina were "friendly" (15). As the book progresses, he depicts them rather differently. Gradually his use of imagery and adjectives changes. Once settled in the Yadkin valley with his wife, they are portrayed taming the Native American forest. Daugherty concludes his scene of settlement, saying, "in a few years [Boone] had a going farm and two fine boys, all busy with crops and cattle and snake fences" (21). The fact that Boone's home was on Indian land is not stressed, but the danger of Indian attack is. Daugherty writes,

> The white families knew only too well how the fierce red warriors would surround the cabins just before dawn, terrible in the ghastly white and black war paint, fearsome images of violent death that haunted the dreams of every border family. Nearing the fort the Boones met other refugees with stories of frightful Indian vengeance. Five savages had hacked in the door of one cabin, desperately wounding the man; but his wife with an ax had killed three as they came singly through the door, and had in the same manner dispatched two more who had climbed down the chimney. There

were hundreds of such stark tales around the border forts and settlements. (22)

Daugherty's omniscient perspective leads the young reader to believe that the Native American peoples are the interlopers, not the white settlers. Further, because Daugherty depicts a woman defending her house and wounded husband against "five savages," he implies that the white male is not the aggressor in the scene and that Indians preyed on women without regard to their being the weaker sex. Later, when describing Boone's explorations in Tennessee and Ohio, Daugherty writes, "He knew that the Kanawha flowed out of the Alleghenies and into the broad Ohio, that perilous Indian-infested highway to the Mississippi" (26–27). Again, he is stressing that the Native Americans are varmint who need to be cleared away to keep the land clean for the trespassing white settlers.

The artwork in *Daniel Boone* has been praised in Sutherland and Arbuthnot's children's literature textbook *Children and Books* for its "heroic illustrations . . . [which] have vigor" (144). Daugherty continually shows white men fighting Indians. The Shawnees warriors are sinewy and fierce. They are depicted with muskets, tomahawks, and knives, often creeping toward their human prey and hacking away at the white settlers. Daugherty's use of perspective places the Native Americans outside civilization. He never shows an Indian woman or child in his illustrations, thus implying that they either did not exist or were not important. Sutherland and Arbuthnot also rely on rhetoric when they defend Daugherty's as a valid interpretation of Boone's life and assert,

> It is true that both Indians and blacks are treated in an offhand manner by Daugherty. But that is how Boone would have perceived them and to criticize Daugherty for not making Boone a twentieth-century liberal is overstepping the boundaries of critical analysis. (460)

The choice of language is significant. By calling Daugherty's treatment of Native American peoples "off handed," these two critics justify Daugherty's style, and imply that it was inspired by real events from Boone's life. Further, they argue that depicting Boone as a man who considered Native Americans in another way would be suggesting that he was a "twentieth-century liberal." Thus, Sutherland and Arbuthnot's discussion dismisses earlier criticisms concerning the inaccuracy of the representation, calling them ideological arguments rather than criticisms expressed by critics who have long studied literature. In the end, such discussion privileges one opinion over another in a way similar to the earlier arguments of the New Critics.

Yet all critics must be taken into account; they give us new ways of looking at books without demanding that we accept their "readings" of a particular text. For instance, Leonard S. Marcus discusses the values of the d'Aulaires' artwork in their picture-book biographies, and he suggests a way of looking at illustrations within all children's biographies. Marcus comments, "in biographies and other books that largely deal with the past, illustrations put a face on the abstraction of *pastness*, placing this concept more readily within the reach of children whose more familiar experience of time is that of continuing present" (17). Put another way, the illustrations of the past often become the contemporary child's interpretation of past events and peoples. If I take Marcus seriously, then I must examine the text for perspective and discuss it with youngsters.

A close look at the illustrations in *Daniel Boone* will show that Daugherty's depiction of the Indians was not "off handed." In fact, not one Indian is shown in a nonviolent scene until page 54. Then two Shawnees from a war party that captured Boone and several other male settlers are depicted with Boone between them at a bargaining table inside Detroit's English fort. Of the scene, Daugherty writes,

> Boone was as persuasive with the British as with the Indians. He showed his commissions as a captain in His British Majesty's army and told of his fictitious plan to capture Boonesborough in the spring. Hamilton was delighted with him. But when it came to selling his prisoners, Black Fish insisted that Boone was his personal property and he was not for sale, even though the general raised the price to the fabulous sum of one hundred pounds. (54–56)

The remaining illustrations of Shawnee images depict Indians at war with the white settlers. It is interesting to note that Daugherty chose never to place Boone in a scene inside a Native American community, though he mentions two times when Boone was held captive in a Shawnee village.

The author's point of view, when he is also the illustrator, is more clearly defined in his pictorial representations. An adept illustrator/writer is capable of shaping his audience's response to the events and people depicted. Marcus warns that illustration does convey messages, and he says that "the experience of fine illustrations remains irreducible. Along with what it tells us about values, temperament and concerns of a biographer's central character, fine illustration also puts us in contact with an individuality—and a form of praise—that is esthetic" (17). Unfortunately, Daugherty's illustrations are stylized representations of reality. His white men are all muscular and rough hewn. His women contain strong, almost masculine physiques, and they too are homespun figures. And throughout the book, Daugherty makes no bones about his responses to Native Americans. Bereft of families and social structures, the Indians are being portrayed as aggressors while the white population is shown as a "settled group."

In 1942, *The Matchlock Gun* won the Newbery Award. A highly evocative adventure story, it tells how a small boy was able to save his mother from Indian raiders while his father was away protecting the fort. Once again, an author concentrates on the imagery of marauding savages who attack innocent children and women. The author's language sympathizes with the plight of early white settlers. He begins by explaining that "The

Van Alstynes were real people. . . . Their lands [in Germany] were dev-
astated by war; they were politically persecuted by both French and Ger-
mans; and they left their homes, going first to Holland, then to England,
and finally coming to America because they wanted to be free" (viii–ix).
Throughout the text, Edmonds paints two enemies for the family: the
French who have invaded their area and the Indians. Ironically, he also
observes that this "free loving" family has slaves, writing, "Gertrude explained that all the place really belonged to Teunis, so that Grandmother's
slaves were actually theirs" (18). The first thirty-eight pages of the story
allude incessantly to the possibility of an Indian raid. Finally, the Indians
arrive and Edmonds writes,

> There were five of them, dark shapes on the road, coming from the brick
> house. They hardly looked like men, the way they moved. They were
> trotting, stooped over, first one and then another coming up, like dogs
> sifting up to the scent of food. Gertrude felt her heart pound hard; then it
> seemed to stop altogether. (39)

Edmonds's climactic scene, which includes the Indians wounding Gertrude and Edward's killing at least three Indians, happens in five pages.
Once again, the author's language implies that Native Americans are less
than human. Edmonds compares the warriors to dogs, thus suggesting
that they are despicable. He tells of the final encounter with the Indians
twice, once from the mother's perspective, once from the young hero's.
Concerning the killing of the Indians, Edmonds writes,

> A tremendous flash, a roar that shook the stoop under her, and a choking
> cloud of smoke removed them. She saw the leader cave in over his own
> knees and the next two flung back on their shoulders. She saw nothing
> else at all, but she knew that Edward had touched off the Spanish gun.
> (43)

The author uses a third first-person narrative to give the story authenticity.
He credits oral family stories of the Van Alstynes as his source. This makes
his book legendary history. It gives the drama a definite point of view.
While the author emphasizes the family's need to defend themselves
against intruders, no attention is given to the fact that the land the family
lives on was once Indian territory. The need to have land of one's own is
stressed, but underlying this ideal is the reality that these people are slave
owners and that they have enslaved others for their benefit just as others
persecuted them for personal reasons when they lived in Germany. Taken
as history, the book implies that slavery was less odious than religious
persecution.

Both Newbery books purport to be based on actual events from the past.
Yet they do not contain the absolute reality of past times. While they
most definitely are recreations of U. S. history, they are not unbiased
recounts. Their use of perspective and details favor one way of looking at
the events. The rhetorical styles of these books will affect the reader's

interpretation of historical information about the relationships between diverse cultures.

A 1955 runner-up for the Newbery Award and the recipient of the Lewis Carroll Shelf Award, *The Courage of Sarah Noble,* is also based on historical legend. Again, the author attests that the story is based on history, and again images of Native populations as savages are used, even though Dalgliesh says her message is that these peoples were "friends." When the female protagonist first confronts the Native American children in *The Courage of Sarah Noble,* Dalgliesh tells her reader,

> The Indian children stared at her. Then they came nearer. Soon Sarah found that all around her was a ring of children, standing and sitting, staring, staring with their dark eyes. The spring sun shone on their brown bodies, and Sarah realized with a shock that they were not wearing clothes—unless you could call that one small piece of cloth "clothing." Sarah, secure in dress and cloak and petticoats, felt very well dressed indeed. (26)

When Dalgliesh explains in her author's note that this is a true story, she adds, "It might have happened in many other places in America." Then she goes on to assert that the settlers of New Milford "dealt fairly with the Indians, according to the standards of their time, and were always friendly with them." Since the book is written for the beginning reader, the qualifying phrase "according to the standards of their time" may be misread to mean that they were kind. For a more sophisticated reader, the phrase raises the question of "what standards?" Dalgliesh's third-person voice is authoritative, and her tone causes the youthful reader to accept this story, to see the events from Sarah's perspective, and to concentrate on the "courage" of a little white girl rather than understand the hospitality and intelligence of the Native Americans she is forced to live with while her father travels back east.

Thus, publishers and authors of books about American Indians and their encounters with the Europeans have often given young readers a distorted perspective of reality. While not intentionally censoring Native American history, these authors have left out the Indian viewpoint in favor of images of New World's early settlers. Furthermore, these early children's literature authors never considered that Native American children might be readers, that if they did read their stories the Indian children would have to accept discussions of events from a different perspective than the one *their* culture's legends would support.

Recent U.S. history textbooks at the college level do relate the drawbacks as well as the advantages of European expansion into the Americas. In *These United States: The Questions of Our Past* (first published in 1978), Irwin Ungar writes,

> Contact with Europeans injured the native American peoples even when Europeans intended no harm. Because of their long separation, the peoples of the Old and the New Worlds had developed immunities to differ-

ent diseases. Europeans encountered a virulent form of syphilis in America, and it quickly spread over all of Europe. . . . The Indians suffered far more. Even European childhood diseases like measles became killing scourges among populations without protective antibodies. Smallpox, too, along with tuberculosis and cholera, hit the native populations hard. . . . In 1656 Adriaen Van der Donck reported that the Indians of New Netherland claimed "that before the arrival of the Christians, and before the smallpox broke out amongst them, they were ten times as they are now . . . ." Indeed, the English and Dutch occupations of the eastern coast were greatly facilitated by the European diseases that had spread to North America from the south even before the Europeans themselves appeared and decimated the native populations. (21–22)

By the early 1970s these conditions were being reflected in children's literature, and American authors were writing a different story. Again, the authors used descriptive language and narrative point of view to stress a historical perspective. Two authors are representative of writing since 1970.

Peter Collier wrote and published the children's nonfiction book *When shall they rest? The Cherokees' Long Struggle with America* in 1973. Collier looks at events with sympathy for the Cherokee, and he brings these events alive by taking into account Native American feelings and perspectives. While Collier's history is an accurate one, filled with dates, writings, and real events, it is also his interpretation of a great American travesty. Collier is outraged at American indifference to Indian treatment, and wants to elicit the sympathies of his reader for the Native American's plight. He carefully recreates dramatic scenes from history to evoke a mental picture of a proud culture. He begins his historical journey in 1775, writing,

At a remote spot on the southeastern frontier called Sycamore Shoals in present-day Tennessee, a tall, muscular Cherokee stood up and looked at the Indians and whites seated around the council fire. His hair was raven black, and obsidian eyes glinted out from a face badly scarred by smallpox. When he began to speak, his hands accompanied his words with angry stabbing movements. After gesturing scornfully at the whites around the fire, he began to reproach the elders of his own tribe who had just taken part in the biggest land sale in frontier history. They had signed over what is today all of Kentucky and much of Tennessee to these white speculators in return for two thousand dollars and a cabin filled with cheap trading goods.

When Dragging Canoe, as whites called this man, had finished his bitter speech, he paused for a moment and then made a last prediction that one of the white men wrote down. "Soon the whole country which the Cherokees and their fathers have so long occupied will be demanded, and the remnant of *Ani-Yun'Wiya*, The Real People, once so great and formidable, will be compelled to seek refuge in some distant wilderness . . . . Such treaties may be all right for men who are too old to hunt or fight. As for me, I have my young warriors with me. We will have our lands!" Then he stalked out, to spend the rest of his life waging war against the white settlers creeping a little farther into his people's country each day. (7–8)

Collier's suggestive descriptions depict a different sort of American drama. He describes Dragging Canoe as angry and proud. In Collier's account, Dragging Canoe's hands stab the air as he speaks, and he scorns the white men in the audience. When Collier describes the pox marks on Dragging Canoe's face, he alludes to past events that have affected the Cherokee. Later, he will use another literary device—flashback—to explain how smallpox ravaged Dragging Canoe's people. Then Collier writes,

> There is strong evidence that whites used this dread disease as an early form of germ warfare in their relations with some eastern tribes, spreading it by the gift of blankets that had been exposed to the disease. But the Cherokees got smallpox that had been incubated in the filthy holds of the slave ships docked at Charlestown harbor with their black cargo, and then spread like wildfire through the whole of the Southeast, a symbol of the moral infection slavery was bringing to the New World. (20)

Although Collier's book is nonfiction, it meets the goals of all good literature. It shapes events into an *aesthetic experience*. It is Collier's ability to place the various types of documentation into a flowing narrative that makes his book successful for his readers. Collier has rewritten the old stereotypes and has asked his readers to consider what happened to the Cherokees who once lived in a country controlled by different kinds of laws and customs. The heroes in *When shall they rest?* are tragic heroes. Collier is retelling history to inform white children about the deprivations the Cherokee faced. Collier's story is based on real events and people; he has turned to documents and personal accounts to prove his point. But he is telling his story out of frustration and anger. His rhetoric has been chosen to influence his readers to believe that his perspective is truer than earlier ones.

In his "Author's Note," Collier comments that Indians have long been an ignored people within America, and he adds that they are usually remembered only during times of crisis. Collier notes, "The eminent American jurist Felix Cohen once commented that this nation's treatment of the Indian is a miner's canary for our democracy: it indicates the amount of poison in the political air at any given time" (151). Peter Collier's stance has political overtones. His writing of history can be termed revisionary, and it is purposeful. He hopes to reaffirm the Native American perspective in American interpretations of the European invasion of the United States. However, because he retells the events as they have been recorded in documents, first-person accounts, anthropologist works, and scholarly historical research, Collier's work is more objective. He is not relying on one family's or one village's interpretation. And, since his first-person accounts include both Native American and white statements, he is not simply presenting "the other side of history."

Collier's adjectives create an attitude about events and people. When he tells of the white hunters and sportsmen, he says they "penetrated to the heart of the Nation," implying that their movement stifled the existence of tribal life. Further, he notes the progression of white settlers into the lands of the Cherokees, calling it "drastic" and an "invasion . . . by hordes of whites." When he mentions the slaves already in the territory, he claims they are owned by "wealthy mixed bloods," implying that the full-blooded Cherokees were not a part of the oppressive society in charge of the countryside. What Collier does is to shape a reaction. Yet his retelling is not dishonest; using documentation and interpretation, he forms a sense of history for his reader just as a fiction writer forms a sense of reality. Collier seems intent to use the ideas that evolved from historical, literary, and anthropological scholarship about the American formation of the Indian as a stereotype in a reshaping of the past that will create a sympathetic interpretation of the Indian in the United States.

Milton Meltzer has continually argued that historical nonfiction is an artistic endeavor, that it relies on the author's ability to shape fact into a sensitive retelling of events. He believes that nonfiction is the expression of knowledge and that the author purposefully controls his language to create a response. Concerning the author's task, he says,

> In writing true history, you are dealing not simply with the what and when of events, but also with the why and how. If you do not always have an easy time determining what happened and when, you are sure to have a much harder time finding out how it happened. For it brings you to the heart of what history is about—human behavior. That is the subject novelists deal with; it is just as much the subject for historians. ("The possibilities of nonfiction," 114)

The fiction writer who chooses to create a reality around past events is involved in a similar process. She, too, is reshaping history to show something about human behavior. Like her historian counterpart, she relies on past events and peoples to recreate the past. Yet she has the ability to create scenes and conversations that bring the past alive in more personal ways.

Joyce Rockwood, an anthropologist who depicts the first European invasion into Cherokee land, decided to place her retelling in a fictional context. Using knowledge garnered in anthropological studies, she concentrated on the daily lives of a village. Her main character in the novel *To Spoil the Sun* is a woman who retells the events. Rockwood begins,

> There were four omens. I was young, only nine years old, when the first omen came. I heard it discussed around the fire, told and retold until it became a part of my own knowledge, until it became as if I had witnessed it myself. . . . When in the same winter the second omen came, it was for everyone to see. I remember it clearly. It began with a thunderstorm that awakened me in the night, a violent storm with beating rain and crashing thunder. I lay frightened in the darkness and heard my mother say to my father, "Thunder in the winter. It is not good." (1, 3–4)

Rockwood's book starts out with warnings and with Cherokee interpretations of foreboding "signs" about future conditions. Her purposeful choice of first-person narrative causes her reader to respond in a predictable way. When the reader listens to the narrator's beginning, a sense of uneasiness settles in. Part of this uneasiness comes from Rockwood's use of flashback to begin her tale. The reader understands that the narrator needs to recreate the past in order for her to come to grips with events that have taken place. Because the narrator does not explain why these omens are important, the reader is left to speculate about their significance. She understands that the narrator will do more than simply retell events as they happened to her; while she is retelling what occurred in her village, she is creating her history. And, since she begins with a cautious tone, the reader expects a tragedy. The heroine has established herself as a tragic hero who will be alienated from her society. Her retelling of the four omens gives another time and place a sense of reality that could not be achieved if Rockwood had chosen to retell her story in the third person. Rockwood has a sympathetic narrator tell her reader about the lives of one group of sixteenth-century Cherokees who were ravaged by a smallpox plague. In her "Afterword," she explains that Rain Dove and Traveler "could not be real, not in the literal sense" because the Cherokees left no written account of their individual lives. However, she argues, their story is realistic because it is based on knowledge of Cherokee life that has been "established by archeologists, historians, and anthropologists." Then, she goes on to say that the events, such as the plague and the invasion of Europeans, are not ones she fabricated; they are based on documented Europeans records describing the discovery and exploration of America (177).

Realistic fiction holds some of the same elements as nonfiction, but it is freer in its interpretation of the past because the author is not compelled to represent actual events and people. Unlike Edmonds's *The Matchlock Gun* and Dalgliesh's *The Courage of Sarah Noble,* Rockwood does not claim that the people in her story really lived. Yet she does say that her interpretation should fill a void in history. Rockwood concludes,

> These are events which have never been regarded as greatly significant in our history books, and perhaps they never will be. They are but obscure sentences in the first paragraph of the story we tell about ourselves. And the Indians, so momentously affected by these "minor" events, are never glimpsed by us at all. (180)

There are those who argue that literary studies has denied diverse cultures the right to speak for themselves. Critics from divergent ethnic groups lament that many interpretations about their people and their literature have been penned by authors who are not members of the group depicted. While they applaud carefully constructed interpretations like those of Collier and Rockwood, they suggest that much is lost by denying the minority its own voice in literature. Many critics link the lack of minority texts with the earlier support of European mythic patterns in archetypal studies. They argue against a canon in literature that lacks cultural diversity. Arnold Krupat, a noted critic who studies Native American literature, has argued, "any proposed canon of American literature that does not include more than occasional examples of the literatures produced by red and black people as well as white people—men and women, of indigenous and African as well as European origins—is suspect" (53).

Native American authors are not represented in the Children's Literature Association's canon, nor are they found on many prize-winning lists. All the representations of Native Americans on the Newbery list, other than the hotly contested runner-up book, *Anpao: An American Odyssey*, written by Jamake Highwater, a self-proclaimed Native American whose ethnic roots have been disputed by academics and Native Americans alike, have been written by white authors. Highwater's strong prose and imagery are rooted in Native American myth and legend, but they do not come from his childhood experiences alone. As a student of Indian cultures, he has served as American Indian consultant for special programs of the New York Council on the Arts and has written about Native American art, music, and myths. Yet his book is not based on the history of any one tribe, and he does not claim it to be a historical representation of Native American life. Highwater writes that his book contains "an Indian 'Ulysses' who could become the central dramatic character in the saga of Indian life in North America" (240). If Highwater's background is discounted, it becomes even harder to find a Native writer who has been acknowledged by literary critics as a fine writer. The history of Native American exclusion demonstrates how some ethnic groups have been treated in the field of children's literature.

Is it possible that nothing noteworthy has been written by Native Americans? Recently, literary scholar Arnold Krupat has pointed out that some representations in literature are available, though they do not hold the same patterns as literature from the European and American canon. He argues that their forms depend on their cultural images in oral stories and adhere to the preservation patterns that work best within their particular tribal cultures. Concerning all standards of cultural literacy, he writes,

> Native American literary production, when we pay attention to it, offers texts equivalently excellent to the traditional Euramerican great books. It is not only that these texts should be read in the interest of fairness or . . . [as] charming examples of "primitive" survivals: they should be read because of their abundant capacity to teach and delight. . . . [It is necessary] to recognize that the ways in which they delight is different from the ways in which the Western tradition has given pleasure. (54)

Native Americans have not tended to write down their stories and their history. Instead, they performed them orally. And often their stories are poetic in form. Performed rather than simply told, listened to at clan gatherings, danced out or re-enacted during ritual celebrations, these stories capture the cultural beliefs and traditions of the various tribes. Because the early white settlers could not understand Native American languages, they viewed these tales as gibberish. And because the Native Americans handed down their tales in oral form, Europeans did not study them. Europeans believed that civilized peoples preserved their histories in written forms, and they defined these Native peoples as "primitive." Yet contemporary museums devoted to Indian artifacts easily dispel such logic.

Artwork and ritual objects that reflect divergent Native American day-to-day patterns demonstrate that while Native religious practices varied from tribe to tribe, the various tribes were rich in traditions and beliefs. For example, Hopi and Papago baskets hold symbols reflecting their deities and legends. The Kachina dolls of these tribes also represent cultural heroes and legends. Carved and painted Indian masks of various Southwest and Northwest Indian tribes that were traditionally worn by those who participated in spiritual impersonating ceremonies are Native American icons derived from cultural stories. When discussing Native American poetry, A. Grove Day wrote,

> Some of the finest American Indian poetry is to be found in the great ritual ceremonials of the various tribes. These religious observances— some of which extended over many days and in which the entire tribe took part—form the only sort of Indian poetry which may be called dramatic in the sense of being comparable to our plays or pageants. . . . The dramatic *katzina* songs of the Hopi tribe were, of course, associated with the tribal religious beliefs. The masked dances of other southwestern tribes also represented the gods come back to earth, incarnated in ritualistic symbol and song, to mingle with men and share in their joys and labors. Therefore if we wish to find any evidence of the origins of dramatic poetry among the Indians, we must seek it—as we seek it in ancient Greek literature and in early English literature in the miracle plays—among the religious ceremonies. (63)

Children's books with Native American poetry were not readily available before the 1970s. However, during that decade several books were released. One of the earliest and most noteworthy collections, *In the Trail of the Wind: American Indian Poems and Ritual Orations,* was published in 1971. Editor John Bierhorst introduces his selections by noting at that time the sparsity of the "record of Indian life" from the perspective of the Native American voice, a voice he said was held in "the so-called oral literature— the songs, chants, and speeches—of the people themselves." Bierhorst acknowledges that part of the problem comes with translating Native American oral texts, and defines his collection as one largely composed of literal translations with "the words . . . rearranged with perhaps a few additions and subtractions to make the text comprehensible" ("Introduction," unpaged). The poetry is chronologically arranged and contains a different point of view of Native American life from the one children had seen in earlier books. Further, the poetry's strong use of imagery and of repetition attests to its literary attributes.

Bierhorst includes several poems describing the creation story, including this one from the Navajo.

First Man Was the First to Emerge

You say there were no people
Smoke was spreading
You say there were no people
Smoke was spreading.

First Man was the very first to emerge, they say,
Smoke was spreading.
He brought with him the various robes and precious things,
they say,
Smoke was spreading.
He brought with him the white corn and the yellow corn,
they say,
Smoke was spreading.
He brought with him the various animals and the growing things,
they say,
Smoke was spreading.
You say there were no people
Smoke was spreading. (9)

The rhythmic text paints a picture of man arriving on the earth, bringing those things that were essential for the tribe's existence. Although Navajo history prior to the European invasion holds stories of a strong and fearsome nation, the reference to corn shows that these were also an agricultural people. Our visions of their past are tempered if we read their ritualistic poetry.

Later, Bierhorst includes a Navajo prayer to the spirit of the owl, an incantation to a spiritual god that resembles the religious prayers of all civilizations. Like the people of the Old Testament in the Bible, these people performed ritualistic ceremonies of offerings and sayings that might help them have better crops, happier lives. The prayer begins,

> Owl!
> I have made your sacrifice.
> I have prepared a smoke for you.
> My feet restore for me.
> My legs restore for me.
> My body restore for me.
> My mind restore for me.
> My voice restore for me.
> Today take out your spell for me. (34)

Again, we are exposed to a poem that holds repetition. The tone is reverent. The speaker is calling out to the owl, addressing him as a supernatural spirit who can understand the language of the Navajo. At the close of this prayer, we are aware that Navajo ritualistic chants and ceremonies linked nature to the needs of the human community. Further, the poem includes a spiritual blessing for those involved. One stanza says,

> Happily may I walk.
> Happily abundant dark clouds I desire.
> Happily abundant showers I desire.
> Happily abundant vegetation I desire.
> Happily abundant pollen I desire.
> Happily abundant dew I desire.
> Happily may I walk. (34–35)

This poem shows that the Navajo expected the spirit of the owl to hear them and help them. It comes from a community of people living in harmony with their surroundings and demonstrates that harvesting and weather are essential to happiness in the Navajo village.

Finally, Bierhorst includes a lengthy poem that has been divided into movements. It reveals the ritualism of the planting and harvesting of corn. Each movement personifies the corn as a spiritual food that replenishes the community. It concludes with a historic perspective, saying,

> Since the ancient days, I have planted,
> Since the time of emergence, I have planted,
> The great corn-plant, I have planted,
> It roots I have planted,
> The tips of its leaves, I have planted,
> Its dew, I have planted,
> Its tassel, I have planted,
> Its pollen, I have planted,
> Its silk, I have planted,
> Its seed, I have planted. (118)

The singer becomes historian and priest at the same time. He keeps his culture's traditions alive, and bestows them with a ritualistic reverence.

Bierhorst's collection is valuable because it is respectful of the poetry's origins. Each poem's source is included. Furthermore, Bierhorst includes a discussion of each poem's meaning and form, referring the reader back to the original sources he used.

In 1972 Doubleday published *The Whispering Wind: Poetry by Young Native Americans*, edited by Terry Allen. The editor has collected the work of promising young Native American poets who attended the Institute of American Indian Arts in Santa Fe, New Mexico. Allen explains the school's founding and its continual commitment to educating talented Native Americans, writing, "Opened in 1962, the student body since that time has included representatives of from seventy to ninety tribes of American Indians, Eskimos, and Aleuts" (xv). Three of the young writers trace their heritage to Navajo roots. These twentieth-century poets reflect their Native American traditions in their poetry. A quick sampling of the works of all three shows their depth in style and tradition.

Gary Cohoe was born in Shiprock, New Mexico. He attended the Institute 1965–67 and then the University of Arizona (23). His poetry contains strong imagery of the Southwest and of nature. Like his earlier ancestors, he speaks of nature as a spirit.

Alone Together

The tree stands, beautiful and valiant.
    She stands alone.
Now, in autumn, she holds out a yellow blanket
    inviting winter to its folds.
In the snow, she stands slim and tall.
    Her bare arms cry and pray for spring.
The seasons bring her snow, rain, and wind.
    Still, she waits for love.

I will taste her kiss and be merry
    because of her sweetness.
My feet will dance to the drumbeats, rattles, songs
    of the wind in her hair.
Her blue shadows are forever.
    The tree is now.
When the tree is gone,
    the blue will be blown into eternity.
I love her so much
    I want to be buried in her shadow
so I can be with her forever. (26)

Calvin O'John is of Ute-Navajo descent. Born in 1946, he attended the Institute during his high school years. Later, he moved to Oakland, California. When interviewed before *The Whispering Wind* was published, he admitted that though he tried to write poetry, "I just can't get started" (59). While at school, he had written about his self doubts and about the nature that had surrounded him as he grew up in Colorado. He also recaptured his past for his readers. His poetry holds the stylistic attributes of earlier Navajo poetry. The imagery of the Colorado mountains in "Dancing Teepees" is heightened by O'John's use of repetition and a rhythmic cadence.

Dancing Teepees

Dancing teepees
High up in the Rocky Mountains,
Dancing teepees
Dance on the grassy banks of Cripple Creek
With laughing fringes in the sun.
Indian children
Play with bows and arrows
On the grassy banks of Cripple Creek.
Indian women
Gather kindling
To start an evening fire.

Dancing teepees
Dance against fire-lighted tree.
Braves returning
Home from raiding,
Gallantly ride into camp
With horses, scalps, and ornaments.
Dancing teepees
Sleep now on the grassy banks of Cripple Creek
High up in the Rocky Mountains. (61)

Born and raised near Shiprock, New Mexico, Emerson Blackhorse Barney Mitchell's father had died in military service during World War II. As is traditional in many Native American tribes, Mitchell was raised by his maternal grandparents after his father's death. Because he was raised in the Navajo community, he struggled to write in English (91). Nevertheless, his poetry is full of poignant imagery. Perhaps because he grew up close to his ancestral traditions, Mitchell's poetry speaks of the Native American vision of past history and the dual traditions of farming and warfare.

The Four Directions

A century and eight more years,
    Since Kit Carson rode from four directions,
Deep into the heart of nomadic Navajos,
    Burning, ravishing the Land of Enchantment.

Prairie grasses are once more
    Growing as high as the horse's belly.
Cradles of wrapped babies in colors
    Of the rainbow again span the land.

I know my people will stand and rise again.
    Now it is time.
Pollen of yellow grain,
    Scatter in four directions. (96)

These writers have a tone and voice uniquely their own. Their poetry is shaped by the oral images they grew up with, and it holds their interpretations (or perspectives) of the country's past. It is far more evocative than Annette Wynne's "Indian Children" because it allows the reader to experience Navajo traditions by recalling the cultural and social icons of Navajo literary patterns. These poems relate a place and a time that is distinctly Navajo. Yet they do not all speak of the same location or the same clan.

Earlier oral chants and songs were stylistically suitable for religious sharing. They belonged to a community. Contemporary Indian poets recreate a sense of this community by using Southwest imagery that alludes to traditional Navajo icons, colors, objects, and cultural beliefs. The poems refer to nature with a sense of wonder. They include death, but they also project hope for their people. Thus, perhaps because he remained close to his family's beliefs and his Navajo language, Mitchell has looked beyond the past destruction of his people and declared, "I know my people will stand and rise again."

Other groups who have not been heard in textbooks find their way into children's books. Their stories are shaped by authors who are retelling history to help shape a new reality. Some authors use a more playful voice and tone than the Navajo poets. Less interested in recreating the past, they include cultural stories and beliefs of a particular group of people. Although their stories contain elements of realism, they may not be writing realistic fiction. Yet each author's use of perspective can convince the reader that the world the author perceives is true to life.

Rhetorical critics argue that authors use language to manipulate our thinking, and that the most effective authors convince us that their vision of the past is an honest one. Authors, they maintain, are politically active, whether they admit it or not. If we know that this is true, then we must learn to read in new ways. The author's cultural and social background, his friends and enemies, and his reasons for writing become more important to us as readers. We listen to his voice to understand his story. We look at his use of descriptive adjectives to determine his point of view. We look at his scene to determine his rationale for presenting the characters involved in his drama the way he does. In the end, we ask ourselves, "What is missing? Who do I like or dislike? Why?" Once answered, we know what the author is about and we understand why his voice has influenced us as it did.

Several of my students have sought to find and evaluate fictional and nonfictional accounts that attempt to recreate the past. One student, Debbie Brunke, wanted to explore writers' accounts of Jewish communities prior to World War I that had been written by Jewish authors. She turned to two children's authors who looked at the European Jewish ghetto experience in very different ways. When she was ready to write, she came in and confided that one author appealed to her much more than the other. She preferred the author whose tales contained a sense of humor and realism without retelling historical events. "Why?" I asked. Debbie decided that she preferred the author's style. Her paper focuses on how the two authors reshaped their history in stories. Because she wanted to teach children, she also considered what children would need to know in order to enjoy the authors' stories, and she addressed children's needs as she wrote.

Understanding the Hidden Secrets in Literature

BY DEBBIE BRUNKE

In Sulamith Ish-Kishor's book *A Boy of Old Prague* and in Isaac Bashevis Singer's book *When Schlemiel Went to Warsaw* the real reader's response and the implied reader's response may greatly differ. Although Ish-Kishor's book is fiction, it is written very carefully, using facts about life in the Jewish ghettos of the sixteenth century. A child who is unfamiliar with the details of the Jewish past may read this story with the attitude that the book was only written to entertain. However, for the child to become an implied reader of this book, he must first learn that historical facts are sometimes incorporated into a book of fiction in order to make history more interesting to read and to express the author's feelings about past conditions—just as Ish-Kishor has done. Singer, on the other hand, has created a collection of eight stories ranging from "devilish comedy, to delicate fantasy, to parable. Some are folk tales which Singer first heard from his mother and which he has retold in his own fashion—totally recreating them in plot, detail and perspective; others are straight out of his fertile imagination" (Naughton 615). Singer's stories are written for children to enjoy—not to teach them about the past. "Singer believes that the only role of fiction is entertainment" (Evory 604). For the child to become an implied reader of Singer's stories, he must understand that not all stories are written to teach; Singer's stories incorporate his childhood experiences and Yiddish practices and beliefs.

Ish-Kishor was born in London, England, in 1896. She began writing at the age of five and has published numerous children's books with Jewish themes. Usually, her books are set in the past (Commire, Vol. 27, 84). *A Boy of Old Prague* is set in the year 1550 in an eastern European Jewish ghetto. The story is told in the first person by a peasant boy who describes his harsh life and his Christian's family's prejudices against Jews. It is not until he is made a servant of a Jewish family that Tomas realizes how very wrong his beliefs have been.

Ish-Kishor uses historical facts to paint a vividly real picture of life in the sixteenth century Jewish ghetto. These facts are important to note if the child is going to be truly sensitive to this book. Ish-Kishor's ghetto is set in Prague, a city built during the sixteenth century. Although the Jewish inhabitants of Prague enjoyed a freer life than most people living in the ghettos at this time, they were often persecuted and massacred (Abrahams 63). At first, the Jews and the Christians were friendly with one another. However, "churches and palaces were gradually removed or divided from the contamination of the neighbouring Jewish abodes by huge and menacing walls" (Abrahams 64), and the ghetto was formed. Ish-Kishor describes this fear of contamination through her protagonist's eyes. Tomas calls the ghetto the "abode of the accursed" and faints from fear for his life when he passes through the gates of the ghetto (34). Ish-Kishor also includes the fact that the gates were guarded by gatekeepers and closed each night as a protective measure (Abrahams 65). The walls both protected and entrapped the defenseless Jews. This is what Ish-Kishor's story is actually about.

When Ish-Kishor discusses the house in the ghetto where Tomas works, she uses language similar to Abrahams. Abrahams describes the houses as "a dark grey, moss-covered, hideous pile of stones. . . . A passage, more than eighty feet in length . . . led to a dark, partly decayed, winding staircase. . . . A well protected door opened, and one entered into an apartment cheerfully decorated" (149). When Tomas first describes the Jewish home where he is to be a servant, he says he is led "into the narrow hallway, that smelled damp and stony as a grave" (36), and that he "climbed up a crooked staircase cut out of the stone, where [he] could see the green moss on the wall . . . ." Then, he recalls, "the old Jew pushed open a door into a large, warm room" that was handsomely decorated (38).

Tomas is allowed to eat with the family, he receives a new suit of clothes to wear on the Sabbath, he is taken good care of when he is ill, and he is given time every week to go and visit his family. All of these details correlate with Abrahams's statement that "the Jew was beyond everything considerate to all with whom he had intimate relations . . ." (153). Abrahams also writes that it was common practice for the servants to eat with the family and that they never looked down upon their servants. According to Abraham, the Jews believed, "A man must never put unnecessary burdens on a servant" (158). It is apparent that Ish-Kishor took pains to demonstrate these ideas: Tomas does odd chores like wood chopping, going to the market, and taking the son to the Synagogue; he is never given chores that are stressful or burdensome.

One final bit of factual information which Ish-Kishor incorporates into her story is the Jewish consideration of the role of the young, unmarried woman in the household. Abrahams says that Jewish daughters were never idle, "For idleness leads to sin, but they must spin, or cook, or sew and be patient in all their ways" (156). Ish-Kishor's narrator comments that Mademoiselle Rachel "kept to her room a great deal, sewing, embroidering, or weaving," and says she is very quiet and subdued (51). Although Rachel comes down for meals, she keeps busy in her room the rest of the time. She is never seen relaxing or going out with friends.

If a child would read *A Boy of Old Prague* without understanding how much Jewish history and tradition have been incorporated, she will simply think this is a book written to entertain, not one written to inform her about another culture. However, if a child realizes that the elements of the story are based upon historical facts, then she will see events in a different light. Instead of just feeling sorry for the Jews who perish in the ghetto fire, she may also feel anger towards the people who caused the fire and were so unjust. If the child knows that the events happened, she will realize that these past events had a strong effect on Ish-Kishor and compelled her to write a children's book which held real attitudes and events. The child should also have a better appreciation of the plight of the Jews in history while learning about sixteenth century Jewish life.

Singer did not write *When Schlemiel Went to Warsaw* to teach the child about Jewish life as it was; rather, he wrote to entertain the reader with imaginative Jewish stories. In order for the child to be the implied reader of these stories, he must realize why Singer created them. Singer states, "My old fashioned aim is to entertain the best readers" (Commire, Vol. 5 205). He says he "dislikes modern fiction that focuses on the writer revealing his inner self and complaining about his problems" (Evory 604). Singer believes that writers should not be cause oriented but should be motivated to write artistically. He adds, "if a book was boring we used to throw it away. Now it is considered that a book must be boring to be good" (Commire, Vol. 5 205). Singer has turned to children's literature because he believes "it is only in juvenile books that a writer still has to tell a story, not discuss social changes or psychological motivations" (Hill 569). In an interview he once commented, "When I tell a story, I tell a story. I don't try to discuss, criticize, or analyze my characters" (Ethridge 872). Therefore, Singer does not write with a lesson in mind because he feels it is needless. Rather, he writes stories that allow his readers to make their own decisions about the stories' meanings. He believes that it is important for children to understand that literature is to be enjoyed.

Isaac Singer was born in Poland and grew up in Warsaw with his father, a rabbi, and his mother. His family lived in the Polish Yiddish ghetto. His father set up a rabbinical court in his apartment, and people came to ask him for advice or to settle disputes. Singer says, "In our house there was always talk about spirits of the dead that possess the bodies of the living, souls reincarnated as animals, houses inhabited by hobgoblins, cellars haunted by demons" (Commire, Vol. 17 204). The locations, mysticism, and rabbinical court of Singer's past are apparent in many of his stories. An avid reader as a child, Singer does not write simplified stories for children. And, he tries to give them happy endings.

Children need to know that a schlemiel is "a gullible and powerless, yet oddly wise, fool that inhabits much of Yiddish fiction" (Friedman 21) if they are to understand that the tales have Yiddish humor and meanings. In many of these stories Schlemiel, the fool, lives in the town of Chelm, a town that "Yiddish people singled out as the place of fools, and is, consequently the source of much humor" (Iskander 341). One example of the Jewish seriousness combined with humor which is reflected in Singer's writing is the plot of "When Schlemiel Went to Warsaw." It is humorous to see that Schlemiel is so stupid that he does not realize there cannot possibly be another town, family, house, and wife *exactly* like the one he believes he left behind in Chelm One. Yet, there is a serious tone in the idea that there are Jewish communities so similar they can be mistaken for one another. Schlemiel is not so dumb after all, because in the end he is happy in his "new" home with his "new" wife, being paid to watch his own children until this town's Schlemiel returns.

Although many of the stories take place in Chelm and Warsaw, some take place in unknown towns with spirits as the main characters. In "Tsirtsur and Peziza" a cricket and an imp who reside behind a kitchen stove are the main characters. Singer tells his audience what the characters are thinking, how they feel, what they eat, and how they act. This exact literalness makes unrealistic characters very acceptable. Singer combines the literalness and the idea of the dead walking and dancing among the living in "Menaseh's Dream," a story which concerns Menaseh's transportation to a castle "where nothing is lost." All of his dead relatives live in the castle, and so when Menaseh arrives there he is taken on a tour by his dead grandfather. Singer goes into great detail to describe what Menaseh sees. For example, when Menaseh enters the second room, he sees "all the toys he had ever owned: the tin soldiers his father had bought him; the jumping clown his mother had brought him back from the fair at Lublin; whistles and harmonicas; the teddy bear Grandfather had given him one Purim" (88). These details create a more believable fantasy for the child.

If a child understands that these two Jewish authors have approached their cultural heritage in very different ways, he will see that each author believes that stories hold different things. For Ish-Kishor, literature can paint a clear picture about how life must have been for both the Jews and the Christians living in Prague in 1550. The story can recreate history to make the child more aware of the early disgraceful treatment of the Jews. Singer, on the other hand, wants his reader to enjoy an unusual story which holds both the familiar and the unfamiliar. Although he uses his personal experience and his Yiddish beliefs, he is not trying to teach children about his past. For Ish-Kishor, story can hold truths, for Singer literature "can have many interpretations, scores of messages, mountains of commentaries" (Commire, Vol. 17, 211).

References

Israel Abrahams. *Jewish Life in the Middle Ages*. New York: Meridan Books, 1958.
Anne Commire, ed. "Isaac Bashevis Singer," in *Something About the Author,* Vol. 3.
     Detroit: Gale Research Company, 1972.

————. "Isaac Bashevis Singer," in *Something About the Author,* Vol. 17. Detroit: Gale Research Company, 1979.

————. "Sulamith Ish-Kishor," in *Something About the Author,* Vol. 27. Detroit: Gale Research Company, 1982.

James M. Ethridge and Barbara Kopala, eds. "Isaac Bashevis Singer," in *Contemporary Authors, First Revision,* Vols. 1–4. Detroit: Gale Research Company, 1967.

Ann Evory, ed. "Isaac Bashevis Singer," in *Contemporary Authors, New Revision Series,* Vol. 1. Detroit: Gale Research Company, 1981.

Lawrence Friedman. *Understanding Isaac Bashevis Singer.* Columbia: University of South Carolina Press, 1988.

Donna Hill and Doris de Montreville, eds. "Isaac Bashevis Singer," in *Third Book of Junior Authors.* New York: H. W. Wilson Company, 1972.

Sulamith Ish-Kishor. *A Boy of Old Prague.* New York: Scholastic Book Service, 1963.

Sylvia W. Iskander. "Isaac Bashevis Singer," in *Dictionary of Literary Biography,* Vol. 52. Detroit: Gale Research Company, 1978.

Frances C. Locher, ed. "Sulamith Ish-Kishor," in *Contemporary Authors, First Revision,* Vols. 73–76. Detroit: Gale Research Company, 1978.

Frank N. Magill, ed. *The Nobel Prize Winners.* Pasadena: Salem Press, 1987.

Frances F. Povsic. "Czechoslovakia: Children's Fiction in English," in *The Reading Teacher,* March 1980.

Isaac B. Singer. *When Schlemiel Went to Warsaw.* Toronto: Collins Publishers, 1968.

5

Understanding Utopian Worlds in Children's Literature

Throughout the years, we have maintained that children who enjoy reading stories want to find books about places they would like to visit, events they wish could happen, and characters they would like to be. We have also argued that they prefer happily-ever-after endings to their stories. If this is so, then reading becomes an activity of self-gratification that allows readers to vicariously explore their inner fantasies without feeling threatened.

Most adult readers who say that they like fantasy also say they like to find stories that help them escape from their everyday worlds. Their pleasure reading brings relief from the day-to-day realities of their own lives. Many adults will go so far as to say that they don't like "realism" because it presents a dark side of life that they don't care to deal with when they are reading for enjoyment. The literary world they prefer presents, for them, a view of *utopia*, a world where they can enjoy the adventures of the main characters without worrying about the consequences. They vicariously journey with their heroes to find a more perfect world. Thus, these readers experience the plot as the main character does. Furthermore, most adults who like utopian fantasy are experienced readers who understand the literary patterns of the genre, and they know that their stories will almost certainly end happily ever after. Often the heroes will complete a circular journey; in the end, they return home safe and sound, and if there are any villains to be dealt with, they are overthrown by the hero. Once again, the world is a safer, better place.

When we read about a hero who survives in a society that values the attitudes we believe in, we put the book down and say, "Now, I liked that book." Many of us would be hard put to explain why we liked it other than saying the characters were ones we could identify with, the story worked out the way we wanted it to, or the writer used good descriptive language. In a way, we imagine that we could have created the author's story ourselves.

I once had a student say that he didn't see anything new in Northrop Frye's *The Educated Imagination*. Perhaps not, I returned, but could he write the book? He admitted that he couldn't write like Frye, but he argued that the book wasn't terribly innovative. Finally, he said, "I just felt like he didn't say anything I didn't already know and agree with." If my student was correct, then Northrop Frye had shown him how utopian kingdoms work. Indirectly, my student had identified with the author's imagery and accepted Frye's conclusions as his own. As he read he willingly accepted Frye's fantasy trip to a desert island and had understood the metaphor about literature and his day-to-day existence.

"For the poet," Frye writes, "the particular literary conventions he adopts are likely to become, for him, facts of life." And he continues, "His life may imitate literature in a way that may warp or even destroy his social personality" (89). According to Frye, literature contains a world that can only be visited vicariously. He argues that literary realism consists of "bigger and more intense experiences than anything we can reach—except in our imagination, which is what we're reaching with" (97).

The writer's imagined world becomes his real world because he lives in it as much as he lives in his everyday surroundings. Each day he spends four to eight hours creating the characters in the world he imagines. At other times, he gets dressed, shops, cooks, eats, sleeps, chats with friends, and observes the world around him. Still, while he does these mundane things he does not turn his mind off. At any time, bits and pieces of his imagined world may intrude into his everyday world. At the same time, his everyday world enters his fiction. He probably keeps a writer's journal where he scribbles bits of conversations he hears that might be useful later on, and he writes descriptions of things or events he observes. These are "field notes" for his other world. They are incorporated into his writing to give his imaginary characters and their world a sense of everyday reality. His imaginary world's events happen as we expect they might because they are a reflection of reality.

Illustrators also live in two worlds. They visually describe imagined scenes and people, but often use people they know as models. Yet they do not simply recreate these people. Instead, they reshape them until they become personalities in another world. Often, though artists know who the people represented in their illustrations are, the people they have recreated do not recognize themselves. They have become a reflection of what they might be like if they lived in another world.

The author's and artist's utopian worlds work for their audiences because they are not the worlds either the author or the artist actually lives in but are ones concocted out of cultural desires and realities. The story's imagery is accepted by the reader because the creator has been involved in two equally real worlds and is reflecting something about contemporary society. Yet, because the author and artist are allowed to piece together materials from their everyday and fantasy lives as they wish, the worlds they create are often richer than the reader's wildest expectations.

Writers use *mimetic* language to convince us that what we read could really happen. They create worlds that seem real but cannot be—everything is too neat and tidy. For instance, an author can use weather to change the story's mood or forecast a possible problem for the protagonist; he can create the story's events in a chronological order with no interruptions; he can invent conflicts between the main characters that end in predictable ways. Authors of utopian stories use the literary devices of romance to convince their readers that the action in the story is logical and that events have a cause/effect relationship. Events happen at just the right moment; people are rescued from outrageous disasters; villains are defeated and heroes rewarded. Everyday observations of the characters' natural world become road signs that suggest the story's mood, structure, and even its ending. All of this implies that life is systematic and all conflicts can be resolved.

The people in these stories are also mimetic, and they often become *icons* or represent a personality type. We recognize their attitudes and ways of acting as ones we have seen in people around us, and we accept them as realistic individuals. They are simultaneously unique and stereotypic.

The author carefully plans his conception of reality to suggest his ideal interpretation of human society, his image of another way of life. Thus, even the most mimetic writing holds some sort of wish fulfillment. Children's author Lloyd Alexander once said that literature concerns "how . . . we perceive ourselves as human beings" and he argued,

> . . . all forms of literature are, in a large sense, fantasy—they are words on a page, not the actual objects themselves. They may reflect reality, and give us valid insights into it; but even the most convincing depiction of reality only seems to be real. The material is selected, manipulated, enhanced. In other words, it is a work of art. I see no essential conflict between the most exacting realism and the most inventive science fiction or fantasy.
>
> They come from the same source, they share the same goals: to help us discover who we are and what we are. (165)

Stories often are concerned with heroic journeys. And all these journeys contain landscapes that set up the limits for a particular hero's journey. The world the hero lives in shapes his journey. In turn, the hero expands the world's horizons by venturing outside his everyday scene. The two worlds where the hero exists are equally important. The writer creates a utopia within those boundaries for the hero, but it need not be in one world or the other; the world the hero enters or the world he leaves behind may both seem imperfect to the reader. However, neither world is represented in a entirely realistic way. Both worlds are mimetic in certain ways, and at the same time they are both imaginary. What we need to consider is the author's intent. Why build two worlds for the hero to travel in and out of?

Utopian writers depend on binary structuralism to set up their two worlds. Novelists who write space and time travel stories often construct contrasting social systems in their stories. These binary societies contrast what is with what might be. Often the stories teach the reader more about her own society than she suspects. She may feel most comfortable with a happy-ever-after ending; the stories are not simply too-good-to-be-true versions of what happens in the everyday world. They are moral, social, political, and/or religious statements by an author who is greatly concerned about the state of affairs in the world around him. The worlds constructed within his stories are not likely to happen in the reader's world. Still, if the reader accepts the author's values and strives to create a similar atmosphere in her everyday existence, the author has helped the reader to create a more utopian world for herself. The worlds invented by an author also suggest something about the society the author lives in. And they reflect his philosophy. If the reader lives in the same society, then she will indirectly learn something new about her own life.

Writers, then, contrive to shape society, and they know that they are doing this when they write utopian books. They use language to reshape the people in the real world where they live. Lloyd Alexander prefaced his explanation of literary worlds and realism by saying that all writing depends on the author's experiences. And, he concluded, "Literature that strives for any level of excellence engages the question: how do we perceive ourselves as human beings?" (164–165).

When discussing utopian novels published in America during 1886–96, Jean Pfaelzer said the authors "created a disjunction—a space in the mind of the reader—between the familiar present and the imagined future, between history and possibility, between satire and utopia" (5). Most utopian societies seem to be timeless. They are not bound up in a particular century, nor are they tied to a particular region. Peter Ruppert has maintained that utopian worlds are not explorations of tomorrow as much as they are worlds designed to explain today's society. He says that utopias "make us aware that our present situation is inextricably linked to our past and that the future depends on our choices and actions in the present" (162). Authors who construct utopias look at the polar opposites found in their everyday world, and reshape these opposites in the plots of their stories. The stories work like parables; they teach as they entertain.

U. C. Knoepflmacher has argued that all journeys in children's literature contain a lesson in metaphor for the reader to ponder at the end. Then, Knoepflmacher argues, the reader must grapple with "the implied author's stance towards these polarities: the extreme of youth and age, of freedom and compromise, of dream and actuality" (48–49). Knoepflmacher has also suggested that critics need to consider whether children's literature can best hold "the polarities of innocence and experience" (49).

Children's literature is often traced back to oral folklore. Early folk literature contains the polarities of innocence and experience in unusual ways. Most often the youthful hero ventures out into a new world only to return home and accept the values of his everyday world. His success on the road can be attributed to his internalized belief in the values of his community. And he comes home to reaffirm that all is right in the contemporary sphere. By the tale's end wickedness has been punished, and rewards have been given to those who have remained "good citizens." Because the main character must learn what is best for him at that juncture in his life, the hero's journey brings a loss of innocence. Both reader and character have changed when the book ends. They know more about the dangers they will face within society, and they know how to experience success by suppressing personal goals in civilization. Indirectly, folk tales teach children about social conformity.

Most textbooks in children's literature claim that utopian folklore shaped what is found in today's stories for youth. And they maintain that the tales were not first intended for adults or for children. In *Children's Literature in the Elementary Schools* Charlotte S. Huck, Susan Hepler, and Janet Hickman point to these oral stories as the beginning of literature, and they allege that the stories were community tales, told to young and old alike (97). Often critical discussions trace the tales through the German tradition, beginning with the collected tales of the Grimm Brothers. Since English translations were available to children in the chapbooks published in the early 1800s, and since these tales have been continually retold and republished in children's editions, it is not surprising that they are the most studied versions of folklore. Usually, literary discussion concentrates on the tales that have become widely accepted as children's fare. These include "The Wolf and the Seven Young Kids," "Rapunzel," "Hansel and Gretel," "Ashputtle," "Little Red Cap," "The Musicians of Bremen," "Brier Rose," "Snow White," "Rumpelstiltskin," "The Golden Goose," "The Goose Girl," and "Snow White and Rose Red." The tales form the literary patterns of plot and characterization so often attributed to the German tales, including a plot that quickly unfolds involving a hero's journey, adversaries who are overcome by virtuous main characters, wolves and stepmothers as villains, young girls as dependent, innocent victims, and a happily-ever-after ending.

Traditionally folk tales are considered good literature to share with children. Donna E. Norton discusses a large number of these stories in her textbook and attests, "German folktales are ideal candidates for story telling. Their speedy openings, fast-paced plots, and drama keep listeners entertained for story after story. In these tales, adversaries include devils, witches, and wolves. The good-hearted youngest child is often rewarded, but selfishness, greed, and discontent are punished. The noble character frequently wins as a result of intervention by supernatural helpers, and magical objects and spells are recurring motifs" (246–247). The stories have been freely adapted and changed for a variety of purposes. For instance, educators have used the storylines to teach a number of lessons, including minding your mother (Little Red Riding Hood), not accepting food from strangers (Hansel and Gretel), and being kind to strangers (Snow White and Red Rose). Yet, not everyone applauds these twentieth-century rewritings or agrees that the original tales depict utopian worlds worthy of the attention of modern children.

Feminist critics argue that these tales hold two distinct worlds—one a supernatural place of spells and quests and one the everyday world where the tale begins—but that neither world is controlled by favorable images of women. The castles are full of wicked women who would rid their kingdoms of young rivals, and the forest is replete with witches who would tempt and kill harmless young children. Young girls do not seem safe in either setting—they usually must depend on someone else to rescue them. Thus, the stories are entertaining because of their fast-moving plots and happily-ever-after endings, but they do not help young female readers discover who they might be. Feminists argue that while the female characters have assumed a new lifestyle at the tale's end, they have not had a choice in their fate. Little has evolved in the plot of a traditional folktale to show the reader that the females in the story will need to change from their childlike ways of passivity and trust in order to be truly happy.

Popular culture has proven that the tales do hold some underpinnings of a modern utopia for some young listeners. The renditions of commonly known folktales often hold images of perfect princes and princesses who are brought together by fate and who marry in the end. Many contemporary young women first see the tales in popular versions, and they prefer the romantic tales that have been recreated in these screen and music versions to new story plots featuring strong females capable of surviving on their own. One of the most traditionally accepted plotlines of the folk tales—the Snow White syndrome—is continually placed into modern literature. It has recently appeared in the popular twentieth-century films *My Fair Lady* and *Pretty Woman*.

As children, most of us watched the story of Snow White unfold in the Disney version. Snow White, the innocent child/adolescent is left in her father's house (without her father) to work and toil like a slave under the careful watch of her wicked stepmother. At last, the queen cannot bear the girl's presence, and she sends Snow White out to be killed by a hunter who, instead, allows her to escape to the house of some dwarfs. It is so dirty and dismal that she determines orphans live there, and she sets about with a group of endearing forest animals to clean the place up, "whistling while she works." Once home, the dwarfs ask her to stay and cook and clean for them. Meanwhile, the wicked stepmother discovers that the princess is alive, tries to kill her, and finally succeeds in putting her into a trance-like sleep. Fortunately, it is "a dark and dismal night" when the queen places Snow White under her final spell, and she slips to her death when the dwarfs pursue her. Snow White's prince arrives, opens the casket, kisses and awakens the girl of his dreams, scoops her up to the back of his horse, and takes her off to live happily ever after. This story holds several literary patterns that have been infused into popular culture. The characterization is stereotypic and the plot predictable.

Americans, used to the Walt Disney versions of the Grimm tale, have learned to accept his interpretation of the American success story. They applaud Snow White when she sings, "Some day my prince will come." They long to enter an enchanted kingdom full of cute animals, stereotypic little men, and fine gowns. In the end, they confuse Disney's utopian image of traditional happiness with perfection. They accept the messages in the film because they want to live happily ever after. They hope to rid themselves of evil adults, and they long to find pleasure in their work.

The original Grimm Brothers' tale of Snow White is quite different. The girl is sent to the woods when she is seven; the dwarfs are clean little men who frighten Snow White on their first encounter; Snow White is never depicted as anything but a submissive woman/child; and the prince seems to want to own her rather than to find pleasure in her company. The Grimm tale ends quite differently saying,

> It happened, however, that one day a king's son rode through the wood and up to the dwarfs' house, which was near it. He saw on the mountain the coffin, and beautiful Snow-white within it, and he read what was written in golden letters upon it. Then he said to the dwarfs, "Let me have the coffin, and I will give you whatever you like to ask for it."
>
> But the dwarfs told him that they could not part with it for all the gold in the world. But he said, "I beseech you to give it [to] me, for I cannot live without looking upon Snow-white; if you consent I will bring you great honour, and care for you as if you were my brethern."
>
> When he spoke so good the little dwarfs had pity upon him and gave him the coffin, and the king's son called his servants to carry it away on their shoulders. Now it happened that as they were going along they stumbled over a bush, and with the shaking the bit of poisoned apple flew out of her throat. It was not long before she opened her eyes, threw up the cover of the coffin, and sat up, alive and well.
>
> "Oh dear! where am I?" cried she. The king's son answered, full of joy, "You are near me," and, relating all that had happened, he said, "I would rather have you than anything in the world; come with me to my father's castle and you shall be my bride."
>
> And Snow-white was kind, and went with him, and their wedding was held with pomp and great splendour.
>
> But Snow-white's wicked step-mother was also bidden to the feast, and when she had dressed herself in beautiful clothes she went to her looking-glass mirror and said,
>
> > "Looking-glass upon the wall,
> > Who is fairest of them all?"
>
> The looking-glass answered,
>
> > "O Queen, although you are of beauty rare,
> > the young bride is a thousand times more fair."

Then she railed and cursed, and was beside herself with disappointment and anger. First she thought she would not go to the wedding; but then she felt that she would have no peace until she went and saw the bride. And when she saw her she knew her for Snow-white, and could not stir from the place for anger and terror. For they had ready red-hot iron shoes, in which she had to dance until she fell down dead. (Crane, 220–221)

The original tale depicts Snow White as a commodity. She is feared for her beauty by the queen, harbored as a laborer by the dwarfs, and married to the prince for her beauty. At the story's conclusion, she has returned to her royal position but is not much better off than she was when the story began. She has not learned whom to trust, and she is still accepting someone else's decisions of what is best for her. In fact, she is not a terribly interesting personality at all.

Why is Snow White's story appealing enough to be continually rewritten? One reason is that the story has an intriguing plot structure. And, of course, the tale is so much a part of popular culture that it has become a piece of the commonly accepted canon of knowledge. But it is Disney's version—not the Grimm tale—that most young people know. Most college students prefer the popular culture notions of folktales because that is what they've been seeing all their lives. Some, however, will view things differently. Their perceptions are often similar to the ones of Amy D. Foster, an undergraduate who took the time to compare the tales in Joseph Jacobs' *Celtic Fairy Tales* to those she remembered from her childhood.

Amy had read *Celtic Fairy Tales* the summer before taking the children's literature course because she knew it was on the required reading list for the fall semester. When the book failed to arrive in time for the assigned reading and was taken off the required list, she decided to use it in her first short paper. Everyone had been asked to explore the differences between popular culture renditions of folktales and those found in the earlier collections. Amy was ready to compare a traditional version collected for children with Disney and wrote the following paper.

Comparison of Jacobs to Disney

BY AMY D. FOSTER

To me, all of the tales in Joseph Jacobs' *Celtic Fairy Tales* were new. I had never heard many fairy tales besides the few Disney ones that children are usually exposed to. There was one tale of the twenty-six contained in the Jacobs collection that struck me as familiar, however. When I read *Celtic Fairy Tales* this summer, I was already doing this assignment. I could not help but see the numerous similarities between "Fair, Brown, and Trembling" and *Cinderella*. The characterizations and plots almost match.

Fair, Brown, and Trembling were three sisters. Trembling was in the same situation as Cinderella was with her stepsisters. Trembling's two wicked stepsisters were like Cinderella's two stepsisters. Trembling had to work very hard in the house, as did Cinderella. The sisters in the tale at one point even said, "Oh! We have her for nothing but to put out the ashes" (193). This is, of course, the same as Cinderella. Both young women were working among the ashes. In Cinderella's case, they gave her her name because of the cinders. The sisters in the Celtic tale even kept Trembling at home, as did the stepsisters in *Cinderella*.

The event that Cinderella desired to attend was the ball at the palace. Trembling wanted to go to church on Sundays. At the ball, the stepsisters thought they would meet a man to marry. Church was where the "action" was for the women in Jacobs' tale. Neither set of sisters wanted their beautiful younger sisters to be seen by the men in the town. They feared she would ruin their chances of finding a husband.

In both tales, the youngest sister does gain the opportunity to attend the forbidden social event. In both tales, a magical older woman gives the heroine the help she needs. In *Cinderella*, the fairy godmother comes to the rescue by providing Cinderella with clothing and transportation. Trembling's savior is the henwife who can magically provide whatever color and style clothing that Trembling desires, along with a horse to match. In both stories, the young women are given curfews and warnings by the old women.

In both stories, the prince falls in love with the young sister. He must search the countryside for her, using the only tool he has—one of her shoes. (At this point in my summer reading, I noticed the parallel plot structures. Trembling lost one of her shoes, just like Cinderella!) In both stories, all of the local women tried to make the shoes fit them. Also, in both stories, the prince and the youngest sister eventually find each other and live happily ever after.

Since I first read "Fair, Brown, and Trembling," I have read other versions of *Cinderella*. All of them have these same major events. I have discovered that when I was earlier thinking of *Cinderella* I was thinking of the Perrault version. (Thank goodness!) I must have heard it somewhere in my childhood.

After getting our assignment, I got a copy of Walt Disney's version of *Cinderella* and re-read it. I did **not** enjoy it at all. I was sure it had been shared with me as a child, but now I wonder. When I read the Disney version, I was angered and offended. There were many, many stupid and unnecessary elements in it. One was a bunch of silly cartoon mice. They talked to Cinderella and they had names. All of the animals were very "cartoonish." It was very distracting. The silly happenings in Disney's plot really took away from the story's structure and mood, and they just completely messed up the adventure for me.

I do have a theory on why Disney's book is like this. He made a movie of *Cinderella*, and these pictures seem to be taken from the motion picture. If produced as a movie, I know that the original story would not even come close to lasting two hours. So, of course, Walt Disney had to do some major embellishing. I am sure that Disney and his team of experts meant well by adding Gus and Jack and the other talking mice. They probably thought that it would add an element of humor to the story. Children probably do automatically giggle at the bumbling mice. But I wondered, "Why does this story have to be funny?" And I don't see how these characters add to the original drama. I am not convinced that children would come away from Disney's book or film version of *Cinderella* with an understanding of the classic tale's moods or events. I can just picture children leaving the theater and talking about those stupid mice. These embellishments could cause some children to completely miss the point.

However, I would not censor Disney. There are values for sharing Perrault, Jacobs, the Grimm version, **and** Disney with children. I know I am really enjoying the comparisons of literature that we do in this class. I believe that when we are teachers we can best help our children to see not only the differences in illustrations and moods of the various versions, but also the changes in the actual story line if we share several versions of a familiar tale.

As educators, we need to learn from children by listening to them. We can ask them for **their** opinions about the various versions. They deserve to see Perrault's, Jacobs's, the Grimm Brothers', and the Disney versions so that they can react and tell us about each version. And we need to listen to them.

However, if I were only allowed to share one version in my class, I would definitely choose Jacobs's "Fair, Brown, and Trembling." Children will see the Disney version on the weekends with their parents. Somehow they will probably hear the Perrault or Grimm version of the tale. But they may never hear Jacobs's tale if I don't share it with them. And it holds unique attributes that are worth discussing. Because school time is limited, we need to remember that there is probably a best time and place for everything.

This reminds me of the time when I was small and my family tried a new church. It was close to Christmas at the time. I went to Sunday school while my parents attended the church service. After church, my parents asked what I had done in Sunday school. I replied that we had had Rudolph the Red-Nosed Reindeer read to us. Needless to say, we did not go back to that church. I have learned that I must carefully select those materials which I am sharing, and I believe that I must pick stories to fit my students' experiences and needs.

References

Walt Disney. *Cinderella*. New York: Gallery, undated.

Household Tales by the Brothers Grimm. Lucy Crane, translator. Illustrated by Walter Crane. New York: Dover, 1963.

Joseph Jacobs. *Celtic Fairy Tales*. New York: G. P. Putnam's Sons, undated.

Perrault's Fairy Tales. A. E. Johnson, translator. Illustrated by Gustave Dore. New York: Dover, 1969.

Amy did not discuss the many picture-book versions that are continually released. Often they do contain the original Perrault or Grimm tale, but each new version must hold something appealing, or it would not be published. Furthermore, people must buy them or they would not be available. Editors and artists often turn to traditional versions. If youngsters grow up preferring Disney, what makes the picture-book versions popular in publishing?

Contemporary critics in children's literature often best appreciate the books that do not contain rewritten versions altering the values found in the original plots. They frequently turn to the picture-book renditions that hold translations of the original tales as they were recorded in the late 1800s. These are the books they want shared with children at story hours and discussed in classrooms. These tales hold the archetypal patterns used in romance literature. The classical stories are popular within criticism because they allow for many different interpretations of the events and characterization. Children like the illustrations in picture books and they like hearing someone read or tell them the frightening tale of a young girl who almost dies, is saved, and lives happily ever after.

Whenever we look into the familiar scenes of some of those fairy tales commonly found in children's picture books, we perceive a reality unknown to us in our contemporary everyday world. The imagery of perfection, of beauty, and of living happily ever after catches our imagination and causes us to believe that this adventure so unlike our own lives is full of realism. We know that the events that happen in these tales are not apt to occur, yet we accept the tales as notions of reality. We see young children defeat wild beasts and wicked enchantments, knowing that real children would be unable to overcome such odds. We gaze at the illustrations of perfect princesses and charming princes, aware that few adolescents could ever maintain such poise or display such heroism, yet willing to accept the picture-book artists' symbolic portrayals of youth. We accept a modernization of "the same old story," just as young viewers of Disney accept his fantasy settings. We, the viewers of someone else's reality, are convinced that the images contain the essence of the original tale and relate to our world.

Usually the artist who creates a picture-book version of a traditional tale has depended on a careful translation of the original folk tale. Artists, however, do not simply recreate another century's utopian dreams. True, the utopia found in the pictures does reflect the original tales, and the translations remain true to the original versions written down in the 1800s. But the artists subtly refocus the events and characters in their illustrations. At first the audience for these books may not notice the refocusing and will assume that this is the original tale reflected for a contemporary audience. The trappings of the tale make it difficult to see how the illustrator has changed the tale's impact to create a modern utopia.

An artist can form a separate narrative within her illustrations, giving us a modern adaptation that holds her interpretation of the story's meaning. Her visuals may reshape the tale. Thus, the illustrations agree with Scholes's and Kellogg's conclusion that visual narratives contain "a specific connection between the 'real' world and the world of the story" (85). These contemporary illustrations link past beliefs with present attitudes and suggest alternative meanings for the utopian world. The illustrator uses the original text, creating new scenes to reframe the story's plot for the listener so that she will see the illustrated story's ironic meaning. The original text gains a new interpretation in the illustrations, one that can be in conflict with the earlier oral rendition. While the oral tales relied on the listener's ability to make sense of the plot, illustrations depend on the audience's visual perceptions. Picture books visually frame the texts and give them new symbolism that will often reshape the stories' views of society.

According to Mary Ann Caws, authors use *framing* when writing fiction to isolate a scene for the story's narrator and his audience and cause both to pause and consider what the scene means. The audience who recognizes artistic conventions considers how they function in the author's story. This also gives the audience time to consider how the narrator becomes the story's interpreter. Framing exhibits a scene; it sets it apart and forces audience participation (18).

Framing theory is particularly important in terms of picture books. Authors create a sense of reality by careful use of imagery in their texts. Scenes or details in the text stick out in the reader's mind, and create mental representations of events. These images shape the listener's understanding of characterization and the outcome of the plot. In turn, the artist places her interpretation of a written story within her pictures; she gives the story a meaning that seems to make it more readily accessible for the viewer. She chooses what to illustrate. When the text and the pictures combine archetypes in contradictory ways and the viewer is forced to consider the ironies displayed in the visual message, she will find a message that conflicts with the story's original implied meaning.

The artist's visual framing of a text can relate directly to her past experiences. Within the illustrations, the artist can resolve events from her own life, allowing the story to have a therapeutic resolution to her inner conflicts. An artist can change the story to fit her personal narrative. When describing twentieth-century female writers of utopia, Frances Bartkowski wrote that these writers do not place their stories in a golden age. She added,

> Feminist utopias also reject the specific naming of where and when of utopia and stake their interests in the interplay of the varying "here" of the writer and reader and the "there" of the fiction. . . . Feminists have chosen to specify the contradictions of the "now" and the intensity with which they are felt rather than totalize in order to make the utopian impulse one of potential, not project. (12)

The trick for an woman artist who uses framing, then, is to be able to reframe the "typical scene" expected in a utopian story from a world where the main character is caught to an idealized world that is clearly defined as the ideal model for the artist's contemporary society. To be successful, she would have to remember that her story in one way or another reframes her own culture. She must show society's potential, not remake it to fit her needs.

One artist who has placed personal meanings within her illustrated picture-book versions of various Grimm tales is Trina Schart Hyman. Often her illustrations depict a psychological conflict that she had faced while recreating the images found in the texts. Hyman has placed the world around her within her utopian feminist's interpretation in order to work out personal resolutions for herself. Two of her early books, *Snow White* and *Little Red Riding Hood,* are twentieth-century feminist utopian retellings. However, because they reflect the author's autobiographical journey toward a feminist understanding, they vary in structure.

Unlike the earlier tellings of the stories, which concentrated on the male hero, Hyman began by looking at the females in *Snow White* and restructured the images to reflect the feminist argument against women's dominating concern about physical appearance in a male-dominated society. The conflict between the aging queen's fear that her loss of physical beauty will mean her loss of power and the young girl's growing need for a self-identity was being enacted in her house as Hyman was illustrating *Snow White*.

Caught between the emotional needs of her best friend and her daughter, Hyman resolved the conflict for herself in her illustrations by using her friend as the queen, Katrin as Snow White. The older woman's resentment of Katrin Hyman's growing beauty and need for independence is revealed in the illustrations. At the end of the traditional Grimm story, the girl survives but the queen disappears. When the book was completed and the illustrations shared with all involved, Trina Hyman's friend and her two daughters moved to California, leaving Trina and Katrin behind to live happily ever after.*

Hyman's story centers on the queen. She is the person most affected by the unfolding events. Unlike the young princess, she leaves nothing to fate. Hyman shows the queen continually stalking the young girl while she is still in her care. Later, when the girl has disappeared from the castle, the queen is seen as a distraught woman who gazes in her magic mirror after she has transformed herself into an old peddler woman, torn with rage and anger when the mirror reveals that Snow White is still alive, and finally single-minded in her determination to cast a death-chilling spell on the younger woman with a magic apple. At first, the queen is a lovely young woman, but gradually her jealousy torments her until she loses her beauty. By the end of the story, the queen is flawed by an almost demonic gaze. Although she is still young and attractive, she is visibly altered. Her outward beauty has been marred by her inner obsession with beauty. In contrast, Hyman continually depicts Snow White as an innocent young adolescent who trusts those around her.

Hyman uses traditional icons to make the story even more meaningful. She places the queen and her mirror in several illustrations and shows how the woman's soul causes a transition in the mirror. As the queen changes, the mirror changes. Furthermore, the mirror's imagery alludes to the queen's pre-Christian training. The faces that encompass the golden frame seem to be held up by a she-devil. At first they all appear calm, but as the queen's drama unfolds, they distort into images of fear and death. These, in turn, change when the young woman becomes queen. Once the old queen dies, the mirror alone is depicted. Yet the princess is not out of the scene.

---

*All information about Hyman's personal motives in her illustrations come from my private conversations and correspondence with the artist.

The faces now surrounding the mirror reflect the young queen and take on a peaceful serenity. Although the figure supporting them cannot be seen, the positioned hands resemble those of Christ on the cross, and the mirror itself is reflecting the dawn of a new day.

Hyman purposely made her interpretation's setting abstract. She dressed her characters in costumes that are unidentifiable—they cannot be traced to a particular century. The queen seems to be caught in a time past. Her clothes are long and flowing. However, they appear more compatible to the 1920s than to medieval days. The princess wears a gingham dress covered with a contrasting apron. Her clothes, which are all in red, white, and blue, look more like Dorothy's in *The Wizard of Oz* than a princess's. For the most part, the dwarfs dress like twentieth-century taxi drivers, though there is one "wizardy" dwarf who appears to know that he is from another place, another time. Still, his clothes do not reflect medieval standards. Only the prince and his servants look as if they are fairy-tale characters. Hyman seems to be suggesting that this is an adaptation for audiences who are not interested in the golden age of chivalry so much as they are interested in the story's potential.

Hyman's reframing of the story's emphasis creates a feminist psychological drama. According to Madonna Kolbenschlag, "the dialectic of narcissism between the queen and the magic mirror is the dominant motive of the action. The wicked stepmother assaults her own soul, demanding reassurance of her desirability. The mirror—so like herself, so like a daughter—answers truthfully, but from a gradually changing perspective" (36).

Hyman uses binary images to her advantage throughout the book. She begins her framing with two scenes prior to the text that forewarn of Snow White's removal from the castle. At first, a young woman is depicted hanging up clothes at the side of a wooden forest dwelling while a fox looks on. Then, on the dedication page, a gnarled tree at autumn reflects a naturalistic view of the world; now an owl and the fox are staring out at the viewer. Thus, the viewer sees the child of innocence and the wisdom of nature. The animals suggest the wisdom of the storyteller who can observe and reconstruct events but cannot alter them. Once the story begins, Hyman concentrates on woman's maternal psyche. She shows Snow White's mother in the castle, dreamily staring out the window. She has pricked her finger and three drops of blood are on the windowsill. The woman looks as if she had just experienced pleasure, yet the prick of the needle should have caused her pain. Like all mothers, the scene seems to say, giving birth is both pleasurable and painful.

Hyman's careful portrayal of Snow White and her stepmother continually builds the psychological drama. As the young princess grows into a beautiful woman, her stepmother's beauty is destroyed. The child's wholesome trust creates a healthy outlook, while the queen's inner turmoil destroys those attributes she hopes to protect. The young woman is happy in nature but can be destroyed by the beauty trappings offered by the older woman. The queen's perception of woman's ultimate value as a commodity erodes her beauty. As the princess matures and develops, we are forced to view the her differently. By the end of the story, she is depicted as a beautiful young woman, not an innocent child.

Time is carefully alluded to within each of Hyman's scenes. The queen is first depicted in front of her mirror with a black kitten in her hands. By the last scene, the cat is fully grown. Snow White shows subtle changes also. At first she is childlike; her body has not developed, and her gaze is innocent of the world's ways. Once she awakens to find herself surrounded by the seven dwarfs, her eyes are wary. By the time the queen arrives to tie her up with a bodice, the girl has become pubescent. Finally, when she awakens in the coffin and sits up, her eyes are questioning. Her familiar apron is now tied around her waist rather than her neck, and her physique is that of a young woman.

Hyman uses the women's physical appearances to suggest a natural binary structure in the two main characters, and they reshape traditional imagery. Snow White and her mother are good women. They have dark hair and eyes, ivory skin. Their clothing is simple and unimposing. They are attractive without being sensual. In contrast, the queen is a striking blonde whose hair billows in the wind. Her dresses are low cut and form fitting. While blondes are known to have more fun, this woman cannot enjoy life in a natural way. In the end, the queen's understanding of the female's value as an object of beauty has caused her to lose her sanity. When the princess's inner beauty exceeds hers, the queen and the mirror become distorted and demonic. Because the princess is never depicted once she is "rescued from death," the reader can never be sure that she will learn to place a higher value on herself than her stepmother did. Since she earlier bought the material trappings of beauty from the queen, the reader is left to speculate about Snow White's fate. The story does not reach closure because the young queen's self-image has not been established.

Hyman's illustrations reshape Grimms' fairy tales and present a female perspective of the past, and they depict her interpretation of a feminist's cautionary view of *Snow White*. Hyman's reframing of the Grimm tale "Little Red-Cap" in *Little Red Riding Hood* is more closely aligned to Bartkowski's ideal. In *Self-Portrait: Trina Schart Hyman,* Hyman confesses that this is autobiographical, writing,

> I was a really strange little kid. I was born terrified of anything and everything that moved or spoke. I was afraid of people, especially . . . dogs (until my parents bought me a puppy of my own), horses, trees, grass, cars, streets. I was afraid of the stars and wind. Who knows why?
>
> My mother is a beautiful woman with red hair and the piercing blue gaze of a hawk. It was she who gave me the courage to draw and a love of books. She read to me from the time I was a baby, and once, when I was three or four and she was reading my favorite story, the words on the page, her spoken words, and the scenes in my head fell together in a blinding flash. I could read!

The story was *Little Red Riding Hood*, and it was so much a part of me that I became Little Red Riding Hood. (unpaged)

Hyman's mother sewed her a red cape and Trina spent a year role playing. In her autobiography, Hyman says, "I think it's a great tribute to my mother that she never gave up and took me to a psychiatrist, and if she ever worried, she has never let me know" (unpaged).

Little Red Riding Hood is a commonly retold story. Its earliest versions have caused grownups to censor the tale. Those versions that have Little Red Riding Hood strip off her clothes and share the bed with the wolf have almost disappeared. Generations of parents have also worried about the severity of the Perrault version, which simply has the little girl eaten, and the gory aspects of the Grimm tale, which has the huntsman save the little girl and her grandmother by cutting the wolf open and removing them from his belly. Trina Hyman chose to retell the story within her rewriting of the text and reframing of the action to fit the story she had heard and enacted as a child. Hyman had heard the Grimm version, and her childhood role playing was close to that story's plot. In her imaginative play, the hunter saved the child. Her conclusion of each day's journey in her own back yard came when her father arrived home. Together, they would re-enter her mother's home, safe for the night. Her visual retelling emphasizes the hunter's role as an outsider who helps the women in the story.

Furthermore, Hyman rejects the common psychological interpretations of male Freudians. She does not depict the wolf as a male aggressor intent on seducing a young girl. Instead she returns to her childhood play where her own little dog became the wolf. Since Hyman's play did not include a bed scene with a naked child and wolf sharing the covers as depicted by Gustave Dore in 1872, she does not develop a theme of sexual aggression in her illustrations. She has centered her story on the child's growing awareness of what fear means. The retelling found in Hyman's version of *Little Red Riding Hood* carefully reframes the story until it is not dominated by male images. According to Frances Bartkowski, this fits in the mode of feminist utopian writers; she says that the significant writers of feminine utopias are not interested in making a place for women within male society or of restructuring woman's place within patriarchal utopia. Instead, they create a world with "implicit reference to the world of the reader" (13).

Hyman has alluded to the fact that the symbolic characters and events in the story had a deep, personal meaning for her as a child. When she designed the dust jacket for her autobiography, she placed a young Trina Hyman on the back cover, dressed in a red cloak and standing next to the household dog. That fantasy, she seems to be saying, has a good deal to do with the adult who is retelling her life for others to read. The child stands behind the adult depicted on the front cover. When the viewer looks at the youthful scene, she notices that less than half of the little girl can be seen, but she is the reality in the scene. The dog Sam is looking at her in an expectant way. They stand on the edge of a colorless room. Their realness is a reflection of the artist's childhood fantasies. They fill an active part in the artist's day-to-day world as she returns the two adventurers into their utopian dream of adventure and survival. *Self-Portrait* was published in 1981, two years prior to *Little Red Riding Hood*. It is a preface for the fairy tale's intended audience.

The artist alludes to the fact that this is her story from the beginning of *Little Red Riding Hood*. When the viewer first encounters the book's heroine in the illustrations, she sees a small girl seated on a bench with book in hand. The book's title page spread shows Little Red Riding Hood reading her own story, and she is deeply engrossed. An adult black cat is standing near her, staring out at the reader. A glance inside the house shows her that Little Red Riding Hood's mother is a tall woman with red hair. Hyman is *foreshadowing* the story's happy ending, and she is suggesting that Little Red Riding Hood already knows what is about to occur, that she has been through this adventure before.

Hyman's *Little Red Riding Hood* reveals what the artist values from her past. It also demonstrates both her loyalty to her mother and her contemporary desire to maintain a self-supporting filial domain. Hyman had already revealed this concern in her autobiography. The last full-page illustration in *Self-Portrait* shows Trina Hyman in her kitchen. She writes,

> There is my good friend Barbara talking with Katrin, who has just come home for a few days from Bennington College. And there is Mimi, my mother, to say hello to Katrin, but Hugh O'Donnell will stop her to talk about getting rid of those maple tree branches. Judith is the one sitting under the catnip, looking amused.
>
> That's Betsy, bringing a basket of apples up from the cellar, and that's me with my head in the refrigerator. Sasha is waiting impatiently for whatever I come up with; Sam is sweetly in the way, and Maggie is barking her head off at Teddy (Hugh's dog), who she sees at least twice every day but still gets terrified at the sight of, and Mimi will praise Maggie for her bravery and good sense. Claudia, the cat, is smooching on Barbara's lap, and that's Lisl next to Sam, and Marty is peeking around the corner of the stove.

The world that the reader views in Hyman's *Little Red Riding Hood* is a twentieth-century female world, not the world of the Brothers Grimm. Part of that world evolves from Hyman's childhood. The high-topped boots and puffy sleeved dress Little Red Riding Hood wears do not come from the eighteenth century. And the house, with its painted shutters and geranium-laden decor, is a typical cottage of Hyman's American past. In fact, since this is Hyman's retelling of her favorite childhood tale, the domestic setting is from the Pennsylvania Dutch countryside of her childhood. The characters also come from Hyman's everyday world. A quick glance at this Little Red Riding Hood and the one on the autobiography's cover shows that Hyman has cast herself as the heroine and has set the story in the 1950s. If the reader is familiar with *Self-Portrait,* she recognizes that Hyman uses her cat and dog as central characters in her story. Little Red Riding Hood's mother is Hyman's mother, and the huntsman is a New Hampshire neighbor.

Hyman also uses symbolism to reflect the story's utopian meanings. The cat seems to represent Hyman as the storyteller. Cats, as cultural icons, represent traits attributed to independent women. They cannot be made to conform to societal demands, they can hunt and take care of themselves if need be, and they are jealously private creatures. Since the book is dedicated "to Mimi," the reader knows that men have not inspired Hyman to retell this story. Yet the huntsman's image is an integral part of the retelling. Because his icon is the American frontiersman, he seems alien to domestic life, willing to flee the female circle of home and security. The male and female worlds are clearly defined and separate; they are not conflicting views of the same world.

This interpretation fits with Kolbenschlag's discussion of early mother-daughter relationships. Kolbenschlag calls this a time of "monopoly," and she explains that a young girl's first responses to pleasure and pain are associated with her mother, causing her mother's ideals to overshadow all early experiences of intimacy, whether they are nurturing or destructive. She claims that the mother structures her daughter's ability "to enjoy the security of symbiosis and to fear the trauma of separation" (45). Hyman's retelling and reframing of *Little Red Riding Hood* centers on the child's relationship with her mother. While in her world and following her advice, Little Red Riding Hood is safe. Once in the woods, she is tempted by unknown dangers, but is not attracted to the wolf himself. In fact, she uses his advice only when she sees how it complements her female-dominated world.

Hyman draws her audience into the traditional tale with her first textual full-page illustration. Unlike the title-page illustration, no allusion exists as to the "story book" characteristics of the tale. A sense of tension is found in the scene. Little Red Riding Hood looks up at her mother with awe and respect. Her mother's clear blue eyes stare down at the child. The picture's perspective emphasizes the mother; she looms over the child, and her presence fills the page. The mother begins with a careful explanation of what the little girl should do, and Little Red Riding Hood responds with a promise. Hyman writes,

"Come here, Red Riding Hood, and listen to me. I want you to take this loaf of fresh bread, some of this sweet butter, and a bottle of wine to your grandmother. She is sick in bed, and they will do her a world of good. Go right away, before the sun gets too hot. Promise me that you won't daydream and stray off the path, and don't run, or you will fall down and break the bottle, and then there will be no wine for Grandmother. And when you get there, please don't forget your manners! Say, 'Good morn-

ing,' 'Please,' and 'Thank you' nicely, without staring 'round about or
sucking your finger. Don't stay too long, or else you will tire Grandmother. And when you have had a nice visit, come straight home."
"Yes, Mama," said Little Red Riding Hood. "I promise. I will do just as
you tell me." (unpaged)

The text is full of warnings, and the illustration reflects the mother's and
daughter's concern that the child do as the mother instructs.

Within the frame, Hyman places the talisman black cat. It is staring out
at the audience, and it seems almost as if the cat is telling the story. Its eyes
glisten with experience, suggesting that the drama is not new. It definitely
is aware that the viewer is looking on as the story begins. And, later, when
Little Red Riding Hood meets the wolf, the viewer notices that the cat has
followed along and is watching the drama unfold. The cat knows what is
happening, and expresses adult concern as it views the scene. Thus, Hyman's retelling holds various levels of experience within her pictorial
frames. The child's experience is one of innocence and first adventure, the
wolf's adventure is one of trickery and intrigue, and the cat's observations
reflect the adult who is returning to an already familiar story.

Hyman's story is not a simple retelling of a cautionary fairy tale. Her
interpretation indirectly shows the pitfalls of trusting strangers (especially
male strangers). The drama between the wolf and the little girl is heightened by Hyman's framing. Her careful structuring emphasizes that the
wolf represents the dangers in talking to and trusting in human strangers as
well as the folkloric dangers of traveling alone in an enchanted forest and
meeting talking wolves. It takes three frames for the wolf to suggest that
Little Red Riding Hood should enjoy herself. Within each ensuing scene
the wolf looks less animalistic, more human. In the end, the wolf stands on
his hind legs and places his paws on Little Red Riding Hood's shoulders,
and he tells the little girl,

> For goodness' sake, why don't you relax a bit, look at the world, and see
> how lovely it is? Why, I don't believe you even hear the birds sing, or
> enjoy the sunshine! You are just as solemn and well behaved as if you were
> going to school. Everything else is so gay and happy out here in the forest.

Thus, the wolf uses seductive male logic to entice the girl away from the
dictates of the mother and cause her to stray from her good behavior.
However, Hyman's text makes it clear that Little Red Riding Hood remembers her task. She writes that the girl strayed to pick flowers because
"They are a sight for tired, old eyes." The little girl tells the wolf good day
and goes on her own into the forest. She does not invite him to join her.
And once she has gathered all the flowers she can hold, she returns to the
path and walks "straight to the cottage."

Hyman stresses that the world Little Red Riding Hood finds comfort-
ing and familiar is the world of women. When she enters her grandmother's house with trepidation, she reminds herself, "I always like coming
to Grandmother's so much. Why should I feel so afraid?" Neither her

mother's nor her grandmother's house contain masculine objects to suggest that a male shares their lives. Hyman's wolf has entered a matriarchal world happily void of men. Hyman's illustrations and text imply that Little Red Riding Hood's inexperience in the world of men causes her demise. Once the little girl sees the wolf in bed, Hyman explains, "Red Riding Hood couldn't help but stare." The wolf plays with the little girl's sense of reality, answering her questions about his physical strangeness with mocking love. He tells her his ears are "The better to hear you with, my dear"; his eyes "The better to see you with, my dear"; his wolf hands are "The better to catch you and hug you with, my dear." But it is his mouth that causes the real pain. His deceitful words mock the child when he explains that his teeth are "to eat you up with, my dear!" Hyman's corresponding illustration shows the child's shock at being deceived and she writes, "As the wolf said this, he sprang out of the bed and ate up poor Little Red Riding Hood."

Little Red Riding Hood's lack of experience has caused her demise. However, the cat is too knowledgeable to be trapped. She is depicted in a small illustration, hiding in the flowers. Once the wolf has fallen asleep, the cat leaves the house and finds the huntsman. Together, they return to rid the house of the invader.

Hyman's huntsman looks into the household, and he understands that chaos has been caused by an unwelcome intruder. As a villager, he knows that Little Red Riding Hood's grandmother lives alone. He wishes to help the old woman and then return to his own world. He does not want to live in a domestic setting. Hyman has depicted her huntsman wearing a buckskin jacket, with a rifle slung over his shoulder and a Bowie knife tied to his side. He is a cross between the legendary frontiersmen and Hyman's own twentieth-century neighbor, Hugh O'Donnell, who has helped her raise sheep and understand the wilds of New Hampshire without expecting more than a cup of coffee in the kitchen. Once the hunter has saved Little Red Riding Hood and her grandmother, Hyman frames him in a domestic scene. Although he is holding the child, he is not giving her much attention; he seems ready to take his leave. The cat is at his feet, looking at him with admiration. She seems to know that his help was needed but that soon he will return to his own world. In the corresponding text, Hyman tells her reader, "They were all quite happy." She continues.

> The huntsman skinned the wolf and took the pelt home to nail to his door. Little Red Riding Hood and her grandmother sat down together to eat the fresh bread and sweet butter. The grandmother drank some of the wine, and Little Red Riding Hood had a cup of blackberry tea. After a while, the grandmother felt quite strong and healthy, and began to clean up the mess that the wolf had left in the cottage.

The female world is restored once again, and the males who caused the confrontation and resolution of the child's drama have disappeared. Hyman's Little Red Riding Hood walks home, aware that she did not closely follow her mother's advice. Hyman concludes, "She was comforted, though, that she had at least minded her manners, and had always said 'Good morning,' 'Please,' and 'Thank you.'"

"Surely," you are possibly saying to yourself, "these women don't expect me to believe all of this? It's just too sexual and political." As a group of critics who are actively revaluing texts, feminists ask all of us to rethink our cultural interpretations by returning to the stories we heard and saw as children and looking at them from a female point of view. However, feminists are not the only ones redefining the utopian worlds that authors create.

Marxist critics who have studied the cultural roots of children's literature are inclined to suggest that folklore did encourage early children's literature writers to create similar plots for moralistic pleasure reading. Some argue that the plot structures have been manipulated to reflect the values of those who tell the stories. Jack Zipes has written that the early oral tales were not created with children in mind, but that children were allowed to hear them. These first renditions, he argues, were "in the hands of the peasantry" and were not the castle tales that later evolved (14–16). The later literary tales found in fairy-tale collections created for educated children differed in content and purpose. Looking at the historical tales of France, Zipes concludes, "the basic function of the literary tale for children was to instruct. Amusement was a secondary goal" (18). These critics hold that the stories are less apt to reflect childlike dreams, more likely to hold a particular adult's expectations and values.

A *literary fairy tale,* or a modern *fantasy* story, might seem like a simple retelling of oral patterns. But it never is. The author is writing a tale that takes his reader on a trip into another realm. He understands that if his reader has been a consumer of folklore, she will identify the traditional elements that have been placed in the plot and will feel more comfortable with the tale. The author is not interested in recreating his everyday world, nor is he concerned with the probability of achieving his ideal in this world. Within his tale, he is exploring the moral and political concepts embedded in his society and is suggesting alternative views. When discussing the aims of utopian writing, Peter Alexander has argued, "the theoretical construction of utopias will be valuable if it helps us to clarify our ideas of sovereignty, freedom, equality, justice, law and related concepts" (35). In other words, utopias allow the reader a chance to see the world's order in another way.

Sometimes modern authors only allude to utopia when they are writing. Their new utopian worlds may be ones that the characters want to find but never truly reach. In the end, the heroes of these novels may settle for home. Often, because the authors leave the heroes in their contemporary surroundings they show their readers that "home" can be a better place if the characters can establish a new sense of realism for themselves in their own world.

I want to return to Lloyd Alexander and Amy Foster. Alexander is a twentieth-century children's author who has carefully reframed archetypal values in his fantasy worlds. If he ever was a consumer of traditional fairy tales, he has long since determined that the females in those plots are not very realistic. Though he would be hard put to call himself a feminist, he once told me that he never met a woman who was not strong. His childhood held many strong women, including his mother and older sister. He met his wife Janine in France during World War Two and brought her and her young daughter to America as a war bride and daughter after the war ended. Janine has talked about living in the rural countryside surrounding Paris and surviving by foraging off the land during World War Two. Obviously, both she and her daughter were strong and capable females.

Although Alexander does not subscribe to the feminist stance in literary criticism, all the women in his fictional lands are independent personalities. Often they are the true heroes of his stories. Yet, as a male author who writes for youngsters of both sexes, Alexander's worlds are not constructed to defy patriarchal society or to fit into the ideals of a world shaped just for women. And so, he probably never created a feminist *utopia* in the purest sense. However, he does reconstruct contemporary understandings of male and female roles in society. His lands are free of sexual stereotypes; his heroines are not always defined by their good looks; and they rarely end up marrying until a new order has been established. Alexander's books hold the skeleton maps for those utopias that Bartkowski has described as "in the speculative mode and organized with conscious wishes and fantasies"(161). And, she comments, these novels "tell of the power of speech and naming" (161). In the end, Alexander rewrites past stereotypes and patterns for a modern audience of adolescents who might have grown up on archetypal fairy-tale patterns by manipulating language in his reframing of old ideals.

This is what Amy Foster discovered when she read Alexander's *The Wizard in the Tree*. As a consumer of fantasy literature when she was young, Amy was struck by the similarities between this twentieth-century children's fantasy novel and the fairy tales she had earlier enjoyed. However, she was also struck by the differences she discovered in characterization and tone. When she began to write her final paper, she decided to look at feminist theory and rethink Alexander's fantasy. She also turned to the writings of Jack Zipes and studied Marxist theory. Finally, she incorporated the research she had earlier done for her first paper. It is important to remember that Amy is close to Alexander's implied reader in background and age. In the end, Amy wrote the following paper.

Lloyd Alexander, the Feminist and Author of
The Wizard in the Tree

BY AMY D. FOSTER

I personally enjoyed reading *The Wizard in the Tree* by Lloyd Alexander very much. This is an action-packed fantasy. Something suspenseful is always happening. The scenes are short and the plot is episodic, which makes the book especially enjoyable for female readers. Almost every chapter has a major cliffhanger at the end of it. Like many good books, the story drew me into the scene, and I wanted to know what happened next. During times when I would pick up the book with time to read only a chapter or two, I would find I had read three or four chapters because the cliffhangers kept me going. They created a lot of suspense.

In the back of my mind, I kept thinking that the plot seemed familiar. It reminded me of an old fairy tale. But it was not. *The Wizard in the Tree* is a very modern, liberated fairy tale/fantasy. I realized that the old fairy tale that this book reminded me of is Perrault's "Cinderella." Perrault's "Cinderella" is a traditional fairy tale. In traditional fairy tales, like "Cinderella," the beauty of the heroine is "the girl's most valuable asset, perhaps her only asset" (Zipes 188). In Perrault's "Cinderella," or "The Little Glass Slipper," references to beauty are made over **twenty** times in a nine-page story! I get tired, as a reader of fairy tales and fantasies, of being bombarded with descriptions of some female's good looks as her great asset. Alexander, on the other hand, never once even mentions Mallory's beauty. This is very refreshing to me. In *The Wizard in the Tree,* Mallory's looks are not at all important. Alexander just writes about a *person*.

Mallory can be compared to Cinderella in many ways. They are both girls who are orphaned, both are made to work very hard for a mean woman, and both are treated very poorly in the household in which they live. In her discussion "Cinderella and Women's Work," Madonna Kolbenschlag says that traditional women have described themselves as "waiting to be chosen, discovered, persuaded, asked to accept . . . hesitant . . . waiting to be told what to do . . . extremely anxious when they have to deal with unknowns" (105). Both Mallory and Cinderella could fit this mold.

There are many differences between Mallory and Cinderella, however. For instance, they behave differently. Cinderella is quite meek. She just cries when she is angry or upset—Mallory kicks! Cinderella waits for things to happen. And her adventures work out because the prince she desires feels that she is pretty enough for him. He goes all over the countryside looking for her. She waits to be found. Mallory never waits. If Mallory wanted to do something, go somewhere, or even date a prince, she would make it happen. She is a modern heroine, a real go-getter.

The villain in "Cinderella" is the stepmother, whereas Alexander's villain is Mrs. Parsel. We all know how cruel and hateful Cinderella's stepmother is. Mrs. Parsel is every bit as cruel and hateful, and she is even more damaging and dangerous. She tricks Abrican and Mallory by displaying unfelt love, whereas the stepmother is openly cruel. Mrs. Parsel beats Mallory and calls her many horrible names in front of others. Cinderella is abused too, but I believe that Mallory is more seriously abused both emotionally and physically. Mrs. Parsel has less reason to treat Mallory cruelly. The stepmother's abuse of Cinderella comes from her true love of her own children. She wants to try to make sure that her daughters get husbands, and she realizes that Cinderella would be very desirable to the men in the area because of her beauty. This is why the stepmother keeps Cinderella hidden away and dirty from her sitting in the cinders. Mrs. Parsel, on the other hand, is just lazy and cruel. She resents taking responsibility for Mallory's care, and she keeps her around only to do the work she finds distasteful. Furthermore, she shamefully takes her frustrations out on Mallory. Mrs. Parsel makes fun of Mallory in front of others: "If you ask me, it's the fairy tales that does it. Her head's so stuffed with those tales; I try every way to beat them out, but to no use" (34). "It's the fairy tales. The fairy tales have burst her brain" (133). "They've chewed away at her mind until there's hardly a rind left" (138). Mrs. Parsel blames Mallory's reading of fairy tales for whatever Mallory says or does that she does not like.

Alexander constantly alludes to the old tales, but his story is not a re-telling of an old tale. The heroine and her wizard friend are not typical of fairy tale archetypes. Mallory is not a docile servant like Cinderella is. She is treated quite unfavorably by Mrs. Parsel, but she still does not do everything Mrs. Parsel tells her to do. Even though she worries about what Mrs. Parsel will do to her, Mallory still takes the basket of food intended for Squire Scrupner and gives it to Abrican. She does what she thinks is morally best, and she makes her own decisions. Abrican is very independent also. He is fully liberated from being a "mythic hero. He is crotchety and sarcastic and not impressed with human fairy tales and legends" (May 76). He is a contradiction to the mythos Mallory has come to expect through her listening to and reading fairy tales. And he tells her so: "You humans have always had the notion that anything important must be accompanied by a great show of nonsense" (52). Abrican brings a new reality to the fantasy pattern because he contradicts society's beliefs.

The male heroes in these two stories are very different. Cinderella's hero is a prince, and Mallory's unlikely hero is the old wizard Abrican. These men both provide the means for the heroine to get away from their unhappy, unfair home environments. However, to me, the modern female reader, Abrican is a more reliable hero. Mallory and Abrican both help each other. They learn about each other through long periods of interaction and conversation. Cinderella's prince's motivation for helping Cinderella is lust. And she waits for him to save her; she does not help him win her away from an unpleasant environment. Magic helps her.

There is magic in both tales, but the magic is very different. The magic in *The Wizard in the Tree* is used to do more important things than to make a girl look pretty for a ball. Abrican uses his magic to save his and Mallory's lives. For instance, Abrican casts a spell on a poker and it hits Scrupnor repeatedly. This gives Abrican and Mallory time to escape from his clutches. However, Abrican's magic often backfires. Then it is common sense that saves the two adventurers.

Alexander's story has many folk tale elements embedded in the plot. There is the absent or weak father figure in this story. Mallory's real father is dead. Her father figure is found in the kind-but-weak Mr. Parsel. Like Cinderella's father, Mr. Parsel seems to be entirely ruled by his wife. And the older female (mother figure) is the heroine's worst enemy. Alexander uses many allusions to other fairy tales also, and he points out that they are *tales*. Mallory is constantly harassing Abrican about what an enchanted wizard should look like and what a wizard should and shouldn't do. She asks him things like, "Shouldn't you have a magic wand?" (52). Mallory even requests three wishes when she first finds out that Abrican is an enchanter. And she is surprised at his lack of "traditional" experiences: "You mean you never changed pumpkins into coaches? Or spun straw into gold?" (48). Mallory has many ideas because of her exposure to and belief in fairy tales. She is so used to the story patterns that she believes they are realistic. I would not have enjoyed this book nearly as much if I had not earlier experienced fairy tales as pleasure reading.

Alexander's wicked villains and heroic heroes make this book more entertaining than "Cinderella." His personalities are more detailed and they seem more realistic. Furthermore, the plot is more exciting for me because I do not know what happens to Mallory after she watches Abrican leave her world.

The Wizard in the Tree leaves me thinking and pondering, unlike "Cinderella." When I was done reading "Cinderella," I was **done** reading "Cinderella." The story reaches closure. Everything is all neatly tied up. When I finished Alexander's book, I knew I was not fully informed about the story's meaning. I had been deeply affected by the awful names that were slung at Mallory throughout the book. Words such as "slut" and "wench" were continually thrown at her. I felt anger at Mrs. Parsel for calling Mallory names. But, don't get me wrong, this did not make me angry at Lloyd Alexander. On the contrary, I believed that Alexander used these words to develop strong characterization. I felt that the reader is meant to feel contempt for the more villainous characters who treat the heroine so poorly. Alexander had his characters reveal their true personalities by their use of language.

I felt that I had to take a second look at the story to truly understand it. I went back and read some criticism on Alexander. And I read some interesting material about feminine imagery in literature. All of the professional reviews I have read about *The Wizard in the Tree* were completely positive except for two. Rosemary Weber writes, "*The Cat Who Wished to Be a Man* and *The Wizard in the Tree* are essentially variations on the standard Alexander theme: proving oneself a person of worth even when one has no family background" (19). I have also read a book by Alexander from the Vesper series, and I am not so sure that there is a standard Alexander theme. Furthermore, Weber is saying that Alexander would treat a male hero the same way he treated Mallory. I cannot believe that he would. I believe that Ms Weber's interpretation of the theme of *The Wizard in the Tree* is too simplistic. I know that she is not as careful with her language as Alexander is when he writes. It is impossible for a person to have **no** family background! Weber goes on to say, "Characters must not be created: they must grow and show evidence of it" (19). I believe that Alexander's story is stronger than the traditional fairy tale because the characters act uniquely within the fairy tale plot.

I also cannot agree with Barbara Wersba's review in the *New York Times Book Review* when she says,

> In the end, of course, all turns out well and the grumpy wizard sets sail for neverland. The girl is left behind, much wiser for her adventures, and the only person who feels cheated is the reader. Perhaps this is because the story has been done so many times before, in various disguises, and done best by Mr. Alexander himself. If he is to continue as an artist, he must find new countries to explore. (18)

Alexander did what was right at the end of the story, and this reader, one closer to the right age for the real reader, was left feeling good about Mallory. She does not need to go to "neverland." She is ready to succeed on her own. Alexander has turned around the standard theme of a heroine waiting to satisfy society's goals and to be married off; it has been replaced with a far better message for the contemporary reader.

References

Lloyd Alexander. *The Wizard in the Tree*. Illustrated by Laszlo Kubinyi. New York: Dutton, 1975.

Anne Commire, ed. *Something About the Author*. Detroit: Gale Research, 1972.

John T. Gillespie and Corrine J. Naden. *Best Books for Children*. New York: Reed, 1990.

Mary Jacobus. *Reading Women*. New York: Columbia University Press, 1986.

Madonna Kolbenschlag. *Kiss Sleeping Beauty Good-Bye: Breaking the Spell of Feminine Myths and Models*. New York: Harper & Row, 1988.

Rebecca J. Lukens. *A Critical Handbook of Children's Literature*. Oxford: Scott, Foresman and Company, 1982.

Jill P. May. *Lloyd Alexander*. Boston: Twayne Publishers, 1991.

Jill P. May. "Lloyd Alexander," in *Twentieth Century Children's Writers*. New York: St. James Press, 1989.

James A. Norsworthy. "The Wizard in the Tree," in *Catholic Library World*, October 1975.

Charles Perrault. *Perrault's Fairy Tales*. New York: Dover, 1969.

Rosemary Weber. "Lloyd Alexander," in *Twentieth Century Children's Writers*. New York: St. Martin's Press, 1978.

Barbara Wersba. "The Wizard in the Tree," in *New York Times Book Review*, May 4, 1975.

Jack Zipes. *Don't Bet on the Prince*. New York: Methusen, 1986.

Amy's discussion of Alexander's book and of his critics emphasizes that the author's implied reader may be someone who will look at the worlds he creates in an enlightened, contemporary way, using a writing style and personal tone often different from the academic stances penned by professors who "do" literary criticism. Yet her ability to read criticism and apply it to her reading of literature suggests that, while Amy is not a scholarly critic, she is doing more complex analysis than typical book reviewers. She has learned to compare the "utopian world" created by Perrault with the ironic realities of Abrican's and Mallory's world, and she has decided that Alexander need not send his central child character to "neverland" in order to entertain and enlighten a modern reader.

6

Realism and Moral Attitudes in Children's Literature

Few authors simply write to wile away the time. And very few authors write strictly to entertain their readers. As humans involved in a contemporary world, writers observe the people and events surrounding them. They react to things that excite them and those that upset them. Writers also read, and they discover how the past has given rise to the present. What they observe becomes important to them; they want to share with others what they have seen or read and thought about. In other words, writers write to tell us about life.

Still, writers usually have a good story to tell, and they aren't simply creating *didactic literature*. Fiction authors often want to entertain their readers more than they want to instruct them about life and they become involved in the story they are telling. As they write, the events come alive, the characters take on new shape.

Most authors say that once they began to write, their characters did things they had not planned for them to do. Much like parents, they explain that they had something in mind for their main characters, but at one point in the story found their characters wanting to do something else. It is hard for us to believe that authors don't simply create a story, that something may happen to make them feel differently about what they are writing.

While writing, an author may read a story or a news report or see an event that changes the way she wants to depict the events in her story. Or she may begin to like her characters as she writes about them and unconsciously create less stereotypic personalities than she had planned when she started writing.

When writing historical fiction, an author will base her story on real events and places, so she is influenced by accounts of the past. She will research that past to write a story for a contemporary audience, and may have a story in mind when she begins. However, that story may change if she finds new information—or her perspective about characterization may be altered by editorial demands. Character development also changes a story's outcome. Sometimes a change in the narrator's perspective about events or characters will change the story's course. Suddenly, the obvious hero is less heroic, the villain a bit nicer. All of this means that a story created around a good idea may seem less didactic because a good author will not allow a didactic theme to dominate.

Children's author Marjorie Filley Stover lived in West Lafayette for several years prior to relocating in the West, and we have often talked together about her writing. Mrs. Stover is married to an American historian who taught at Purdue University, so she might take her research efforts a bit more seriously than other children's authors. Still, most of the historical fiction authors I have met and talked with like to talk about their research, so her experiences don't seem atypical.

Many of Marjorie's stories have originated from family experiences. For instance, her book *Trail Boss in Pigtails* is based on the real-life adventures of an actual family. Emma Jane, the heroine, was married to Marjorie's grandfather's cousin, Elijah Filley. The two cousins settled on Nebraska farms only a few miles apart. When Marjorie's father was a boy, Emma Jane told him the story about her cattle drive adventure. One night, when Marjorie and her husband were visiting with her father, he retold the story. He said that he had been doing research at the Nebraska Historical Society and had run across a brief account written by Emma Jane's husband for a book based on true pioneer experiences. The next morning Marjorie went to the library and copied the complete story. She recalls, "Typed, it made one single-spaced page, but that furnished the bones for my story, and my father was able to add a few details."

When Emma Jane's father discovered that he was ill with tuberculosis he decided to leave Texas and take his family back to Illinois where they had relatives who would be able to help them. He determined to drive his cattle to the Illinois stockyards where they would get a fair price, and he began the trek with his family. However, he died in Waco, Texas, and Emma Jane was forced to lead the drive herself.

Emma Jane, the oldest of the children, faced the responsibility of getting her ailing mother, younger sisters and brothers, and eighty-two longhorns all the way from Waco, Texas, to Avoca, Illinois, in 1859. She presented an unusual, but realistic, picture of frontier situations. This was a brave, unusual thing for a young woman to do, and Marjorie was eager write about it. Marjorie wanted to tell how one youngster faced life after the family crisis of her father's death. Emma Jane was not yet fifteen, but she became the head of her household when her father died.

Since Marjorie is constantly reading children's literature, she probably knew that if the book were published, it would fill a gap in children's historical fiction. When she completed her book at the beginning of the 1970s, it was not like the other frontier stories previously published. It had more realism than the typical girls' historical novel that depicted survival in frontier times. Most young girls in American schools were used to reading books like those by Laura Ingalls Wilder. Earlier books contained romanticized retellings of a family's survival in the prairie country during the 1800s. Wilder's own memories were of growing up in a loving family that was dominated by "Pa," the male hero, and nurtured by "Ma," the quiet female who wanted a secure home of her own. Books like hers seem to suggest that pioneer children generally grew up in loving two-parent families. However, those pictures of pioneer family life do not represent all prairie families in the late years of the 1800s.

In fact, women survived in various family situations. Historians Joan M. Jensen and Darlis A. Miller have pointed out that many women homesteaded on their own, without a husband, and that in some areas of Colorado women were more successful at homesteading than men. In addition, they have noted that women who were married had more children if they lived in the West than if they lived in the East, that they often died at an earlier age. Historically, children often lived without a two-parent family; often one of their parents would die and leave them with adult responsibilities before they reached their teen years (183, 190–191).

Marjorie Stover's story holds a sense of realism not found in much of the children's literature published earlier. It is about a young fourteen-year-old girl who listened to her father's dreams of relocating his family back in Illinois where they had started. She decided to take her family's cattle to a faraway market in order to support her family and rebuild their lives after her father's death. Like Wilder's books, *Trail Boss in Pigtails* is based on Marjorie Stover's family's experiences. However, Marjorie's family remembrances were not ones she had lived through, and they were not detailed enough to sustain an interesting book-length story. Since they didn't take long enough to retell, Marjorie created a story that centered on Emma Jane's trials. Emma Jane is a carefully developed character; her struggles reveal what a young girl's reactions to the dangers would be as she faced the problems of a cattle drive across the Southwest and on to Illinois. Emma Jane is pictured as a youngster whose personal goals and common sense help her accomplish the things she sets out to do. From the beginning of *Trail Boss in Pigtails*, Emma Jane is facing the realities of early settlement in the American West.

Part of the story's reality is constructed by Marjorie's choice of episodes used to reflect social attitudes of the time. *Imagery* is built into this story, and it focuses the reader's understanding of this historical interpretation of the past, allowing the reader to feel events as they probably happened in the past. Furthermore, Marjorie uses foreshadowing to establish her drama. For instance, in the fifth paragraph of the opening chapter, she begins to develop a sense of realism when she *foreshadows* the father's death and writes,

Emma Jane's hands clenched the loose reins in her lap until the knuckles showed white. A fear that had been inching along in the back of her mind for weeks suddenly loomed over her like a hovering giant. She had to face it. She could no longer avoid it. Pa wasn't going to get well. *Pa wasn't going to get well!* (4)

Although the use of foreshadowing helps the reader accept what happens in the story, it does not romanticize Emma Jane's feat or create details that do not fit within American history. It was possible for women to take on male roles during that time. Women on the plains were outspoken heroines in U.S. history. Jensen and Miller note that there are records of women who could "outride, outshoot, and outcuss the best cowboys in the West" and they point out that these women were the heroines found in the dime novels and wild west shows of the 1800s. (181) Still, Emma Jane's role as the fourteen-year-old trail boss on a cattle drive was unusual for a youngster, and Stover knew that if she hoped to create a positive image of this youngster, she would have to depict her as resolved in her interactions with the men and the American Indians she met on the drive and to show Emma Jane's growth toward maturity as one that was admirable in her own day as well as in contemporary times. Emma Jane's personality had to be consistent; her experiences needed to reflect the attitudes about women and cattle drives held by the ranchers at that time.

Marjorie Stover read all the books she could about cattle drives and family life in the area of Texas where her heroine's family lived. She needed to be comfortable with her depiction of the countryside, so she read accounts kept in logs by the men involved in cattle drives. She determined what the weather and locale would be like by reading about the year she was recreating, the year of 1859. Even as she wrote, she continued to read. At one point, she found out that Queen's Anne lace had not yet been introduced to the countryside and she went through her story to eliminate her references to it. She read in the men's journals that they had to barter with the Indians as they passed through Indian territory, that they had antagonistic feelings about the Native Americans they came into contact with, and she had her characters talk about the Indians they met on the trail.

Emma Jane is a fictional female protagonist, but she is not portrayed according to traditional children's literature stereotypes of the frontier. She does not live in one home with a complete family, she has no one to give her advice on the trail, and she must interact with grown males to succeed. In fact, Emma Jane is closer to the historical reality of women in the frontier who acted as "the chief civilizing agents . . . whether they lived in mining camps, ranches, or sod-house prairie shanties" (Jensen and Miller 179). As Emma Jane meets the Native Americans one-on-one, she learns to barter with them and understand them. When Emma Jane trades with the first group she encounters, she says, "We take to make new home in land far beyond Indian borders" (151). Stover continues:

"New home." Emma Jane watched closely. Had she detected a glimmer of understanding in this proud man who only two decades earlier had been

forced to leave the land he called home and come with his scanty posses-
sions to a new land? She could not be sure . . . .

As the Indians turned into the draw and disappeared from sight, Emma
Jane whispered in half-wonderment, "I wasn't afraid. Oh, Pa, I wasn't
afraid. They're just people—displaced people like us." (152)

Emma Jane does not hold the typical distrust of the Native Americans or
regard them as savages who have no right to be where they are. Indirectly,
she gives the frontier settlement a new perspective.

Marjorie also hoped to depict a growing girl's desire to be a respected
female in the West. Thus, when Marjorie Stover first wrote her story, she
began it with a scene of Emma Jane dressing.

Emma Jane tapped one foot impatiently and pulled her brown gingham
skirt farther down over her black stockings. Maybe next winter Ma would
let her wear her skirts longer. After all, she was thirteen, going on fourteen. She'd soon be a young lady and able to wear her hair done up instead
of in two brown braids flopping down her back. "Pigtails," Pa teasingly
called them.

She ended her story with Emma Jane thinking about her future, and wrote,

Emma Jane pulled a brown pigtail over her shoulder and flicked the wispy
end between her fingers. No longer was she a pigtailed trail boss. Next
month she would be fifteen—almost a young lady.

Satisfied, Marjorie mailed her story to her editor. She was pleased with
the realism in the portrayal. Her heroine was nearly fifteen, the age when so
many young women were expected to accept the responsibilities of adult-
hood. Her interest in hair and clothes seemed natural. However, Stover's
editor explained that the ending had to be changed. Though it might have
been conventional for females to give up their braids, their high spirits, and
their rough-and-tumble ways then, this was the twentieth century. Her
editor wrote back, saying,

This is a perfect women's lib book and to have her suddenly content to be
nothing but a young lady seems to dissipate the effect of the whole. It is
undoubtably what she would have felt in that time, but it is not quite the
right approach for today's world. Is there something to end the book that
would be logical for that time, but that wouldn't seem like a cop out to
today's kids? [Maybe when you see the book in galleys it will come to
you.]

The editor wanted to realign history so that Emma Jane would appear to
be "modern." Since Emma Jane needed to stay her high-spirited self in
Marjorie's mind, she changed her ending so that it fit within the editor's
needs and her own. She has explained her rewriting, saying,

When I stopped to think about it, I knew that the length of her skirts
weren't the most important thing in Emma Jane's life either. She had just
spent weeks and weeks working very hard to get those cattle to Chicago

so that her family would be able to buy a farm where they could be together and support themselves.

I went back to the typewriter and rewrote the conclusion. This is a much stronger ending and far more logical for a girl who had shouldered the responsibility of being the leader of her family and brought them and her herd of longhorns a thousand miles up the trail.

When Marjorie considered the editor's suggestions and changed the book's ending, she let her plot be shaped less by history than by a twentieth-century perception of how history should be reflected for a contemporary audience. Her editor also suggested that she write an *Epilogue* explaining Emma Jane's life after she was the "trail boss in pigtails." Marjorie was able to place the earlier image of Emma Jane into her story, but the emphasis was changed.

Emma Jane pulled a brown pigtail over her shoulder and flicked the wispy end between her fingers. The Burkes would be an independent family. She had fulfilled Pa's dream.

Or had she? Her fingers, clutching the wispy end of braid, were still. Maybe buying the farm was really just the beginning of Pa's dream. And what did she, Emma Jane, know about running a farm?

She had been too young to pay any mind to the planting and harvesting of fields before Pa pulled up stakes and moved to Texas. Shucks! All she knew was trail driving. . . .

A familiar quiver rippled along the curve of Emma Jane's face. Next month she would be fifteen. No longer was she a pigtailed trail boss, but managing that eighty acre farm was going to be a challenge. (218–219)

In the end history wins out. Marjorie's epilogue tells us that Emma Jane was married before she was twenty years old, and that she and her husband moved to Nebraska "where once again Emma Jane faced the hardships of frontier life" (219). Then she explains that Emma Jane and her husband sometimes hired over twenty hired hands, and that Emma Jane often had to drive in her wagon to the bank. Once again, Marjorie paints a word picture of a courageous woman, writing,

The return trip was not without its dangers because of the possibility of a hold-up—especially at a narrow bridge part of the way home. Therefore, Emma Jane always drove a team of fast mules. The money bags were securely stowed in the buggy so they could not jolt out. The mules set a good pace, but as they approached the bridge, Emma Jane braced her feet and lashed the mules to cross at break-neck speed. (219–220)

The ending of Marjorie Stover's book is successful because Emma Jane's personality remains intact. Not curling her hair and donning a dress does not make her less appealing as a heroine, and it doesn't change her growth from a young girl who is afraid that she might not be capable of leading her family and a herd of longhorns across the southwestern territories and into the Chicago market to a young woman who readily embraces the challenge of setting up the family farm. Still, Marjorie had placed enough scenes in her story to foreshadow Emma Jane's change from pants to skirts, from pigtails to curls, and the reader aware of the fact that foreshadowing gives clues to the story's ending might be surprised not to see Emma Jane change into a dress. After all, hair styles and clothing had been continually alluded to in the text. The earlier scene about changing her hair from braids was in the opening chapter, and once they reached Waco, Texas, Emma Jane had reflected on her attire and her "unladylike stance." Marjorie writes,

> But Emma Jane wasn't watching Captain Ross anymore. Instead her eyes were riveted on a girl wearing a pale blue dress sprigged with tiny pink flowers. Her dark hair was caught at the nape of her neck with an enormous bow, which fluttered like a huge pink butterfly.
>
> Emma Jane was suddenly conscious of her own disheveled appearance. Her boots and pants were muddy, and her jacket was spotted. The two brown braids hanging from beneath her battered hat were tied at the ends with bits of old string. Well, it couldn't be helped. (67)

A few pages later Marjorie says,

> How good clean clothes felt. Emma Jane pulled on a blue calico print that she had taken from the trunk. Skirts again! She brushed her shining brown hair and plaited it into two smooth braids. But she didn't get out her hair ribbons. The string was good enough for every day. (70)

Marjorie alludes to Emma Jane's desire to dress like a "lady" again at the end of the book. The last two paragraphs before the epilogue read:

> Emma Jane paused outside a small shop window with a display of ribbons. Suddenly she remembered a big pink bow bobbing up the street ahead of her in Waco. How long ago that was! She remembered Pa's words, "You're almost a young lady now." She thought of Elijah Farley's admiring glance.
>
> Turning to Uncle Oscar, she said, "May as well shop in here. Easter does admire pretty ribbons." She grinned. And maybe she'd just have one herself, too. (215)

For the reader who reads on and discovers Emma Jane's future, this is another foreshadowing scene. Elijah Farley, Marjorie tells her listener, becomes Emma Jane's husband before she is twenty years old.

Marjorie Stover has talked about the editor's change in her ending, and she has said that she thinks it is perhaps better than the first ending she wrote. She has added that if she were to do it again, she would have saved the epilogue for a sequel so that she could have developed Emma Jane more completely, showing her change from trailboss to frontier wife. Still, this was her first children's book and she wanted it published. Authors are aware of their audiences and realize they will need the support of editors if they hope to be published.

In fact, the addition of the "Epilogue" adds to the "authenticity" of Emma Jane's characterization as an independent, courageous woman in modern terms. But it is not necessarily a truer ending for Emma Jane's saga. Historian Everett Dick notes that while on the westward wagon trail to California, women riders "discarded their silks, satins, laces, flounces, and pantalets for riding habits made of dark-brown denim" (290). However, there is no reason for us to believe that they had **permanently** discarded their female attire. Historians tell us that women were the "civilizing influence" on Western and prairie society. Old pictures show us women in skirts, even when they are homesteading. Furthermore, there is no reason to assume that Emma Jane's desire to look like the other women around her would change her personality. Nor is there any reason to believe that Emma Jane wanted to remain single. Marjorie indirectly tells us that this is not true when she tells us in the epilogue that Emma Jane married Elijah Farley, the cowboy she thought of when she determined to buy ribbons for her hair.

Marjorie Stover was telling a good story about someone she admired. She may have wanted the reader to see Emma Jane's plucky attitude and emulate it, but I doubt that she really began to write the book as a lesson in feminism. She was more interested in showing young readers what the Western movement was like for one family. Furthermore, she never intended to write a modern story of realistic fiction. Her research was not concerned with contemporary attitudes about women as heroines. She concentrated her research on the historical accounts of trail riding. Her realism involved the conditions of life in 1850.

Marjorie's editor, on the other hand, hoped to sell the book to an adult audience looking for stories about "liberated women" that they could give to young female readers who had already heard about girls who let down their hair and turned into young ladies. Her audience wanted stories that were less "romantic." Though the editor may have felt that the new ending never changed the "reality" of life on the trail, she had not done her historical research to see that women in the mid-1800s were expected to dress in a particular way if they were to enter society. What she did know was that the ending she suggested would appeal more to contemporary book reviewers. If the ending held a dominant impression that Emma Jane never quite became a "lady," the book would probably get better reviews. And so, Emma Jane did not join her historical sisters in the clothing she was probably wearing when she drove to the bank. For all the modern reader knows, she still wore pants. While the editor hoped to make Emma Jane more modern and liberated, she failed to see that young girls were being presented with a new romanticism, a romanticism of women who acted and dressed as their male equivalents did. Indirectly, by suggesting that Emma Jane's ending must comply with modern standards, the editor was implying that the clothes make the woman, and that is exactly what feminists have tried to disavow.

Perry Nodelman argues against the "rewriting" of history to present a more acceptable modern image, stating that this creates a reader who is self-indulgent, who expects things to work out in stories in a way that is similar to her life. He suggests that readers need to learn to do more than simply identify with the main characters, and he argues,

> In training children to identify, to read only themselves, we sentence them to the solitude of their own consciousness. Less significantly but just as sadly, we deprive them of the pleasures of genuinely admirable fiction— the ability of carefully chosen words to evoke experiences we have never experienced and to show us lives we have never lived. The more we teach children to read about themselves, the smaller will be the audience for writing about people different from ourselves, and good writing, whether for children or grownups, is never about anything else. (152)

If authors know that their books won't be published unless the editors can see a modern audience for their stories, what sorts of stories must they write? How can they write the future while they are looking at the past?

Whenever we read a story, someone is telling it to us, even if we fail to see the narrator in the story. The narrator "talks" to the reader, and that person "narrates" an adventure for us. As we become the listeners, we are experiencing the story while allowing the narrator to tell the story without interruptions. We are "hearing the narrator out." The story becomes a simulation of "ordinary talk." The narrator is our confidant as we enter into another world and share the adventures the story contains by looking at the scenes through another person's eyes. We trust the narrator because the narrator is assuming that we want to be friends, to hear about "the best of times and the worst of times."

Authors who use first-person narrative depend on the same sorts of audience reactions as storytellers. They expect the audience to react to the narrator in a positive way, to learn about the events and outcome without having to hear a didactic moral overtly preached. If a moral exists, the story acts as an oral *fable,* a tale told to reveal a particular attitude or value. This is the writing style Ann Turner used when she wrote *Dakota Dugout.* Turner's short narrative is published in a picture book, but it would work as effectively if it were simply read out loud to a group of children because Turner is using the storyteller's tricks of direct communication and controlled descriptive language. It is a story that fits into the realm of realism because Turner discusses a seemingly disjointed series of scenes. And she creates a storytelling vernacular that suggests a woman speaker who has lived her life in the prairie. Her language is direct and sparse. It seems that the narrator is remembering the past as she speaks. And so, Turner's narrator creates a believable world for her listener. Turner begins her tale by addressing the reader as if she and the narrator were engaged in a two-person conversation. She writes,

> Tell you about the prairie years? I'll tell you, child, how it was.

> When Matt wrote, "Come!" I packed all I had, cups and pots and dresses and rope, even Grandma's silver boot hook, and rode the clickety train to a cave in the earth, Matt's cave.

Built from sod, you know, with a special iron plow that sliced long earth strips.

Matt cut them into bricks, laid them up, dug into a hill that was our first home.

I cried when I saw it.

The text is broken into segments to facilitate the picture-book format. Each separation is complemented by a lifelike black-and-white drawing that depicts a realistic scene. When the text and illustrations are viewed together, the bleakness of Turner's description of the prairie years is softened. And while the two flow together to give the remembrances a feeling of plot, there really is not a traditional beginning, middle, and ending like those found in the typical stories in children's picture books.

The text creates word impressions of events. Turner says the two lived "snugged like beavers in our burrow," that the woman "pasted newspaper on the walls," that the wind blew across the prairie with a "*shoosh*-hush, *shoosh*-hush" sound. A feeling of realism evolves, though the listener is never sure how long Matt and the woman lived alone on the prairie, how many crops failed, how they found the money to go on. The narrator retells her life, and we believe in her retelling because it is poetic, descriptive.

Ronald Himler has reflected the spirit of this woman in his illustrations. Throughout, the narrator is never directly portrayed in a dejected stance, even when Turner tells about the summer when the couple faced ruined crops, and "Matt sat and looked for two whole days, silent and long." The double-page illustration for this simple statement shows Matt sitting in the ruined cornfield on the right-hand side of the illustration while the narrator looks out over him and the field, back turned to her audience, apron tied around her waist, and laundry basket resting on her left hip. This is an honest retelling of the pioneer past, both in text and illustrations. Turner and Himler have created a sense of survival, a narrative image of strength, and have evoked a feeling that this is oral history retold for new audiences. The didacticism in the story is placed at the end when Turner's narrator sums up her past by saying,

Talking brings it near again, the sweet taste of new bread in a Dakota dugout, how the grass whispered like an old friend, how the earth kept us warm. Sometimes the things we start with are best.

Turner's story is found in a picture book, but it is as complex as Marjorie Stover's story because of its imagery, its sense of the past, and its implications concerning values. There are loose ends that are left up to the reader. If the reader knows about mail-order brides, she can sense that the narrator might have been one. When she begins to explore the prairie woman's importance in the westward movement, she will benefit from Turner's narrative and Himler's illustrations. Together they have created a vignette of a society long ago, a place where isolated men and women depended on themselves and the earth for their future. Afterwards, if she wonders what sorts of adventures women had in the West, she can look for further first-person accounts.

When discussing the importance of story-making in society, Barbara Johnstone commented, "there is nothing more complex, structured, and revealing of our human nature than ordinary talk, and nothing more interesting than learning to notice it and understand it as an object of beauty. . . . Shared voices help to create communities of people and reflect the texture of the communities" (2). Using the first-person narrative, the author always strives to create a bond between herself and her listener and give her reader the feeling that her central character is a real person. Indirectly, this creates a shared experience for the character and the reader, even if the listener never hopes to live in a similar situation.

Many authors probably use first-person narrative in order not to seem didactic. The narrator says, "Let me tell you all about it," and the reader listens. If the narrator says, "I've learned something from my experience," the listener can pause in agreement and appreciation or consider that the teller might not have learned as much as she suspected. Often, however, the reader simply takes in the story and moves on without relating the narrator's experiences directly to her own life. The experience expands the reader's understanding of the past and the present without placing moral judgments in the story. The author recreates a world that explains the past and its relationship to the present.

Almost all children's historical novels for older children hold a *dominant impression*. The introductory scene or the closing scene where characters are involved in the beginning or ending of a conflict, the descriptive scene that creates the entry into a new world, or the scene that introduces the story's conflict may capture the reader's attention and can later resurface when the reader returns to the story and rethinks its characterization, plot, setting. The author of fiction uses language to draw the reader into her story. While she may want to create a sense of the ordinary that allows her reader to believe the story could be true, the author can also create an unusual twist in her story to capture her audience's attention and heighten reader interest. Sometimes it is the stark realism that causes readers to reconsider if the book might be realistic. Something true to life may not seem credible in a story. Yet when it is revisited within a plot it may seem more realistic, and may say something not said within the conventional story patterns of romance.

George Levine, when discussing the elements of realism, stresses that writers of realistic fiction tend to write against traditional literary conventions. These writers try not to create a stereotypic hero or villain, and they strive to recreate events in ways that are not romantic. Their endings are not necessarily happily ever after, and their characters don't always understand why things happened as they did. Writers of historical realism hope to give their readers some insight into the past events they are recreating. Thus, they form characters who are anti-heroic and they write about social conditions as they really existed. Even so, these authors choose the events they wish to use, and they create the characters they want involved in their story. Such writing, Levine suggests, is not an actual projection of the past. It is always suspect to "the recognition that the reality it most adequately represents is a subtly disguised version of its own desires" (15). Put another way, we can look at realism as a way of rewriting the past in order to change the reader's interpretation of it. That means that the reader who meets a character's unromantic ending will understand why the past needed to change, why societal beliefs and behavior evolved as they did.

Realism often leaves the reader with a sense of uneasiness because she sees things in controversial ways and because the writing is puzzling. The books that cause readers to pause can cause them to reread the accounts. Writers of realism often allow for different responses to the same story. They do not hope to didactically reshape history for moralistic purposes, but they do strive to create a new awareness and need for reflection for their audiences.

English children's author Jill Paton Walsh once wrote that literature is not simple, that it does not contain a "neat little . . . moral" (38). And she went on to say, "it is possible to read a realistic book as though it were not really fiction at all, but a statement of fact of some kind—a narrative chunk of autobiography, reminiscence, eyewitness account, or some such" (38). Walsh argues against teaching one interpretation of a story. She denies that realism holds "one-horse rides, with only one drift, one meaning" (38). An excellent writer of children's historical fiction, Jill Paton Walsh strives to create complex stories that allow for multiple reactions and interpretations. This is the sort of realism we should look for when we are sharing children's literature.

One year when I was teaching the undergraduate children's literature class, I assigned two books about children and their wartime experiences to my students. Both books were written by women. One, however, chose to have her narrative told by a male protagonist while the other used a female. One book contained the realistic events of death and family separation, the other chose to allude to the family's return to their "normal life" after the war. One produced a narrator/confidant, the other created an unreliable narrator. Both concentrated on the horrors of war. Both were written for older children and adolescents who are beginning to question the everyday morals of their lives. These representations of past experiences imply that society is not always ruled by moral or just attitudes. Because both authors used first-person narrative, they were able to depict an adult society with questionable values from a child's perspective, leaving final value judgments to the reader.

Andi's War, by Billi Rosen, tells of a Greek family torn apart immediately after World War Two when civil war broke out in Greece between Communist partisans and loyalists. Rosen herself was living in Greece when she wrote the book, and she begins by talking directly to the reader. Her foreword explains Greece's history and the background of the war. Her personal warning that the past contributed to the present problems of the Greek people and that "the present may be prologue" to more change is placed in the foreword's conclusion:

> Now, in 1987, Greece is at peace with itself. It has a democratic (socialist) government, which came to power in 1980, and there is freedom of speech and political freedom for all. Thanks to tourism, Greece has become prosperous to a degree unimaginable even twenty years ago. These days all children sit down to three square meals a day, and wear shoes every day of the week.
>
> Me, I look at the hills and keep my fingers crossed.

For the reader who is astute enough to interpret the foreword, a tone of foreboding has been set. For the reader who skips the prologue and begins with the first chapter, a second warning is placed in the text. When Rosen begins her fictional story, she opens with a parable; a grandmother is telling her granddaughter a legend about a bold young woman who defied the country's Sultan and was put to death. Rosen switches her scene back to the protagonist and begins her first person narrative as she continues:

> "So she didn't live well and we still better?"
>
> "No, not in this story."
>
> "And she didn't get a dress which was as the sky with all its stars?"
>
> "I'm afraid not."
>
> I swallowed hard. "I don't like that story," I said, my voice thick with tears.
>
> Grandmother pulled the sheet up around me and bent down to kiss me good-night but I turned away. "Andi," she pleaded, "all stories can't live happily. Besides, it was you who insisted on a different kind of story wasn't it?" (2)

Rosen's story begins with a powerful scene between grandmother and grandchild. The grandmother tells of a legendary young woman who helps the leader of a rebellion and faces death rather than betray him. The young narrator says, "That was very brave of her, wasn't it Grandmother?" Then the grandmother explains that fear is the only thing that keeps one from being brave, and she recalls how she kept the girl alive when she was near death as a baby. Finally, Rosen ends the chapter with the narrator saying,

> Now I was sleepy and content to lie back in bed and let Grandmother go. Later, when she'd given Aunt Hercules a hand with cousin Aki—he'd got so big it needed the two of them to carry him to bed—she'd come back. Careful not to wake me she'd creep in beside me, and I, who would not be asleep, would throw my arm across her broad back and only then would I close my eyes, safe at last from the night and the sounds of war filtering down from the brooding, thyme-covered hills that surround our village. (4–5)

The reader trusts the narrator and is ready to accept the account placed within this book. Yet the reader should not feel secure. The dominant impression is one of turmoil. Rosen loads her first chapter with unanswered questions that the reader must ponder. Who is the narrator? How old is she when the story is taking place? Who is Aki? Where are her parents? Whose war is this? How old is the narrator now? In addition, Rosen's style creates a sense of foreboding for her reader because it contains several clues that "this is a different kind of story."

Jill Paton Walsh's *Fireweed* is set in London during the World War Two bombings. As a British citizen, Walsh is weaving her country's history into her retelling of that wartime action. Although her book does not include a foreword, she has left clues about the book for the thoughtful reader. She dedicates the story to her father-in-law and writes,

> My thanks are due to almost everyone I know who is old enough to remember 1940; to many other authors whose work I have consulted; and to Miss Elizabeth Almung, who gave me invaluable assistance.

Thus, Walsh implies that she has done a good deal of oral history research as well as book research prior to her writing. Because her narrator is male and her book is dedicated to her father-in-law, the reader might imply that this is a story told by father-in-law (expanded of course) and that these are experiences she first heard about from him or encountered herself.

Walsh's narrator reveals that he is less honest than Rosen's Andi is when he tells about his past, and the reader can view him as a less reliable narrator. His narrative implies that the reader must continually question what he is saying by thinking about what he is not saying. He must deconstruct the story to look for missing pieces. Walsh's male narrator begins as if the reader had just asked a question. The protagonist sets up a scene in a British underground railway station and tells his listener that it was an appalling place to be because it was overcrowded with people, it smelled of urine and perspiration, and it was unfriendly. Then he continues,

> I was fifteen that year, and she seemed sometimes younger, sometimes older. She looked older now because she had that air adults have, of knowing exactly what they are doing and why. Now I come to think of it, lurking is the wrong word for her; I was lurking—she was just staying put. But I knew she was playing some game like mine, because she hadn't any bedding either. (3)

The uncertainty in the text causes the reader to be slightly uneasy. This narrator seems less sure of himself.

The narrator tells how the two young people stumbled out on the streets of London together and hurried to the back streets, away from crowds and police. All this time, the narrator is following the girl he has just seen, observing and evaluating her. Finally he strikes up a conversation and the action begins. When she asks him his name, the narrator continues,

> "Bill," I said. That isn't my name, but I decided in that split moment to lie about it, just in case, and then I couldn't bring myself later to admit I'd not trusted her, and tell her my real one. "What's yours?"
> "Julie," she said. (6–7)

When the reader learns that the narrator lied to a person who must have made a great impact on his life, he begins to sense that perhaps he isn't hearing the complete story either, especially as soon as the narrator confesses,

> I told her a bit; I can't remember how much. After all this time it's no good trying to remember just what I said; when I try to remember I remember very clearly what it was like, what I might have told her; and I remember trying to impress her, thinking that if I made out that I had had a rough time she would see what a brave, tough type I was. And pathetic though it seems to me now, I really *did* think things had been rough. (8)

The dominant impression is one of uncertainty. The narrator seems foggy, and the reader senses that the story is being told in monologue that is a stream-of-conscious rambling. The narrator is returning to a scene he left behind long ago; he may or may not remember all the details of the past. He has already assured his reader that he will remember London more than he will remember conversations and events. The scene of his story will dominate. And that scene is precisely what the reader wants to know about: What, exactly was happening in London? How can a narrator who has hazy recollections about his past conversations and who talks about his father and aunt in vague ways tell an authentic story? Why does he keep so many secrets from those he meets? Will I be included among those people to whom he tells half-truths?

The next dominant scene for both novels concerns the effects of war on the country. The narrators recount how they first discovered what the war was doing to their home, and they have the reader see the war through their eyes. Andi tells her listener about the Greek problems, and she says,

> The big war was over. The Germans and Italians had gone home and so had our friends, the English, who'd helped to rid us of them, and here we were working up yet another war, one that had begun in the mountains but was coming closer to our village every day. Our mother and father, Paul's and mine, had both been in that other war, the one against the Germans and the Italians, but no sooner had they come back from that one than it was time for new farewells. It seemed to Paul and me that we had spent most of our lives saying good-bye to our parents. (7)

She explains that she, her brother, and her cousin have been sent to "the *stani,* the sheepfold," and she tells how the three children accidentally find a hiding place used by the partisans. The reader enters into the world of war with the narrator, reading,

> In the narrow band of grey light that poured in through the low opening, we began to take stock of our discovery. The floor was hard and smooth, the walls uneven with sharp rocks sticking out of them, and the ceiling as high as the dome of a church. To begin with, that was all we saw, but as our eyes became more accustomed to the gloom, we picked out an old pan, a *brikki,* and a small rusted spoon. At the very end of the cave we

stumbled over a thin wooden box, a bit like a coffin but not quite. I ran my hands over it and around it and felt the padlock. A locked box that looks like a coffin but isn't. . . . Well, one only locks things that are either very precious—or that one wants to keep a secret. It wasn't necessary to put two and two together to realize that others had been to the cave before us. Others, with secrets and things to hide. . . .

It was a big, heavy lock, the kind used to lock up shops and warehouses. It would take more than just a stone to crack it open.

"We'll have to come back, that's all," Marko said, as if getting up here were the easiest thing to do in the world. Still, if we wanted to find out what was in that box, a return trip was the only answer. (18)

Walsh's narrator flashes back to an earlier time when he was in London in order to explain how he ended up on the London streets alone. The reader learns that he had been sent off to live in Wales, that he didn't like it there because he wasn't allowed to attend school, and that he returned to London and to his neighborhood. He recalls,

I caught a bus to go home. I sat on the upper deck, looking at the streets. In two places on the way I saw collapsed buildings lying in a heap of rubble behind some hoardings. The wood of the hoarding looked new, still raw and clean. It carried posters. I remember one of them said, "A grand use for stale bread!" And I shuddered and felt a brief twinge of regret for Mrs. Williams's kitchen and soft Welsh talk in the suffused fragrance of new baking.

Then suddenly the bus took a wrong turn. It rattled away in a new direction, and I looked up and said to the conductress, "Where are we going?"

"Don't ask me, mate," she said.

"Well, what's up?" I demanded. "We're going the wrong way."

"Haven't you heard there's a war on?" she said. "For all I know, the street ain't there no more." (25)

The narrator casually tells his audience that everything is chaotic, yet he observes that things around his aunt's house almost looked normal, that the flowers are still in bloom in the yard. The area also looked unnatural and unkempt. He recalls confronting a man in his yard and telling him that he's going to enter his house. Then he recalls what he's told:

"Look, son," he said, still wearily but with an edge on his voice, "there's a bloody great bomb down there that's maybe going up any minute. You go across that barricade and you'll maybe set it off; well, you would have asked for it, wouldn't you, so never mind what would happen to you; but you'd wreck a whole street of houses and maybe kill somebody else who hadn't asked for nothing. See? Now get moving." (27)

Both authors use descriptive narrative to take their readers into their war zones. And both set up the idea of the protagonist's need to return to discover how the changing landscape changes the protagonist.

Andi's real conflict comes when the children are told by the schoolmaster

that anyone harboring a partisan will be shot without a trial. Andi's parents
are partisans, and she says,

> That made Paul, Marko, and me wonder whether we should tell them, at
> home, about the crate of rifles we'd seen in the cave, but somehow we just
> couldn't. The way things were made us feel there was more safety in
> silence. One day Stavro, a man from the village whose wife had just died,
> came to buy flowers for a wreath. We had a lovely garden, thanks to Aunt
> Hercules having such green fingers, and Stavro said that someone had
> told someone else, who'd told him, that an order had come from Athens
> giving the Chief of Police free powers of arrest. . . .
>   "Rumors," our aunt insisted. "You'd think people would have other
> things to do than go about spreading rumors. We live in a democracy,
> don't we?"
>   "But there is a war on. You can't deny it."
>   Aunt Hercules snipped off another white carnation. "Not a war," she
> said. "Not a war, Stavro, just a skirmish." (27)

Andi tells the reader that this war is everyone's conflict, right down to the
schoolmaster and the villagers. Andi's own enemies, however, are closer to
her own age, and she talks about them next.

Andi explains that her town has a new Chief of Police whose son is
attending her school. His son is her age, and he is "tall and handsome in an
arrogant kind of way" (28). Andi adds,

> Most village children kept clear of Aristo. He was a bully and did not care
> who knew it. Like most bullies he had to have someone to hide behind
> when things got rough, and so he had put together a gang of ruffians like
> himself. They called themselves "The Warriors" and out of school they
> carried shields to drive home the point. Father and son, they were one and
> the same. Yes, I thought, that's when the change had begun. Shortly after
> they'd come to the village. (28–29)

Billi Rosen's drama builds as Aristo's and Andi's conflict builds.

Because Jill Paton Walsh's story has so many conflicts embedded in it, it
is difficult to identify one crisis scene over another. The scene picked will be
the one that fits the reader's own interpretation of the story's meaning. For
me, the real conflict comes when the narrator sees his father. He says,

> "I'm going after my Dad!" I called to her, still sitting on the slowly
> revolving boards.
>   "Goodbye, then, Bill," she said, and gently the roundabout turned her
> face away.
>   At the sound of the emptiness in her voice, I stopped. I froze there,
> suspended. And it came to me very clearly that if I went after my father it
> was goodbye; it was just another way to Wales for me, and Canada for
> her, or somewhere else for both of us, but, wherever we went, not to-
> gether. (69)

The narrator chooses to stay with Julie, and they live a "free life" in the
ruins of bombed-out London until Julie and a waif they have picked up get

caught in the rubble of the condemned house they are sharing. They are living on the edge of society and are confronting two problems: the war and their survival as independent people.

It should not surprise the reader of *Fireweed* that the two are separated in the end. The narrator began his story by telling the reader, "Remember? . . . I was fifteen that year, and she seemed sometimes younger, sometimes older" (3), and he goes on to say, "and then I couldn't bring myself later to admit I'd not trusted her, and tell her my real [name]" (6). He was forewarning that his existence with this young woman in war-torn London is a memory; that he never really had to tell her his real name or learn how old she really was.

And the reader of *Andi's War* should not expect the family to remain unscathed by the war. Billi Rosen's development of the conflict dividing the adults and the children into two hostile camps is built up until the tension goes into the family itself. If the reader carefully follows the story, she should not be surprised when Andi's mother and her brother are killed by the enemy.

However, Rosen's final conflict is not between insiders and outsiders. Andi's cousins come from Athens; their father is a soldier, a man who works with the enemy. When he is killed in ambush, the oldest son joins Aristo's gang, and the children turn against each other. In turn, the gang kills Andi's brother and her mother is caught and killed. In an "Epilogue," Andi says,

> [Mother] was laid to rest beside Paul in the warm, thyme-scented soil of Greece, in the little cemetery between the mountains and the sea, and it is good to know that nothing will ever separate them again.
>
> Father and I often talk about them and of Greece and our village, and when the pain gets too hard to bear anymore, we cry, because although things will change some day, they are bad now and we must stay here to live. Father says I'll feel better once I start school here and get some friends of my own age instead of always being with him and his refugee friends. But I don't know. (135–136)

We react to realism in different ways, and we always look at it from our own world. We combine what we know about the past and what we understand about ourselves as we interpret all texts, especially when we are forced to face the realities of a situation different from our everyday experiences. If the author uses a subjective voice, we will become more involved in the story. First-person narratives place the reader in the story. When discussing how first-person narrative works, Avon Crismore has suggested that it requires the reader to look at the text in more complex ways. Concerning the subjectivity of such texts, he argues, "readers become deeply involved with the beliefs, attitudes, opinions, and intentions of real and implied authors as they determine how their own beliefs, attitudes, opinions, and intentions relate to the authors'" (125).

I purposely chose not to discuss the books by Rosen and Walsh with my undergraduate students. I wanted them to react to the story on their own. I hoped they would take time to mentally compare the two books. At the end of the semester, we formulated some essay questions for the final exam. One of those questions concerned the two books. When exam time came around, I had several answers to the following question:

> The books *Fireweed* and *Andi's War* have been shared in this class; both can be used to introduce young people to the realities of war. Both are set in another country, and both concern twentieth-century strife. Discuss how each author uses the countryside as an integral part of the plot, how each author builds credible characters into a tense drama. As a real reader, which book had the most impact on you? As an implied reader, which book most affected your thinking? Why? How might you share these books with youngsters ages 10–14?

The students were allowed to choose between this question and one that discussed popular culture literature. Students who chose to write about *Fireweed* and *Andi's War* wrote carefully considered essays that read more like formal papers than answers to an examination question. They also wrote about how the first-person narrative had affected them when they read the books as both real and implied readers. Three women who had chosen to answer the question demonstrate how literature allows for multiple perspectives. Their essays show how three readers can look at the same children's historical novels and evaluate them very differently.

Katie Oplawski had spent the semester developing a strong feminist stance in her writing. She continually questioned the traditional role of women in stories and struggled for a personal way to interpret literature. She had begun to consider how realism fit into children's literature. For this question, she wrote,

The books *Fireweed* and *Andi's War* focused on the difficulties in people's lives during times of war. Both of these pieces are aimed at the young adult reader. The topic of war is not an easy topic for anyone, but introducing historical fiction concerning war topics is an important aspect in my helping to broaden young adult knowledge and expand their critical thinking. Preteens need to break out of their egotistical bubble and realize their differences as well as their similarities to others.

Both authors present the reader with young adult characters who are faced with independence and hardship. The characters in *Fireweed* are a young boy and a young girl who seek refuge in each other's company because they are in the middle of a war zone with no other relatives. The young boy, who had lived in the country, fled back to London in order to seek independence. He felt as if the country was imprisoning him, so he took it upon himself to leave. Once he was independent, he had to accept the realities of being alone, feeding himself and finding shelter during a time of turmoil. The young girl met the young boy and clung onto him, but she insisted that she, too, was independent. The young girl then took on a caretaker role when she befriended an orphan child. She seemed to want to prove her independent "female" role by caring for the child while having "her man" to take care of them both. The characters in *Andi's War* are a girl, her brother and cousins, and her grandmother. This book focuses on the main character, Andi, a teenaged girl who is living with her grandmother because her parents are out on a mission as partisans. Andi has not seen her parents for a long while and she, being the oldest and only girl, has to take care of herself and her emotions. She lives in a town in Greece, but she uses the countryside as an escape from her problems. One day she and her brother and cousin discover a cave with artillery for the war, and fear threatens her in this once peaceful countryside. Andi now begins playing the female role of mothering her cousin and brother, but she does not need a strong man to back her up. Andi finds comfort in her grandmother instead.

In both of these books the authors used the war to develop a theme of insecurity and fear. All of these characters were constantly running away from their opponents and trying to fight for their "reality" as well as their lives. The families were torn apart, and other bonds were formed. During these hard times, the characters faced more change because of the horrors of war and the horrors of a "reality"—everything always comes to an end. In *Fireweed,* the two young people are split apart, and in *Andi's War* death leaves the main character with new perspectives and heartaches. These stories represent reality in children's literature.

While reading these two books, I found that as a real reader I enjoyed *Andi's War*. This book was a fast paced war story that had a girl struggling in her society. I didn't have to analyze or predict too much as I read the story because it was told from Andi's point of view. She told the story as it had occurred, and there wasn't a lot of room for speculation. The book was fairly straightforward, so I think a young reader could relate to some of the plot, but I don't think that any reader would go into great depth in analysis of the writing. When I read *Fireweed,* I found myself becoming the implied reader. I found myself trying to predict what would happen to this young couple. At times I felt the characters were difficult to figure out and I wasn't sure what they were trying to say to each other, something I feel is common in many female/male relationships. The book made me delve into myself and ask myself how I would feel if I were living on the streets. Then, I had to think how I would feel with adding the problem of a sick child. I found that it was fun to analyze the characters—what they said, how they acted, especially after the child was in their presence. There was a lot of description in the story, and this gave me a chance to recreate things in my imagination.

If I were teaching young adults today and we were learning about wars in history or literature, I would introduce either of these books to supplement textbook knowledge. . . . What these young people need to see is that in war there may be a supposed "winner," but in reality everybody loses something. I feel the young readers could benefit from reading these books as real readers. Somehow I think that even as "real readers" they will automatically become implied readers because they will compare and contrast the young people's lives with their lives, will learn about another culture, and will see similarities and differences. Young readers will note these things in their own minds and do what they wish with that information. By giving them the opportunity to read this type of book, we, as teachers and parents, are giving them a perspective on what independence means for their own lives and for the lives of others.

Lisa Buening also looked at the two books from a feminist stance, but her reactions were slightly different. Lisa wrote,

Fireweed and *Andi's War* are both adolescent historical fiction novels. The devastation of London during WW II and the Greek Revolution really did happen. The feelings, moods, and events in these books are derived from the way things were in the past. But the characters Bill and Andi are fictional and they didn't really exist. They are "everyman"—showing how any child might have felt in that situation at that time.

Both stories are told through the child's eyes. It is Bill's and Andi's interpretations of things and their feelings that we know. The authors personally involve the reader so that she sympathizes with and understands what Andi and Bill are going through. The child reader can easily identify with the young narrators in *Fireweed* and *Andi's War*.

In *Andi's War*, the actual fighting cannot be seen—it takes place in the hills. But the effects of the war are seen in the village with the growing mistrust of the villagers and symbolic war between Andi and Aristo. In *Fireweed*, the bombing and devastation surrounds Bill and Julie daily. It has become almost commonplace and seems to have little effect on the people of London.

Both Andi and Bill fight their own little war against city officials in order to keep their freedom. Both have families involved in the war and feel its effects through the absence of father (Bill) and parents (Andi). But the war doesn't really "hit home" for either of them until the people they are living with are hurt.

The authors' credible characters are built through lots of natural dialogue. Because the stories are told through first-person narrative, we get to know what and how Andi and Bill think. By hearing about the characters' actions and reactions, we get to really know them. We believe they possess certain beliefs and qualities, and we expect them to act in certain ways. What makes each drama tense is that unexpected things occur, and the characters have no control over them. Bill could not foresee the falling of the house, and he could not dig out Julie. Andi could not be with Paul twenty-four hours a day, and she could not keep him alive.

I was affected most by *Andi's War* as a real reader. I identified with Andi, an independent, strong young girl. I admired and respected her for being liberal and mature. Also, there were more characters in *Andi's War* who appealed to me. I didn't like Julie in *Fireweed*—she was snobby and too wimpy. In *Andi's War* Andi fought her own battles—she didn't need a boy to do things for her. And nothing seemed easy. Andi lost her mother and her brother in the outbreaks. This created a sadder ending, but it was more realistic. War is not a pleasant time and it does not have a happy ending. I thought things fell into place too easily in *Fireweed*. There was always enough money, food, and shelter. The young couple always got away from the officials and barely escaped near death *every time*. It wasn't realistic that both Julie and Dickie were found alive in the rubble. A war was going on, but Julie and Bill never really suffered.

As an implied reader, I went back and tried to figure out why I liked *Andi's War* better. I realized that the feminist point of view was what appealed to me. The women characters in the story were strong and non-traditionally independent, daring, and risk-takers. The grandmother, mother, and Andi were all feminists. They sacrificed for a cause, something usually thought of as a male role. Andi and her mother were both physical fighters. I liked/agreed with Rosen's depiction of the women in her story. There was an absence of strong males which supported the feeling of feminine superiority and the feminist point of view. The gender roles were less traditional, and being a "modern woman," I liked that.

I would share both of these books by reading them, perhaps a chapter at a time to the students. I'd read *Fireweed* first and then *Andi's War*. I'd have the students compare and contrast the two, looking for similarities and differences. I'd have the students keep response journals that held their daily reactions and feelings (to refer to in discussions and to use later in compare/contrast activities). I would encourage the children to think, to figure out how each book affected them. We would discuss conventions and characteristics of historical fiction and the adolescent novel. I'd try to give them the literary tools they needed, but their judgments and how they reached them would be up to them.

Joan Blessing was a mother and a full-time student when she sat in on the class. She viewed the stories from a more experienced point of view because she was more familiar with the historical aspects of World War II. Joan wrote,

Fireweed uses the city of London as the backdrop against which two adolescents survive in a war torn country. The author describes the bombing raids as they destroy people's houses, lives and century-old buildings. The narrator leaves the safety of Wales to enter this city of strife. We learn the layout of the city and the surrounding countryside where he can easily get to places of safety when the bombing raids occur. This story does not delve into ideas of right or wrong or politics but only shows the struggles of people to survive when their homes and lives are in shambles.

The boy "Bill" is initially a typical, bland teenager. His egocentric attitude is shown when he explains his attitude towards his aunt and the family in Wales that takes him in. From there, we see his character grow and change as he accepts responsibility for the safety of two other people. He spends his days trying to meet their needs. The culmination of his personal change occurs when he sees his father and stays with the girl instead of going to him. Each day of survival is obtained at a cost of physical effort and psychological fear that they will be discovered by the authorities. His sacrifice is undermined by what he thinks is Julie's reaction. He develops into a strong, compassionate character.

Andi's War is a painful story about a young girl's loss. The children in this story seem more politically aware of the cause of the war and more involved in it. Their parents are freedom fighters who must remain hidden in the countryside so that they won't be executed for their part in the rebellion. The children are aware that there is fighting going on around them and at one point they see a hidden cache of guns in a cave. Since both sides are using the countryside to fight or hide in, this is very much a part of the plot. The serene land hides death and strife.

Andi's character is more intense from the beginning than Bill's. However, she undergoes terrible personal sacrifice by losing her brother and mother. There is a lot of symbolism and foreshadowing in this book. The shepherd in the hills who is an intermediary between the freedom fighters and the village people is fore-shadowed to die. When the children first see him, one feels his death will eventually come.

Andi's character grows because of her experiences and she gains strength, but it is not the same as Bill's. She is strong and accepting but there is a hopelessness about her future that one doesn't feel about Bill. He was hurt, he grew, he changed.

She was hurt, she grew, but her change is shadowed by the uncertainty of the future. Her strength is gained at a high cost.

As a real reader *Andi's War* had the greater impact on me. I had no need to know where she was, what caused the war, what the political implications were because I was involved in the painful, sad mood of the story. I was satisfied not to discuss the book with others but only to feel and respond to the text.

As an implied reader, *Fireweed* had the greatest impact. I had knowledge of that war. I knew of the politics, and my country was a part of that war. My interest in and knowledge of the outcome allowed me to know more about the story than I knew about *Andi's War*. I could visualize the bombing of the landmarks of London, and I knew where Bill and Julie were sheltering in London because of my knowledge of London's history.

Either book could be used with youngsters to show how war affects the average person who is part of it. Too often children hear about wars or see the news stories but have no idea about what happens to the people being bombed or living in fear or losing loved ones. In addition, *Fireweed* could be used in a history lesson that covers the second world war. While children are getting the dry, cold facts of war they could see that it isn't all glory and winning. They can be shown that people actually suffer, lose their homes, and die during wars.

Each of these women had personally responded to the experiences depicted in the two novels, though none of them had ever lived in a war-torn country. Each had reacted to the characterization and the settings. In Joan's case, the book by Walsh was plausible because she already understood the realism of the social struggles that happened during the bombings of London. She found the sights and scenes compelling and believed that she had experienced the reality of this particular war because it fit her earlier experiences. Katie projected the past into the present because she saw similarities between herself and the young people involved in London's day-to-day activities. She became the characters in Walsh's book, and she considered the possibilities of her behavior in a similar experience. She asked herself, "What if I had to live on the streets? What if I was responsible for protecting someone else when I was fifteen years old?" Lisa rejected the realities of *Fireweed*. She did not have the historical background that Joan did and was not drawn in to the harrowing scenes. She felt uncomfortable with Julie's personality and could not identify with the male narrator. In the end, the book seemed unrealistic to her.

These readers had given the books a great deal of thought before they came up with their own decisions, and they each had a personal reading for the books. However, they do have some common themes. Each discusses the authors' ability to recreate war-time conditions, cultural differences, and the personal uncertainties that war generates. When they discussed sharing the books with youngsters, they commented that the books could help contemporary youngsters see that war does not allow anyone to completely win. Beyond that, they wanted to let their students examine the elements of literature that created the stories' sense of realism.

Authors of realistic fiction want their readers to live through the experiences in their books and see the problems another person or culture faces. Good writers succeed because they draw their audience into their stories. They write to evoke a response to the plot. However, response is not enough. Good authors hope that the narrator's voice will haunt the reader enough to cause a second reading, further study, and, finally, a new reader's interpretation to the questions their stories pose.

7

Poetic Language and Literary Style

A few years ago, while attending a writer's conference I listened to a young African-American author describe the biography she had been working on. It was about the first black astronaut she explained, and it included interviews of his family members as well as a summary of the man's life and accomplishments. In some ways it was a disjointed story because she had not placed the man's life in perfect chronological order. Also, she was less interested in telling a hero's tale than in discovering why this man had become an astronaut while his brother had gone to prison. So far, none of the publishers she had approached had been willing to consider publishing her manuscript. The author running the session nodded in understanding. "Publishers aren't interested in black biographies," he answered. "I wanted to write a biography about African-American sports heroes, but my publisher discouraged me. The argument I got was books about African Americans don't sell." Why, I wondered as I drove home, aren't stories about African Americans selling?

Today there is growing awareness that Anglo-Christians will not be the dominant U. S. population in the next century, and educators are voicing an interest in reaching the at-risk student population, many of whom are minority children living in substandard conditions. I feel there should be a growing interest in all divergent literature. White Americans need to read about the experiences of others. They should grow more comfortable with the images of people who by choice or chance live a life apart from mainstream America. Publishers need to give children books about life outside the middle-class setting. Yet, unless we look beyond traditional literary patterns, minority voices will not be understood or published. Diversity in literature will be a reality when we know how to read diverse writing styles and learn to listen to new ways of expressing cultural realities.

There are unofficial canons published for children's literature, and they have helped to define what is good in children's literature. The most prominent ones are the Newbery and Caldecott lists, founded and supported by the American Library Association, and the Touchstones list, founded and supported by the Children's Literature Association. On the whole, these lists hold "safe" titles depicting wholesome white children struggling to secure a self-identity for themselves. Rarely does the child have a physical or mental handicap. The children are usually learning how to live inside their mainstream culture, even when they live in different ethnic or social neighborhoods from those around them. Since most of the authors have never lived in poverty in the ghetto or experienced life from a minority or diverse cultural background, they are looking at an alien experience as they write their stories. Furthermore, when authors in children's literature deal with controversial issues, they are usually dealing with issues society has already begun to discuss. Traditionally, children's literature has fit so well into the fabric of American society that it will not cause loud outcries of concern about story pattern, tone, or dialect. Critics argue that "inferior" children's literature will not fit "the patterns of good literature" and they often place books with diverse literary patterns outside the winning circles. While award-winning children's literature is well written, the books selected generally reflect the state-of-the-art in children's writing instead of innovative or divergent writing.

I believe that the author who hopes to speak to his children must consider the activities, sayings, and beliefs of the children from his region and ethnic background. That author will write stories reflecting the inner workings of his community, and will produce books that will be important literature for children who share similar experiences.

Everyday experiences influence the way authors tell stories. Family stories are fables about community traditions, beliefs, hopes, and fears. Authors using their family's cultural roots will not tell a story that is a misrepresentation of themselves. Their stories will reflect their community; minority writers will write books that will be important literature for children with similar experiences because they are relating experiences that seem realistic within their cultural world. Minority writers who write for their children know why Uruguayan writer and editor Eduardo Galeano says,

One writes, in reality, for the people whose luck or misfortune one identifies with—the hungry, the sleepless, the rebels, and the wretched of this earth—and the majority of them are illiterate. Among the literate minority, how many can afford to buy books? Is this contradiction resolved by proclaiming that one writes for that facile abstraction known as the masses? (113)

If Galeano is to be answered in the affirmative, the cultural writer must carefully use rhetoric so that it contains his world while suggesting that his story follows the standards set by the earlier established authors.

Storytelling styles differ from one group to another. The acceptable plot structure, for instance, of the European folktale is very different from the structure of Latin American literature. The interweaving of supernaturalism in stories told by Latinos is significantly dissimilar from traditional European religious tales published in picture books for small children. The tellers of the oral Hispanic tales share transformation stories, tales of spirits wandering the earth and mingling with mortals, and narratives that flash back and forth between time periods. These storytellers are not "making up fantastic stories"—they are relating legends they believe to be true. While the story structures are often alien to the Anglo-Christian tradition, they are valid interpretations of cultural standards.

Cultural stories have been published in the past, and they offer some insights into other literary patterns. For instance, picture book stories by African Americans can be traced by surveying the winners and runners-up of the Coretta Scott King Award given by the American Library Association to an outstanding picture book depicting African-American culture. Looking at the winners during the 1980s, we begin to see patterns in African-American children's literature. Ninety-five percent of the texts were written by African-American women. Ashley Bryan is the male most often honored. His stories concern black music and African folklore. The uses of perspective and narrative in all the winning picture books fit into current research about African-American literature. These tales reflect Black Aesthetics.

Patricia McKissack is a past Coretta Scott King winner who has discussed why she writes about the African-American experience. I often recall her remarks at the opening session of a two-day conference for aspiring writers. McKissack explained that she has chosen to provide stories about black history that contain positive images for African-American children. "Young blacks need a reality that is not depressing," she said. And she explained that language is an important issue: "The words used to describe scenes should be positive ones which do not present modern stereotypes or rely on modern adjectives." Patricia McKissack is continually concerned with the author's use of *rhetoric* to shape an experience for her audience.

McKissack has divided her story creations into two categories: those that come from Athena and are born out of someone else's ideas and experiences, and those arising from a mustard seed in her imagination and grow into full-fledged stories. She said that when she wrote the children's story *Mirandy and Brother Wind* she combined the two categories. Patricia McKissack's "Author's Note" for *Mirandy and Brother Wind* tells her reader,

> One of our family treasures is a rare picture of my grandparents dated 1906, five years before they were married. They were teenagers at the time

and had just won a cakewalk. As winners, they'd been awarded an elaborately decorated cake.

First introduced in America by slaves, the cakewalk is a dance rooted in Afro-American culture. It was performed by couples who strutted and pranced around a large square, keeping time with fiddle and banjo music. As the dancers paraded by, doing flamboyant kicks and complicated swirls and turns, the elders judged them on appearance, grace, precision, and originality of moves. The winning couple took home a cake.

It's never been difficult for me to imagine my grandparents strutting around a square with their backs arched, their toes pointed and their heads head high. . . . They were full of life's joy, especially Mama. Papa used to say he believed Mama had captured the Wind. I believed it too. (unpaged)

McKissack's autobiographical stance in her author's note is consistent with the archetypal rhetorical style of earlier African-American writing. Literary critic William L. Andrews explains that since the nineteenth century African Americans have self-authorized their stories in order to convince that "facile abstraction known as the masses" that they were writing a certain kind of reality. During the 1800s, the story, or "fable" within the narrative would be released by publishing houses controlled by white publishers, editors, and booksellers only if the author made the who-what-where-when information seem factual. Andrews claims that early African-American writers had to produce a story that sounded "truthful" or "risk suspicion" from the publishers concerning their "sincerity" (23).

To some degree this is also true in today's publishing for children. Teachers and librarians usually like authors and illustrators best who tell them where they got their ideas and what their stories mean for them. They want the story validated. McKissack's stance fits with Black Aesthetics, black history, and children's literature. It is important for us to see how these three elements combine.

Literary critic Valerie Smith has argued that book learning is less significant in black culture than oral storytelling, that black narrators, both writers and storytellers, display the ability to impose a narrative order onto events and manipulate autobiographical experiences into a literary whole (5). This, then, allows authors to use information in creative ways. I watched Patricia McKissack address a predominantly white adult audience the night she explained her writing. She told them that the cakes in her story *Mirandy and Brother Wind* were highly prized because slaves rarely had such delicacies. Furthermore, they were concocted out of pilfered ingredients, garnered from the "main house." She added that there was a conjure woman in this story and explained that this was a part of her culture when she grew up. Yet McKissack does not tell all of this in her book. This is the background she has used when weaving a believable story that will entertain her youthful audience. McKissack employs an active voice to bring the past alive. She doesn't explain how the slaves made their cakes in the introduction for her picture book. Furthermore, she only indirectly shows children the significance of the conjure woman in African-American tradition when she writes,

> Talk had it that Mis Poinsettia wasn't a for-real conjure woman like the ones in New Orleans. But didn't nobody mess with her, just in case talk was wrong. Mis Poinsettia welcomed Mirandy inside. "Your people don't approve of conjure. Why you come here?" she say.

McKissack recreates African-American cultural patterns while placing her story in a more recent African-American southern community. Details from history and from her family are interwoven into her tale. Historical scenes—some personally remembered, some recalled from her family's history—are part of *Mirandy and Brother Wind*. Her own childhood experiences at her grandmother's farm in the South are carefully woven into the tale. Her grandmother fed chickens just as Mirandy's grandmother does, and the air seemed to rush out of her grandmother's chicken house when McKissack opened its door as a youngster. When she has Mirandy capture Brother Wind, McKissack writes,

> . . . Mirandy was moping on the front porch swing when Brother Wind swooped over the hedges, kicking up dust. He leaped over the lilacs, around the snowball tree, and into the barn.
>
> While he was inside shaking the rafters and scaring Ma Dear's hens, Mirandy slipped up quiet-like and slammed the door. There was no way for him to get out, 'cause Pa had stuffed all the cracks.

Metaphors are important to African-American literature because they imply more than a simple but enjoyable plot structure. Although metaphorical language may seem simple, it can function as a controlling image in the story. McKissack's use of the wind as a personified element is metaphorical, suggesting meanings that will only be understood by those who know the African-American history of slavery. McKissack has explained that while she was growing up she listened to her grandparents talk of the wind and soon aligned "chasing the wind" with "going for the impossible." When she wrote *Mirandy and Brother Wind,* she remembered the cultural personification of the wind. McKissack probably knew that the wind is an archetypal metaphor in African-American literature suggesting the slave dreams for freedom. The wind could come and go as it pleased; it answered to no one; it could not be caught. And the wind is also representative of twentieth century African-American idealism. Colorless, devoid of stereotypes, it represents spirited freedom, a bold and proud behavior that defies cultural boundaries. McKissack begins *Mirandy and Brother Wind* with metaphorical language:

> *Swish! Swish!*
> It was spring, and Brother Wind was back. He come high steppin' through Ridgetop, dressed in his finest and trailing that long silvery wind cape behind him.
> *Swoosh! Swoosh! Swoosh!*

Her tale sounds like an oral storytelling experience, and it implies that she is retelling a story she knows to be true. Her imagery does not need a particular time or place to work. And there is no need to set up a "once upon a time" feeling. Her audience is immediately carried to a particular scene with her *imagery*. McKissack is an excellent storyteller; she enthralls her audiences when she tells *Mirandy and Brother Wind* to them. Her voice, diction, and expression bring the tale alive. The book itself is like her oral retelling; it is rich with regional *idioms* and *dialect*.

The use of conversation as an integral part of an author's plot can be traced to earlier literary traditions found in African-American literature. It has given African-American authors a way to directly communicate with their own people while sharing a story that can be enjoyed for its entertaining qualities by others. African-American critic Valerie Smith explains that since slavery blacks have been conscious of their ability to subtly use rhetoric in their conversations to suggest something different from what the audience might first believe has been said, and she argues that African Americans have consciously manipulated language and nuances of speech. Concerning their use of language, Smith comments,

> Whether possessed of book learning or not, the dissembling slave was a confidence figure who displayed a profound consciousness of language, created a space for the expression of his or her will or identity, and seized the opportunity to escape. (4–5)

McKissack's story is significant for American children if literacy is to have real meaning. It fits with Myron Tuman's argument that literacy requires the reader (or listener) to negotiate a meaning from stories. He explains, "While language can and often does affirm our interpretation of the world, in metaphor it exhibits the power to unfold before us a new, unexpected way of understanding" (17). McKissack's story allows all children to better understand an event from the past, and the African-American tradition of the cakewalk. As such, its primary intention is to give African-American children a positive image of one of their traditions. However, it is not a cultural story that will appeal to a limited audience. McKissack has used language to create highly evocative and well-chosen images. The dialect should appeal to the auditory senses of all children. The child's goal of becoming a hero is common among all children, and helping those within the community is not alien to any group. The reader/listener who stands outside the African-American literary tradition should learn to respect the ideals of family love, community support, and high-spirited adventure, and may even want to share in that tradition once the story is read. Both the intended and the interloping audiences have much to gain by hearing *Mirandy and Brother Wind*.

Writers for adolescents also use cultural literary patterns in their stories. They help youngsters identify other motifs found in literature. For instance, Walter Dean Myers introduces the adult autobiographical tradition of *signifying* in *Fast Sam, Cool Clyde, and Stuff*. This careful manipulation of language is used by black Americans when they want to "readjust realities" in oral language. Myers has placed dialect and regional idioms within the descriptive and conversational scenes of *Fast Sam, Cool Clyde, and Stuff* in order to capture the imagination of the reader while he validates his story. Myers has carefully integrated cultural beliefs and values in his characters' conversational scenes. The characters come alive as we "hear" them speaking.

Three times the winner of the Coretta Scott King Award for his writing, Walter Dean Myers has spoken of his desire to write positive stories about the African-American experience for black children. His storytelling is more contemporary than McKissack's. Because he grew up in New York City, he has chosen to create a story about contemporary African-American youngsters living in the inner city. *Fast Sam, Cool Clyde, and Stuff* is set in New York City.

Myers begins this story with a "Prologue" that establishes the narrator as an adult who wants to recall the past, to retell his youthful experiences. He writes,

> *This is a story about some people I used to hang out with.* It's funny calling them people. I mean they're people and everything, but a little while ago I would have called them kids. I heard that one of them, Gloria, got married about a month ago. Her father and mother have gotten back together, and they moved into one of those rent-controlled places where the State tells you how much rent you have to pay. Since her father got a decent job the guy really changed. I can dig him changing like that. (7)

Within his "Prologue," Walter Dean Myers uses rhetorical devices to draw his reader into his story. He uses the first-person narrative to establish his narrator as the reader's confidant and friend. The listener is told that the narrator has grown up and that the people he is going to talk about no longer live in the same neighborhood. The listener begins to view the narrator's past from the narrator's perspective; he will have to trust the narrator's version of events. Since the narrator is grown, he is looking back at the past, seeing how some characters' lives have improved since the story's beginnings. When the narrator mentions both Gloria's father and subsidy housing, he suggests that the story will concern social issues effecting the black community.

Myers's narrative style fits with Henry Louis Gates, Jr.'s explanation of the "quasi-autobiography" used by early slaves in their stories. In this format "life is at the same time revived and judged, presented and remembered." Gates says that the narrative is prejudiced toward one interpretation of events, but is also "reflective, philosophical, and critical on moral or religious grounds" (*Figures in Black*, 81–82). Myers uses this traditional stance within *Fast Sam, Cool Clyde, and Stuff*.

Once Myers has established the authority of his narrator, he describes the neighborhood and his family's readjustment. He writes,

I first moved to 116th Street when I was twelve and a half. I moved into this building about halfway down the block, which, I found out later, everybody called the safe house. (If someone from another block was chasing you and you made it to the safe house they would never chase you inside. That was because they'd have gone too far to get off the block if your friends started after them.) Anyway, I moved into this house . . . into Apartment 4S. I really liked the apartment because I had a separate room. In fact, that's why we moved to 116th Street in the first place. I was twelve and my sister was ten and my mother said it was high time I had my own room. So finally my father found the place and we moved. My room was small but it was all mine . . . It was just early fall when I moved in and I'd started school already, but I had to transfer to a new school called James Fenimore Cooper. It was an older school than the one I'd gone to, but that was okay because they had a really good music department and I played saxophone. (9)

Within a short space, Myers has established that the neighborhood is an isolated community that rules itself, that it is at once a step up for the family and a step back for the children: the apartment is bigger, but the school is older. Then, Myers has his narrator tell his listener that the school has a strong music department, which is one of his main interests, and he ties the narrator to his cultural traditions of jazz and rhythm music.

The multiplicity of Myers's narrative voice shifts again when the narrator begins to recall his first encounter with his group of school friends. He describes the youngsters who have assembled on the stoop as wearing "dungarees" with patches on the knees. Since no one calls jeans dungarees anymore, the scene has shifted into the past. Finally, the narrator ends his introductory description with slang, saying, "It was a cool-looking group. All the guys wore sneakers and the girls had on sandals" (10).

Immediately after the narrator confides in the reader, the story switches to a conversational scene:

"Hey, man, what apartment you live in?" one guy with a real long head asked me.

"Four S," I said, trying to be cool.

"Can you play any ball?" Long-head asked.

"He can't play no ball," another guy said. "His feet go the wrong way. Look at him."

I looked down at my feet. They looked okay to me.

"Man, the cat that used to live in 4S sure could play some ball. You should be ashamed to even move into that apartment." Long-head shook his head and looked at me like I was smelly or something. "Can you stuff?"

"Do you mean dunk?" I asked. I knew what he meant. I could play basketball pretty well, but there was no way I could jump over the rim and stuff the ball. No way. I couldn't even come close.

"Yeah, turkey, can you?" They all looked at me.

"If I get a good start," I lied, asking myself why I was lying.

"I'll go get my basketball," a girl said. Later I found out her name was Gloria. A girl! I figured if girls had basketballs around here, the guys must be fantastic. (10–11)

The narrator's story takes on the storyteller's stance. Scenes are being recreated as if they were happening before the reader's eyes. The dialect places the characters within a particular culture. Dialect, Gates argues, has a "capacity to carry imagery compactly, its separate language not only conveying the image but focusing it, strengthening it by contrast with its standard English reflection" (189–190). Myers carefully integrates dialect into his story and begins to create a text that holds two grammars. His narrator still talks in a straightforward, grammatically correct style when he is speaking directly to his audience, but as he recreates the scenes from his past, he uses the social dialect of the young people involved. The dual language structure reinforces the feeling that the story is being told to the listener by a grown-up remembering his past. Throughout the book, there are two voices involved in the action—the older, more assured teller and the youthful actor of the events, not fully aware of the consequences of his life story.

Myers uses a double linguistic structure and creates a binary interpretation of the events depicted. Both adult and youthful attitudes are consciously reflected. The plot contains the devil-may-care abandon of youth, but this is tempered by the narrator's cautious observations. Myers uses the linguistic code of African-American language with its double meanings and suggests to his audience that black dialect has a richness of its own, that it adds meaning to his story. He builds his drama by relating the cadences and word play common to the contemporary African-American community he is depicting.

Aware that street blacks have an oral literacy that often surpasses the more controlled linguistic patterns of educated whites, Myers builds his scenes using realistic, symbolic conversations. And, because he believes that his primary audience is in the African-American community, he does not change his metaphoric imagery or embed the text with explanations of his characters' dialect to appeal to white readers. He incorporates African-American linguistic structures and meanings within his text, showing the vitality of black speech.

Myers's style demands that his listener acknowledge his story as an honest cultural experience within the African-American community. His audience must accept the narrator's black voice as the authority, must acknowledge that his culture is significant. Myers allows the youthful listener a chance to revel in the outrageous adventures of the hero while he warns of the actions' consequences. When Myers has two block gangs meet with one leader accusing the other of talking behind his back, he writes,

"Your name's Robin, right?" Gloria asked. Gloria was one of those girls that was always signifying—saying something to get something started or get somebody mad.

"That's right," Robin said, rolling his eyes in Gloria's direction.

"You know, Binky, I think you were wrong," Gloria went on. "Robin looks like a nice cat. I don't believe half those things you said about his mama."

"Say what? What you say about my mama, man?" Robin's scar was twitching and the veins started standing out on his neck.

"I didn't say anything about your mama, Robin. She's just signifying, that's all."

Now everybody knew that Gloria was just signifying, but we didn't figure Binky to back out. If he got beaten it was one thing, but if he backed out he'd be letting down the whole block. I mean, is you're the baddest dude on the block you've got responsibilities. If you got the weight you got to take the freight. (19–20)

Myers is using a scene that includes a *trope*, in this case used as a uniquely African-American rhetorical pattern where speech repeats, or reverses, an earlier statement. Myers incorporates it in his story, allowing his scene's hero to win the first verbal bout of signification by finally retorting,

The worse thing I could say about your mama is that you're her son. And hasn't anybody told you yet that that toe-jam you keep between your teeth don't do nothin' for your breath? If you ask me you must be the retarded son of the Heartbreak of Psoriasis. (21)

Southern slaves learned to signify in their conversations with their white masters on the plantation, and then they turned their linguistic banter into a cultural strength both within and without their community. They re-phrased arguments until their meanings changed. Linguistic tropes gave the slaves a momentary victory in their existence. Thus, when Myers recalls the verbal battle of an inner city neighborhood, he relates a tradition that began in the days of slavery and is still practiced within African-American culture.

Myers is depicting a strong African-American community that is not dependent on others. Stuff's best times are inside his tightly knit African-American and Puerto Rican community in New York City. When Gloria's parents have marital problems and Gloria's father deserts the family, the neighborhood group gathers together to discuss how to survive their day-to-day existence. Again, Myers draws his listener into the scene with his conversation. Once the reader is caught, Myers has his protagonists deliver a sermon about community concern. He writes,

"Dig it, care for each other, then we'll always know that we have each other to fall back on. We can do it as just friends, but if we agree to do it *before* things go *wrong*, then we'll know that we have something else."

"What's that?" Angel asked.

"Somebody who cares for us all the time. Whether things are right or wrong. So when things go wrong we don't go around looking for some-one who'll like us and understand what we're all about. We'll have people we can turn to. We'll have each other. And we should be able to dig on each other's problems."

"Yeah, and we always get the same kind of problems. Somebody is sad because they don't have any money or something like that or they got family troubles or school trouble," Angel said. "Everybody in this whole neighborhood gets just about the same kind of problems." (75)

In fact, Walter Dean Myers portrays the world outside the ghetto's isolated neighborhood in negative terms. The scenes involving the outside world contain sharp criticisms of mainstream society while the inner-city scenes reaffirm the community's strengths. Myers's interpretation of the inner city has become as important for the contemporary African American child as McKissack's depiction of southern family roots and community values in *Mirandy and Brother Wind*.

Both McKissack and Myers present isolated racial communities. McKissack's heroine never sees a white face; Myers's three male heroes come to grips with the outside in their scrapes with the law, but they always return to the protection of the African-American neighborhood. His heroes bond together and support one another. Yet in the end their community has established a sense of pride that allows them to leave their surroundings and change. The two older boys go on to college. The neighborhood's old buildings are torn down to make the way for housing projects. Myers's narrator tells his listener,

> This didn't seem like much but it was a really important thing. The neighborhood started to change. When all the new people moved in we ended up going to school about a half mile away. We had to take a bus to get there. And slowly the things that made the neighborhood changed and it wasn't the same . . . .
>
> The one thing I won't forget is how close we all were. How much we cared for each other. I just hope I'll always have people to care for like that and be close to. And I'd like to teach somebody else that feeling. (190)

Henry Louis Gates, Jr. has said that the task of the black poet has always been to create a reality for the members of his community, to allow them to see their world in a new way. Authors like Patricia McKissack and Walter Dean Myers are fulfilling that task. They are willing to carry on the literary traditions of the African-American community and are rebuilding the past into a valued present by extending its traditions and explaining the past through a rhetorical style that is a part of their culture's traditions.

My students have continually been interested in African-American literature and in its acceptance by all readers. Some have submitted essays on Black Aesthetics in children's literature to the English Essay Competition at Purdue University and they have won awards for their thoughtful arguments. These students have usually centered their critical discussions on two African-American writers and their rhetorical styles. Both Julius Lester and Virginia Hamilton rank among favorite authors with many of my students. Students admire their language and their ability to break story barriers in children's publishing by writing in new ways about the African-American experience.

Even before I encouraged my students to submit their essays to the

English awards, however, I had received thoughtful and carefully re-searched papers that discussed how African-American writers adjusted their rhetorical styles to fit with the expectations of the publishing indus-try. One student who wrote an essay in the early 1980s, Derek Arrowroot, placed the following note on his paper when he gave me permission to try and publish his piece:

Prof May,
Thank you for the opportunity of writing this paper. It was one of the few papers I have written at Purdue that I have enjoyed and put forth a genuine effort to write at the same time. I would like to teach in the inner city and hopefully by scratching the surface of racial difficulty/differences I will be a better prepared teacher. Also, I honestly believe that Lester can make a student really want to know more about his/her heritage. Since reading his autobiography, *All Is Well,* I want to know more about the black heritage; I can only imagine my feelings if I were black.

Derek's essay looks at the use of language and plot structures from a historical standpoint.

Scratching the Surface of Racial Differences

BY DEREK ARROWROOT

Lorenz Graham and Julius Lester are two authors who write in order to educate. While many authors write for the same reason (to educate), these authors have a unique curriculum they wish the young reader to learn. That curriculum is black heritage, for Lester and Graham are black authors trying to explain the roots of the Negro population. This is not to say that Lester and Graham write only for young black audiences. On the contrary, they write for the youth of all races so that they may better understand the plight of the American Negro not only during slavery (Lester), but also during the 1950s (Graham). In their writings, these two authors bridge a sociological gap that has been neglected or glazed over for many years. While Lester and Graham have the same intentions, they go about these intentions for different reasons and in different ways.

Lorenz Graham is respected as one of the earliest writers for young people to portray black American and African characters and cultures realistically (*Children's Literature Review* 101–103). While in college, Graham had the opportunity to travel to Africa and teach at a small mission school called Monrovia College. He left with the idea of bringing light to a dark land, only to find that Africans were very much like the people in any other land. This was his initial reason for writing: to write books that showed African people as people and not some sort of wild group. He did this in *I, Momolu* and *Tales of Momolu,* books with African characters and settings. While writing these books, he found that there were few books that described black Americans realistically. This led Graham to write books that did attempt to portray black Americans realistically. Graham decided to write books with a purpose, to show that people were people no matter what their race (*Elementary Education* 185–188).

Graham's writing career has been devoted to writing literature with a message that if one wants to succeed, one can. A quotation from one of his book's main characters, David Williams, a black teenager coping with growing up in an integrated school in the North sums up that message very well: "I've learned that whatever happens you don't just quit! You keep going forward, pushing, driving, you don't quit" (*North Town* 101). This is Graham's message for black youth, but also for all youth who want to succeed in life. Keep trying and eventually you will succeed.

Julius Lester is nearly forty years younger than Lorenz Graham. Lester could be said to be following the path that Lorenz Graham blazed in writing about American blacks in a realistic way, but this would only be partially true. Where Graham focused on the American black in the 1950s and 60s in his Town series (*South Town, North Town, Whose Town,* and *Return to South Town*), Lester focuses on the American blacks who experienced slavery and the Reconstruction period of the Southern history. Graham wrote what he did because he felt there was a lack of literature about blacks; Lester, on the other hand, wasn't concerned by the **lack** of literature about black slaves. He felt that the earlier writers glazed over slavery. When reading testimonies of slaves he found in the Library of Congress, he said that since "the whites [who interviewed the ex-slaves] came from the same area in which they were interviewing, they never got a straight answer" ("Julius Lester: Newbery Runner-up" 2070). This led Lester to write fictionalized history of that period; he wrote stories based on historical fact and added details of characterization and setting consistent with the period. He did not write about the great black leaders of that period but, instead, focused upon the "great figures" of the mass who he said were

> individuals who embodied in their lives and actions the ethos of their times, and for that reason stand out above the mass . . . they were the movers of history. While Frederick Douglass organized against slavery, he would have been an isolated figure if hundreds of thousands of slaves had not run away, eventually threatening slavery's survival to such an extent that the South was forced to go to war. (*Long Journey Home* Foreword)

This is what Lester concentrates on, trying to give the reader not only the sense of hardship that these people faced but also the spirit they faced that hardship with.

The fathers of Lorenz Graham and Julius Lester were both Methodist ministers. But Lester came away from his childhood experiences with a much different philosophy than Lorenz Graham. Graham said, "try and you will succeed," Lester said, "work without regard for the fruit of your labors for pain and pleasure are the same" (*All Is Well* 39–40). This is the major difference between Lester and Graham; Graham believed one could triumph over color but Lester thought otherwise. Lester didn't believe that being black was unconquerable; he felt that it was something that had to be constantly dealt with. He wrote of the black heritage to teach all youth where blacks had come from and what they had overcome. Lester wrote, "My race is not a disease which needed curing, but a blessing to be defended from all who seek to regard it otherwise" (*All Is Well* 14).

In *Long Journey Home* Julius Lester portrays blacks who fought because of their race but didn't necessarily win, although they continued fighting just the same. In *South Town* Lorenz Graham writes of a black family who fights not to win but to survive. This is the difference between Lester and Graham, one writes of a fight to win, the other of a fight to survive.

Long Journey Home is a collection of stories which describes the plights of slavery and Reconstruction blacks in a realistic way. This book is sociologically significant because it fills a gap in the history of blacks in children's literature. In this collection of historical fiction stories, Lester gives the reader stories about live people who actually existed. This captures the reader, making the stories not only believable but enlightening as well. The book has been highly acclaimed. One reviewer stressed that the stories help black youths "understand their roots because they recapture the spirit of a past generation of black people authentically" (Goddard 8). Another reviewer pointed out that Lester broke literary ground, saying,

> Children's literature of race has so far been, at best, mostly of a rather tentative kind. Even when they have known their minds, writers have hesitated to speak them forcefully. Julius Lester makes up for all that now in a forthright collection of true stories told in controlled passion. (*Junior Bookshelf* 409)

Lester was one of the first black authors to speak to black youth in such a direct and honest way to make black youths want to run out and read more about their heritage.

When *Long Journey Home* was published Lester was on the verge of being an angry black writer. He controlled that anger for the most part and usually turned that anger into passionate writing. But sometimes the anger slips out. In passages such as, "Ain't nothing here [America] for us black folks but bad luck and trouble" (*Long Journey Home* 147), that bitterness slips out. It is covered transparently, but it is still noticeable. Some critics have felt that the anger "dulls the edge of the story" (Smith 10). I believe that it was this anger, although veiled, that set Lester apart from other black authors writing for children. It is this anger that boldly proclaims the heritage of Afro-Americans and induces his reader to want to know more about their heritage.

South Town is the first in the Town series by Lorenz Graham. *South Town* tells of a young man's trials and tribulations while growing up in the South during the 1950s. It was published during the 1950s, a time when racial tensions were high. Because of these tensions, Graham did not write an indictment of racism; he signaled that racism existed. His warning of racism, in itself, was a giant step forward for a black writer to take at that time, especially since he was writing for a youthful audience. This story was written to build better understandings about contemporary black attitudes and problems by a contemporary black man.

In his book, Graham attempts to do justice and to present both sides of the racial problems in the South during the 1950s. He represents the black people as a people who wish to free themselves from the guardianship of the rich white people. He shows the whites as a people who must first get rid of the idea that blacks are an inferior race and then must deal with the need to change the status of the "inferior race." Graham attempts to show the problems of both sides; he does not blame one group for the racial problems. He paints a picture of the South as a place where things are getting better, slowly but surely. In *South Town* the white racist reforms and the white doctor argues, "progress is being made all the time. . . . In spite of what happened last week, things are better now than they were" (247). Graham's message for blacks is "pull yourself up by your bootstraps" and whites will grant you acceptance. For whites, the message was to treat people as individuals and learn that blacks are just as good as whites are.

Lorenz Graham wrote what could be acceptable for a time with racial tensions. *South Town* was not meant to upset the society of that time; it was meant to shed light on some of its problems. Graham's approach was as simple as his message. He was as direct about the problems as he could be without being censored. He accomplished what no other writer in children's literature at that time could. But he also painted a glossy picture of what would become an ugly nightmare. A contemporary wrote

> [*South Town*] is an admirable choice, and in this day of heightened racial tensions, a courageous one . . . a moving picture of Negro children growing up in a South where the survival of mores of a slave era color attitudes and points of views, an authenticity, an integrity that could only come from experience, understanding and wisdom. (*Kirkus* 272)

Lorenz Graham and Julius Lester are extremely important writers who added new social realism to the reading afforded black children, and for that matter all children. Graham was a trailblazer and groundbreaker in writing about racial problems. Lester was one of the authors who not only wrote about black Americans, but who created vignettes from history that evoke a lust for more knowledge about the real story of the black man's heritage.

Lester and Graham wrote with somewhat the same intentions. Both wrote to show what black Americans could do. Graham showed that the black youth of the 1950s could fight and survive the racism of the time. Lester showed that the blacks of slavery and Reconstruction times were not just Uncle Toms. He depicted them as fighters who not only fought against a system designed to keep them captives, but as fighters who ultimately won personal battles against oppression.

Lester and Graham wrote to evoke different emotional responses. They wrote stories for their contemporaries that fit societal needs at the time they wrote. Graham, writing during the conservative 1950s, wrote passively. He wrote in a style that wouldn't alienate readers, black or white, that showed all readers that blacks could fight and hold their own. Lester, writing in the politically active 1960s and 1970s, spoke with the activist's voice. He showed his readers black pride, and he demonstrated that blacks didn't just fight to survive; they fought to win moral victories within an immoral social system. Graham wrote to teach and enlighten contemporary people about current problems. Lester wrote to inspire young blacks to go on a quest for their heritage. He dared them to search for their history, using the words of an ex-slave:

> In all the books that you have studied you never have studied Negro history, have you? You studied about the Indian and white folks, but what did they tell you about the Negro? If you want Negro history, you will have to get it from somebody who wore the shoe, and by and by, from one to the other, you will get a book. (*To Be A Slave* 11)

Lorenz Graham passed the literary shoe to Julius Lester. Both men have created books that give us some idea of what life as a black American really was and is like.

References

Lorenz Graham. "An Author Speaks," in *Elementary English,* Vol. 50 (February 1973).

Ibid. South Town. New York: Follett, 1958.

IBID. Whose Town. New York: Crowell, 1969.

Rosalind K. Goddard. Review of *Long Journey Home. New York Times Book Review,*
    July 23, 1972.
"Julius Lester: Newbery Runner-up," in *Library Journal,* Vol. 94 (May 15, 1969).
Virginia Kirkus. Review of *South Town. Virginia Kirkus Review Service,* April 1,
    1959.
Julius Lester. *All Is Well.* New York: Morrow and Company, 1976.
Ibid. Long Journey Home. New York: Dial Press, 1972.
IBID. To Be A Slave. New York: Dial Press, 1968.
"Lorenz Graham," in *Children's Literature Review,* Vol. 10.
Review of *Long Journey Home. The Junior Bookshelf,* December 1973.
Jenifer Farley Smith. Review of *Long Journey Home. The Christian Science Monitor,*
    August 2, 1972.

Derek's paper shows us how a close analysis of an author's style and his time will explain the author's carefully constructed divergent view of the world and how it fits into the values of middle-class citizens. He argues that some of the outstanding authors will be passionate about telling the truth, even if it is not the truth that middle-class citizens believe. Derek is suggesting that the author who creates a countercultural message usually follows another writer who has established that such themes have legitimacy in children's literature. His analysis of Graham's and Lester's place in the history of children's literature helps us see how each author's work builds on earlier works. This is one of the ways that rhetoric helps to shape literary content, but there are other ways.

Writers of poetry are often explored within rhetorical criticism because they are masters at metaphor, *simile,* allusion, and imaginative language. All poetry might be labeled "rhetorical" because it contains persuasive language and attempts to create a response to an *illusion* of reality. When discussing how poetry should be analyzed, Maud Bodkin wrote,

> . . . one should read a page of poetry, or distilled prose, and wander with
> it, muse, reflect, and prophesy, and dream, upon it. Some such element of
> absorbed musing, or reverie, must be present if there is to be real contact
> between the poem and personality. . . . For such absorption, moreover,
> a certain spontaneity is necessary, incompatible with the laboratory.
> . . . On the other hand there is needed, in addition to spontaneity of
> subjective response, a sharply objective and precise observation of results;
> if the knowledge sought is to be observed. (28)

Her description of poetry and its analysis suggests that a poem should be viewed as both an aesthetic experience that causes the reader to "dream" and to "muse" and an efferent one that requires that the reader "make sense" of its meaning in a precise and "sharply objective" way. She implies that our making sense of someone's rhetorical style comes from our individual objectivity.

If we are looking at a poem in an aesthetic way, we can respond to the sounds and images within the poem, and we can rely on our past experiences to evaluate the poem. Later, we will need to return to the poem to see what the writer has placed in her imagery to evoke our response. The poem becomes a work of art as we learn to appreciate how the poet has embedded layers of meaning in one short piece of writing.

Children's poets often try to "write like a child," and because they have not been there for some time, they write simplistic verse. They fail to understand that children can listen to and enjoy poetry that is much deeper than a simple rhyme or a humorous verse. Children like the sounds of poems first, but they also like to look for their own meanings for the "word puzzles" in the poetry they hear.

Some years ago I shared poetry once a week with my daughter's third grade class, and I quickly discovered that when we read and talked about a poem together, we all grew to appreciate it all the more. During the year, I shared the works of adult and children's poets. And we all wrote poems. As far as I'm concerned, the children's poems were always better than mine. They were not stifled by imagery, and they felt no need to rhyme or count meters.

My daughter Beth had begun to write poetry the year before, and she had written several rhyming poems. One of her early poems was "The Clock."

The Clock

> On the clock upon my desk,
> it says, "6:00, it's time to rest."
> I watch the hours go by,
> The numbers change before my eye.
> 12:00 clock says, "Time for lunch.
> Where at your table you munch, munch, *Munch*!"
> So digital or face,
> Party or race,
> I'll tell the time with a clock!

Up to the last line, the poem contains an aesthetic reaction for me. It has a sense of rhythm and it rhymes; it also has some nice childlike qualities. It seems to reflect a child's perception of a clock. Beth begins with personification. When she describes her clock, she writes about it as if it were a personal friend or perhaps an intruding mother who calls her child away from play to eat or rest. It engages her in a conversation. However, the poem does not sustain this mood. Beth's last three lines suggest that she looks at her clock as one of many, that it has no particular significance to her. Her mood of companionship with a personified object is replaced with a feeling that any old clock will do. When I look at the poem in a sharply objective way, it doesn't work.

A year later, after listening to lots of poems and discussing how they made us feel, Beth wrote very differently. Often she wrote poems that contained mysteries I could not easily unravel. She played with language and sounds. And she created unusual *imagery* in her poetry; in addition, her poems did not always contain a story. That made them more aesthetically appealing. For instance, she wrote "Owls" with one verse that is easily understood and "story-like," followed by a second verse that seems only to be concerned with sounds and rhythm.

Owls

Owls
looking out in the night
Searching,
To make a deadly flight.
"I have found one!" they cry
Goodbye,
Blinking their eyes off one by one.
    Mo-om
    Derylumcha leisina,
    Mosakite
    Ritenut oulcha,
    Swista,
    Teriah Sakato,
    Sho-sak,
    Elia elio qwarter whista sakato.

The poem works for me when I am musing about its meaning. The first verse contains definite imagery that builds a mood. I like the lines "Searching, / To make a deadly flight," because they convey a somber image of death and remind me that owls are night predators. When I read "'I have found one!' they cry / Goodbye, / Blinking their eyes off one by one" I mentally compare their trips to those taken by pilots who fly night missions during wars. I personally see the first verse as one containing both an image of real owls and an allusion to war missions. If I use this interpretation, the second verse reflects the senseless rhythm of death and of war. It is patterned and controlled, yet it is not rational. But if I remember that the poet is an eight-year-old girl who didn't read war stories, I realize that the second meaning is mine alone. The poet didn't purposely put it there. When I asked Beth about her second verse, she simply said, "Oh, I wanted to write in a new language." Does that mean that I must give up my interpretation? Probably not. After all, she had read very little about owls either. So it was less a poem about owls than a poem about something that Beth had thought about—predatory animals and night.

Beth had used her imagination and thought about the owls as if they were humans on a hunt, and that had inspired my reading of her poem. She had sustained her mood in the first verse, so I could accept the second verse as consistent with her first one. Today the poem gives me new puzzles to ponder. By the time Beth was in the fifth grade she had become a vegetarian. Perhaps this was an unconscious musing about carnivores. Today she composes music and creates visual images in art. Was her second verse a natural response to the sounds and rhythms that she now places in her music?

Perhaps very young children can naturally understand poetry in a rhetorical way. Leonard Clark, when discussing poetry once wrote,

> . . . poetry is one of the arts which has an immediate connection with imagination. Imagination, which all children are born with, and have in such astonishing measure, is the means by which they apprehend before they comprehend. They will often get to the heart of a poem without necessarily being able to understand all the meanings of all the words which a poem uses. At no period in their later lives will they have a greater divining power. It is not difficult for children to make a bush into a bear, an upturned kitchen table into the "Hispaniola," terrifying city streets into something like Dante's *Inferno,* the small hillside outside their back door magnified to the height of Everest. . . . [Poetry] enables children, and indeed all of us, to enjoy and appreciate patterns in sound as well as content. (135)

Indirectly, Clark helps me understand how reader response works for readers when they explore new literary patterns. Authors employ good imagery in an artful way to help their readers muse, imagine, and determine meanings for themselves. The images are refocused by the reader's own experiences. Thus, even when I am being "objective" I will draw personal conclusions from "impersonal" analysis. The objectivity found in musing comes from a reader's personal sense of the world.

All analysis places the aesthetic and the efferent experience side by side. We cannot read for one without looking for the other if we really want to experience the piece we are reading, whether it is a book, a poem, or a retelling of history. We must listen to the language and consider the author's rhetorical style in order to appreciate and understand how each piece of writing works for us.

8

Reader Response in Children's Literature: Listening to Determine Audience

Although I first worked as a children's librarian, preparing story hour programs and working with teachers and elementary school classes and later took a job as the Public Library Bookmobile Coordinator and Outreach Program Coordinator for Head Start and the housing project in Madison, Wisconsin, I did not appreciate children's responses to literature and my responsibilities to them until I began my second set of careers. Heather was born the same year that I began to teach children's literature at Purdue University, and I became a professional mother and educator at the same time. Both jobs have reshaped my thinking about reader response.

One of my colleagues who has been at Purdue since my career started likes to remind me that when I arrived at Purdue I taught like a New Critic. I would write literary terms, names of books, authors, and illustrators on the board at the start of each period. These became the parameters for the day's lecture. I would refer my students to the opinions offered in one of the standard children's literature textbooks and talk about the importance of certain genres and classics in children's literature. In turn, I expected that the students would be able to repeat the major ideas on test questions. I allowed them to freely select books from the bibliographies in the book's chapters, but insisted that they read a certain number of Newbery and Caldecott titles. Every book read was to be annotated for the students' personal card files so that they could refer to them when they began their professional careers. Indirectly I was suggesting that these titles would somehow always be the core for their teaching about or sharing of literature. This established a personal canon of children's literature for each student. Furthermore, I had every student tell a story, create a bulletin board, and design lesson plans and games so that they would consider how to instruct in entertaining ways. All of this was designed to help them develop an understanding of what children would want to know about their literature.

None of these activities are bad in and of themselves, but they imply that children's literature should be manipulated for classroom exercises and that it is important because it fits into the elementary school's curriculum. Since I used a textbook about the subject without referring my students to other ways of thinking, I forced the class to come to didactic conclusions supported by one argument. In reality, I was suggesting that an authorized opinion exists about children's literature that every reader should share. On the other hand, at home I was learning that this is just not the way literature works.

By the time Heather was six months old my husband and I were daily reading out loud to her. At first we read the books I knew to be good. One of my favorite books was *Where the Wild Things Are,* and it was already on her library shelf. So were *Goodnight Moon* and *The Snowy Day.* I didn't like board books, so I didn't buy them. But someone else did, and a copy of an ABC board book sat on Heather's bookshelf. I'd never heard of *Pat the Bunny,* but another mother had and she gave me a copy. Heather's bookshelf was growing, and her own tastes for books were developing.

I learned that Heather enjoyed participation literature. For instance, Heather loved *Pat the Bunny.* She could interact with us as we read it to her, and it became a favorite before she was one. When asked to pick a book from her shelf, she would pull off this book and bring it over to be read yet again. Furthermore, it made her aware that certain words complemented the illustrations. She listened carefully to our readings, and soon she was saying the words along with the reader.

As I watched Heather choose her own books from her reading shelf, I learned that Heather liked books for different reasons than I did. She loved the board book because she could sit on the floor and "read" it on her own, pointing out the animals and naming them as she went along. She was striving to develop her own literacy patterns that fit within her daily experiences.

I was pleased to see that we also shared some interests in similar stories. I liked repetitive stories for their natural rhythm and predictable outcome. Heather liked *Goodnight Moon* for the same reasons, and in no time she was "reading" that book along with the reader. I liked books that related to the child's real world, and so did Heather. *The Snowy Day* became a favorite because she liked to go out in the snow and do the same things that Peter did. I was beginning to discover that Heather had definite preferences. She liked books that invited the reader to actively relate to the story.

I also began to learn that children will alter their reactions to please the adults who share their literature with them. When Heather didn't like a story but knew we did, she had problems telling us. For example, she didn't like *Where the Wild Things Are*. However, she didn't tell us directly that this wasn't a book she enjoyed sharing with us. Since she knew we both liked it, she would always say it was lost, or "I can't find it" when either her father or I would ask her to bring it in and share it with us. Later, the book would be found behind the curtains in the living room, under the sofa, or at the back of her closet. Eventually we realized that she was purposely losing it.

Furthermore, I began to understand that every child wants to learn how to manipulate reading on her own. When Heather was four, she told us that she wanted to learn to read, and her father started teaching her against my better judgment. We found a book with rhyming phrases but no discernable artwork, only abstract illustrations to go along with the text. Furthermore, the story was stupid. It went something like "Tim can spin. Tim can spin on a tin." I thought it was terrible. Heather must have too, because about halfway through the book she rebelled. She simply wouldn't read with her father unless he picked a "real book." I admonished him to quit pestering her, and he did. By the time the two quit their lessons, Heather had what she needed to be a solitary reader, but she didn't tell us that. We discovered it by listening to her. Heather began to read street signs to us. Realizing that she probably wanted stories to read, we switched her from signs to books she could read on her own. *The Cat in the Hat* joined her library, and so did *Johnny Crow's Garden*. Both offered satisfying challenges.

When Beth was born we were already a library family. Every week we went to the public library and allowed Heather to pick out her own books. We also took her to the public library's story hours, and she listened to storytellers share oral tales with her. Because Beth was always there with us, she never knew a time when she was not surrounded by books. Some of them were the family books found on the bookshelves in the girls' bedroom.

They shared their library experiences. However, when Beth began picking out books to have read to her, it became apparent that she liked different stories. Beth's favorite book was *Where the Wild Things Are*. She continually brought it over to us when we were reading together. In fact, she was a Sendak fan, and while she was busy carrying Sendak's Nutshell Library around (a present for Heather from her grandmother that Heather had ignored), she picked up the phrase "I don't care!" from *Pierre*. Although she liked *Pat the Bunny*, she preferred to hear nursery rhymes. And she began to sit still and listen to chapter books with her sister before she was two years old.

We learned that adults should share what they like with children. Bob liked *Alice in Wonderland*, but I didn't. He read it out loud to the girls, and they loved it. I liked *The Lion, the Witch, and the Wardrobe*, and we read that book out loud. And as we listened to our daughters' responses to familiar literature, we began to understand that children saw literature differently. They perceived characterization and events in ways we were not expecting. For instance, we saw a British television production of *Little Women*, and Heather, though she was only five years old, took the book out of the library and began to read it on her own. She wanted to be Beth; I was appalled. How could she want to be so submissive, to languish and die? Why didn't she want to be Jo as I did when I was young?

I decided to return to see why the book continued to appeal to so many young girls, why Louisa May Alcott had written the book, and how each of the sisters fit into the story. That research resulted in one of my first published articles. I started having my students read the book and write an essay that discussed which sister was the most interesting character and why. I discovered that all the sisters had fans, that one ideal of female responses did not exist. All of this happened because I listened to Heather. If Heather hadn't picked Beth as her favorite sister in *Little Women*, I would never have reconsidered one of my childhood favorites and my didactic ideas about reader response.

By the time Beth was born, Heather was in nursery school. My career at home and at work had changed a great deal. The girls had made me aware that all literature and literary responses belong to individual readers. However, I was not sure how that fit in with what was being published in the field of children's literature as I knew it. When I went to library and education conferences and listened to speakers, I heard professionals tell me what "children liked" rather than talk about the child's interpretation of her literature.

Before Beth was two, I left my children and husband and ventured off to a Children's Literature Association annual conference. I had never met people who looked at children's literature the way the speakers at this conference did. Most of the people at ChLA taught children's literature in English departments, and they talked about their family experiences more often than they proclaimed what they knew about "children's tastes." Because they listened to their children respond to stories, they discovered that children's tastes are unpredictable. I began to acknowledge that there probably never would be one book that would appeal to every child.

As the years flew by, I listened intently to literary experts talk about their children's likes and dislikes in literature. I also continued to consider how my own two daughters differed from each other in their selections, even though they shared the same parents and loved to play together. Much of my research became child centered. I worked with one class of children for four years, and I discovered that the children had very definite tastes that often conflicted with the adults who read to them. Furthermore, they knew why adults wanted to share certain books with children: they realized that adults hoped to shape children's attitudes through literature. What I inevitably learned from this class was that literature can open up new horizons for readers, but it cannot be used as a tool to change their attitudes. Literature about the Holocaust may make readers more sympathetic to the people who suffered during that time, but it will not keep children from accepting cultural prejudices about Jews. What, then, does literature do?

As my girls grew older, I discovered that literature changed them when they became active consumers of the characterization and events. Both Heather and Beth began to internalize the stories they liked best. Although *The Lion, the Witch and the Wardrobe* didn't create a secondary world for Heather's imaginary adventures, Beth role played the book for months when she was four years old. Furthermore, as I watched her play, I found that she wanted to control her interpretation, to determine how things worked for herself. Beth walked around the house, creating dialogues and scenes in her head. Whenever she re-created *The Lion, the Witch and the Wardrobe,* she cast the same people in the same roles. Her father was Aslan, her sister was Susan, and I was the witch. She, of course, was Lucy. In many ways her play was solitary. She would walk around us and would only involve us indirectly. In fact, although we would occasionally interact with her, she did not need anyone to say any lines in order for the story to work for her.

In some ways reading and imaginary play affected her social growth. She went to nursery school for a short time, but did not enjoy the "rough and ready" play with trikes and toys and soon became a nursery school drop-out. By the time Beth was three, she was independently creating music, illustrations of imaginary scenes, and writing stories. Much of her time was spent in solitary activities.

I also began to understand that I could not pick out my children's pleasure reading unless I paid attention to what their earlier favorites were. I tried to get Heather to like fantasy, but she preferred realism. I thought both girls would enjoy sharing Laura Ingalls Wilder's books because the two oldest sisters were good companions, but I was wrong. Neither of them liked Laura Ingalls Wilder's books. After reading *The Little House in the Big Woods* and watching a few television episodes together, they dubbed the Ingalls girls "the little fairies on the prairies." And I discovered that even when I thought an earlier book might trigger an interest in a later similar one, I could not be sure. Heather liked *The Little Princess* when she was seven years old. She also liked wearing dresses and looking neat. I gave her Frances Hodgson Burnett's children's classic, *The Secret Garden,* thinking she would like it as much as she did *The Little Princess,* but I was wrong. She was polite, but she never finished the book.

Since the 1980s, members of the Children's Literature Association have continually considered the role of the child as reader and interpreter. At first, professionals expressed concern that the individual child's interests had not been more closely studied. In 1980 Peggy Whalen-Levitt edited a special section of the *Children's Literature Association Quarterly* on children and their literature. "Literature and Child Readers" addressed the then growing concern for child-centered criticism. She wrote,

> It must be admitted from the onset that, beyond intuition, we know very little about the aesthetic communication process as it involves children. . . . As the relationship between child and book generally begins in the lap of an adult reader, we wish we could have introduced you to

ethnographies of these story-reading events. Unfortunately, the work in this area is all but nonexistent. Theoretical models exist for the study of socially situated meaning, but to date they have not been applied to the story-reading context. (9–10)

Several trained critics began to consider how their perceptions of literature differed from children's and to admit that contemporary books were created for reasons not often considered or discussed in professional journals. Furthermore, they had to concede that children's books and toys were often created for reasons that had little to do with the interests of children. Marketability had become a driving force in children's literature.

Critics started looking hard at popular culture and its ability to reflect values. The dichotomy between children's likes and adult values became even more obvious as early criticism evolved and took on new topics. In 1982 Perry Nodelman edited a special section in the *Children's Literature Association Quarterly* called "Commercial Culture for Children: A Context for Children's Books." Perry wrote that his own three-year-old daughter seemed to like her toys and books for reasons different from his own. He reported that her favorite book was *Outside Over There,* and admitted that she liked the goblins in the book "at least partly because one of her records has a song on it about g-g-g-goblins" but that she probably preferred her favorite objects to her favorite book. He concluded, "She has taste, but it's not always good taste" (2). Patricia Dooley, a literary critic trained in the English department at Yale University, reported her personal frustrations when sharing literature with her baby. Dooley wrote,

> It struck me that an infant whose fascination with his toes sprang from the uncertainty as to whom they belonged was not, perhaps, ready for a plot. I realized, albeit with a pang, that my son, who regarded paper as a delightful means to making tearing and crumpling sounds (and a pleasing mess), could not be given a book with paper pages—i.e. what I thought of as a "real" book. And although I had long been accustomed to think of words—i.e. print—as another indispensable part of a book, I rapidly saw that here, too, I had something to learn. The objects offered to my inspection *were* called books; but they had leaves of laminated cardboard, or cloth, instead of paper, and if any words at all were to be found within there was rarely more than one per leaf. Sentences were at a premium, plots almost unknown. (7–8)

I contributed a piece about toys for that issue and found that the new toys out for Christmas were spin-offs from television and movies. Were these the favorite toys of children, I wondered, and sent my graduate students out to randomly interview children ages two to twelve. Few of the 190 children interviewed chose the spin-offs as their favorites. Several children between two and eight named a stuffed animal as their favorite, while only two children chose a board game as their favorite toy. Interestingly, only one child in the entire sample chose books as a favorite toy. Toys seemed to reflect parental ideas of childhood more than child play. One of the graduate students doing the survey was from New Zealand. She concluded,

After interviewing preschool children and discovering their favorite toys were stuffed animals, dolls, puzzles, and even a clean juice container, I am appalled to find the same children have closets crammed full of toys. U.S. families seem to have a fascination with owning things. (6)

Today I must ruefully admit that both Heather and Beth preferred to take books to bed over stuffies when they were young, but that I kept dumping the stuffies in, hoping they would take. Of course, the books went in along with the toys, and they remained long after the last stuffie was thrown to the floor.

The adults involved in ChLA were not experts in education; they were willing to acknowledge that their choices of books, films, and toys for children held literary values unappreciated by the children they shared them with. And they admitted that when they shared literature found in popular culture with their children they were influencing what children could read and see without really changing their children's real responses. Indeed, contemporary children are influenced in their book selections much the same way children have been influenced throughout the ages. Adults pick books that "seem suitable for children," and they suggest morals for children that may not be childlike. However, children's response journals and personal diaries show that they read the books they can the way they want.

In 1984 Norman and Angela Williamson studied the 1893 diaries of a Canadian adolescent girl and discovered that although she had definite tastes in literature and she loved to read, she sometimes found her literature selections frustrating. The library available was housed in the church, and Mamie Pickering had to request books from a female librarian. Often she was forced to take out a book more than once. Furthermore, although Mamie was thirteen, her selections were controlled by her parents and the church librarian. In order to read "secular literature" or magazines, Mamie had to get permission from her parents. Concerning Mamie's entries about one secular book, the Williamsons write,

> Mamie was ecstatic when, as she tells us, she "got hold of" *How He Won Her*. The characters of this romance were the type Mamie liked. Above all they out-stripped the bounds of the role of virgin. There was Alfie who dies in a war—a "good death" usually reserved for men. Elfie, "who was a little fury and Britomarte who was so brave that she disguises herself" as a boy and joins the army just so she can be near Justin Rosenthal, her lover. . . . In every case we have virgins who do what boys get to do in boy's literature. Mamie and her girl friends loved it all . . . Mamie's excitement at it all literally bursts from the diary. (Part Two, 58)

Sylvia Patterson Iskander's insightful study of Anne Frank's reading, as mentioned in her diaries, depicts a similar scenario: Anne's reading in the attic was controlled by her parents and the people hiding the families. Anne commented that her parents allowed her to read almost all the books that came into the attic, and Iskander concludes that the shared readings afforded the adults and adolescents recreational and educational fodder.

She says that the books were mainly contemporary titles, that they were written by authors of various nationalities, and that "they represent a wide diversity and a broad spectrum and reflect Anne's reading in Dutch, German, French, and English. Perhaps they contributed to her tolerance for others and her hope for the future" (140). Nevertheless, the titles that Anne read and critiqued were chosen for her, and her reading was influenced by adult values and morals.

When a group of ChLA professionals delivered papers on children's reading interests at the Modern Language Association's meeting in 1987, two speakers looked back at their childhood readings for patterns, two looked at their children and their choices. Once again, all stressed that children's preferences are controlled by their social needs.

Children's author George Shannon told of his adult search for his favorite childhood books. He explained that six books from his childhood had affected his adult writing. Three were children's books, three were adult books belonging to his parents. None were chosen for Shannon as "moral education," but the children's books were introduced to him by his parents and read to him as entertainment. The adult books were part of his parents' book collection. Two were art books, one of cartoons and one of famous paintings. These were books he liked to look at. No one guided his interpretations of the art, so he did not like them from an efferent sense. He liked them because the people in the illustrations drew him into their worlds. The children's books all contained characters unhappy with their lot, heroes in search of their true identities. Looking back at his selections, Shannon says,

> My selections, as are all children's, were based on emotional need and felt connection rather than any awareness of quality or stature of the writers and illustrators. Two were Little Golden books by Richard Scarry. The third was by Moore and Leight who made few other books. What sent me back to these books was again visual. (122)

As a writer and former children's librarian, Shannon examined his childhood literary repertoire and concluded that his storytelling and writing experiences contained many stories that were similar to his early favorites. He added,

> . . . what we write is always shaped by our primary perspectives and forms just as paintings are informed by the visual artist's personal dictionary of color, line and form. And what formed the basis of my personal dictionary was the pattern and image of my three treasured picture books from childhood. (123)

Nancy Huse, a feminist children's literature critic, returned to her childhood and recalled that her early influences were from "the work of Olive Beaupre Miller and the women who taught her" (114). She further observed that her early reading was controlled by her mother's careful determination to give her daughter one book a year from *My Book House,* a series of anthologies designed to entertain and inform children about the best in children's literature, the most important ideas and attitudes needed to become "genteel." Huse's mother never read to her daughter; that job was relegated to her father. And she never allowed her to randomly select one of the books from the set to read from. The remaining books were kept under lock and key until the appropriate birthday rolled around. The books became a central factor in Huse's childhood. Looking at the books and recalling her favorite stories, Huse concluded, "my preferences seem to have backed up Miller's conviction that literature and life are intertwined. As one of the significant insights of feminist criticism . . . this connection seems obvious to me now as a critic" (119).

I recalled the reading patterns of Heather and Beth and argued that children who learn to manipulate stories are more apt to grow up to be writers or illustrators. Concerning Heather I wrote,

> Heather is almost eighteen now, and she is busy getting ready to go to college. She spends a good deal of her spare time writing college essays. Most of them contain a story, and almost all of them are circular in pattern. They start out with quotations from favorite philosophers or authors or lines from favorite poems. . . . All are used to capture the reader's imagination. She seems to believe, much like Perry Nodelman, that the reader's attention can be caught best in a narrative that allows him to interact with a scene. (129)

Virginia Wolf discussed her daughter Nina's reading of *Alice's Adventures in Wonderland*. She recalled that Nina "insisted" her mother read the book to her when Wolf was certain "that she was too young." She remembered how this and its sequel, *Through the Looking Glass,* remained two of Nina's childhood favorites. Based on her adult perceptions of the stories and her daughter's personality, Wolf had earlier concluded that the books would be most appreciated by "demanding, aggressive, curious girls . . . clearly, very few children would be readers of *Alice*" (135)." Wolf explains that her attitudes changed when she shared Louise Fitzhugh's *Harriet the Spy* and Madeleine L'Engle's *A Wrinkle in Time* in her college class and noticed that the books' heroines read Alice and were affected by the story. L'Engle's Meg is not aggressive, and she did not fit Wolf's earlier analysis. Looking at Meg as the "typical" child reader, Wolf began to see that youthful readers might like the *Alice* books because they are ego-centered idealists who want to control the world and make it behave as they wish it to, and they perceive Alice as liking to do the same thing. Fantasy, she concluded, appeals to these young readers because is allows them to believe that the world can be reshaped.

All these ideas lead us back to the reader and refocus our attention on the real audience for children's literature. They work like mini-ethnographic studies of childhood reading and they also fit Peggy Whalen-Levitt's call for a new perspective in literary studies and sharing children's literature. However, they still do not allow real readers to respond for themselves.

What would happen if we shaped our opinions about childhood reading around children's responses, if we allowed them to tell us what really worked and why? This is a question many critics have begun to ponder.

In 1988, Rod McGillis considered his two daughters and their playtime activities, asserting that they were not readers. Yet, he added, they were critical readers. Looking at Nancy Huse's article, he wrote,

> . . . each of us, no matter what our training, reading habits, or interests, is a critic; none of us simply reads. We learn to expect certain things from our reading. We become critics in the sense that we all have notions about what kinds of books speak most deeply to us.
>
> For me the mystery remains. What makes a reader? Certainly, our training has much to do with the theoretical assumptions practising critics employ, but just as certainly, our desires and attitudes, our deep desires and early formed attitudes provide a context for our reading. (107)

Perry Nodelman has spent a good deal of his time talking about children's literature as a didactic field. He has continually argued that children's stories are written by adults who are no longer children; that the books, therefore, are never really "childlike." And he says that the childhood we remember is probably not the childhood we experienced. He asks, "How is it that we adults know better than children do how to act as children?" In the end, he suggests that critics need to think less of children as "the other," the group of people who can be analyzed and categorized by a description of their "sameness" in attitudes, needs, and reading habits. Instead, he argues, critics who turn to children's literature have intriguing questions that they must address.

> What claims do specific texts make on the children who read them? How do they represent childhood for children, and *why* might they be representing it in that way? What interest of adults might the representation be serving? Perhaps above all, how does it work? How does children's literature make its claims on child readers? (34)

All this suggests that the real readers are the children and they should be telling adults how children's literature entertains, instructs, and reflects their lives. For those of us who hope to practice reader response theory in children's literature, this is exactly what we must do. When we learn to listen closely to real readers responding, we will end up discussing literature with them in literary ways and will help them become implied readers who are somehow different from when they first put their books down.

Several of my students have listened to young readers and have explained their preferences in student essays. However, they have usually come away with conclusions about the appeal of a particular children's book rather than with theories about the values of reader response criticism. Recently I watched one of my students form her own questions about reader response criticism and children's literature that echo the ones Nodelman later formulated.

Nodelman often struggles with the duplicity of keeping children "innocent" while allowing them to explore their texts in interpretative ways. He is troubled by adult tendencies to view children's literature as a way to teach adult values. However, I believe that Thespena has suggested a practical way to share literature that is both enlightening and informative. Thespena Cappas's paper calls for a responsible teacher who is willing to take on a new role. This teacher may be more knowledgeable than the students she is working with, but she must remember that the children's personal responses can help her define a story's classroom meaning. While she is sharing new information about literature and its patterns, she is relearning about childhood reactions to the ideas authors place in their stories. Together, they construct meaning for a shared literary experience.

Thespena Cappas spent a good deal of time in my office talking about the book she had read for her final paper; during that time she gradually turned her thoughts away from the values of that particular book. She became more and more intrigued with the idea that she would best understand the book's childlike appeal if she talked with a "real reader." Finally, she determined that she had to find a youngster to speak to, one who would confide her thoughts. Since she was interested in the author's use of females in his story, she wanted to talk with a girl. Her final paper makes a strong case for all reader response theory.

"Will the Real Reader Please Stand Up?": Reader Response and Literary Interpretation

BY THESPENA CAPPAS

Do children notice folkloric patterns when they read a story that uses conventions? Do they try to predict outcomes as they read? How do young readers determine if characters are realistic or stereotypic? What do they get from their books—pleasure, a point of view on male/female relations? All of these questions, and more, came to my mind as I read Bill Brittain's *The Wish Giver*.

At first, I simply wanted to see how reader response theory actually works, so when I read the book I kept a response journal myself. As I read *The Wish Giver*, I felt that Thaddeous Blinn was either the devil himself or someone who can twist dreams into nightmares. Furthermore, the story seemed predictable to me. After reading through the first wish, I felt confident in predicting what would happen throughout the rest of the story. The heroes seemed unable to foresee the future, yet, I could see their tragic outcomes. I continued to read the book just to see if my predictions were right, and they were. As I continued reading, I found myself not relating to the characters. I did not really empathize with the children. However, I liked the plot; I found the adventures curious, predictable, and satisfying.

I enjoyed reading *The Wish Giver*. When I looked back in my reader response journal, I noticed that I had noted many interesting things. For instance, the characters' literal interpretation of advice was a key element in the story. I also saw that Bill Brittain used many conventions in the story. It fits with other fantasy stories. First of all, the number three is used. There are three children and who are given three wishes. But *The Wish Giver* is not only a fantasy; it is an adventure story also. The plot moved quickly, and the adventures are more interesting than the characterization. Also, foreshadowing is used when Thaddeous Blinn says that the wishes will be granted exactly as they are asked. Brittain uses irony. When the children make their wishes, they say one thing, but they wish for something else. Brittain uses many stereotypic patterns also. He portrays men who are strong, women who are weak. Also, his women change personally while his men change the world around them. I considered how feminism tied to the book.

Many conventions were obvious to me, but I wondered if they would be obvious to children. I realized that my point of view might not be similar to a child's. I wanted to know how a children's book that held many conventions worked for a child, and I decided to have my twelve-year-old cousin Georgia read the book and keep a reader response journal.

After I read Georgia's journal, I noticed several similarities and differences in our journals. And I realized that children do not necessarily react the way we think they will. First of all, Georgia thought Thaddeous Blinn sounded "really ugly and scary looking." Georgia also said, "When reading Thaddeous Blinn's sign, it seemed impossible because nothing like this could happen in real life! But after reading his poster, I really wondered if this man could give someone what they asked for." I also felt like Georgia did after reading Thaddeous Blinn's sign. There was something about this poster that made Georgia and me want to believe it was true, even though we knew it was impossible.

I asked Georgia to predict what she thought would happen after reading each wish. After reading the first wish, Georgia wrote, "I think that Polly won't become friends with Agatha and Eunice because she'll see that they're snobs just like the twins said they were." After reading the second wish, Georgia wrote, "I think Henry will go back to where he came from, and Rowena will realize he's a jerk after all." After reading the third wish, Georgia said, "I think Adam will get the water he wished for, but something bad will come out of it." Before the last wish, Georgia guessed, "I think Polly, Rowena, and Adam will go to Stew's Meat store and argue over who will get the wish on his card. At the end, he will probably wish that all three of the kid's wishes will be changed around."

The Wish Giver was predictable to me from the very beginning because I was aware of the conventions held in the book. After reading the second and third wishes, Georgia was unable to correctly predict what would happen, but after reading about the third and fourth wishes, she could. I discovered that books are not as predictable to children since they are not aware of literary conventions. Sometimes, though, they will begin to predict outcomes that fit within an author's pattern. Georgia unknowingly figured out some of the conventions in this book. Therefore, she was able to predict the final outcome of the book, and she will probably be able to predict future books with similar plots more easily.

What I found most interesting was the fact that Georgia related to the characters. She often commented about them in her journal. First of all, she thought that the mud fight Polly, Lenora, and Leland had sounded like a lot of fun. Secondly, she thought the twins sounded like brats. Georgia liked the way Lenora and Leland talked about Agatha and Eunice. She thought it was hilarious. She also noticed that Polly did not stick up for herself enough. Georgia thought it was very cruel of Agatha to slap Polly across the face. Finally, Georgia thought Henry was a jerk. She said, "If I was Rowena, and Henry was talking to me that way, I'd leave him there all by himself until he appreciated that I was trying to help him." Georgia concluded this entry by saying, "Most books for my age (12) don't even write about this fun stuff."

Georgia's reader response journal gave me a new outlook on the characters in the book. I did not originally identify with the characters because I was more concerned with predicting the outcomes of the wishes. I now realize that different readers respond in different ways. Just because Georgia's response is different from mine, it is not wrong. Furthermore, Georgia's responses might have been different if she knew about conventions in literature.

One question still intrigues me. What is the best way for children to read—as a real reader or an implied reader? The person who reads without knowing about literary conventions, the author, and/or the illustrator is the book's real reader. She will pick up the book, read it, and leave it alone when she is done, whereas an implied reader will read the story through and then ask questions about the elements to try and figure out what the story means. Is real reader response the best way for children? Or is implied reader response better? Should children read books for their own enjoyment or should they discuss their books after reading them in order to find out why stories are written as they are, what meanings the authors have placed in their plots?

The child is a natural real reader, but I have come to the conclusion that she should also be an implied reader. However, I believe that the adults who help children discuss their books should not lead them to certain answers and demand that everyone reach the same conclusions. Adults may help children analyze their texts, but they should not conclude that there is a right way to read.

Yet, throughout my education my literature teachers have followed the practice of New Criticism, stressing "the perfect reading" of a story. In my classes we discussed many stories together, but in the end the teachers told us which interpretations were best. After a while, I found myself not caring about the literature we were reading. I didn't participate in class; I just waited for the teacher to tell me what the story meant. When I was tested on the stories I read, I wrote down what my teachers wanted to hear. I didn't hear the author out. I became a passive learner who sought a teacher's interpretation of what I read.

We must get away from New Criticism. How can children understand the many conventions in literature if the "correct" answers are always given to them and are expected to be repeated without any exceptions? I have begun to consider how critics view reading.

I agree with Robert E. Probst and his theory of reading. According to Probst, knowledge is constructed by the reader as he is reading; the meaning of a story is not in the text alone. It is created by the reader who "self-defines" the text's meaning. Throughout *Response and Analysis: Teaching Literature in Junior and Senior High School,* Probst demonstrates ways that a teacher can encourage students to respond to texts in their own ways. I like his discussion of reader response criticism the best. Probst says, "The teacher's role is to view reading as an act of creation, rather than a search for one true meaning" (53). I strongly believe this. However, because of the way literature is shared in the schools, many students have come to believe that they must obtain "right" answers from their teachers. They have not learned to trust their own interpretations.

Perhaps if college students in teaching programs begin to think and formulate ideas on their own they will begin to see how children can be encouraged to do the same thing. Then, the teachers will become participants in their own classes. Probst says, "If a class begins to work well, the students may accept the teacher as a participant in the same processes of responding and thinking, able to contribute as another learner" (54). When a teacher achieves this stature in her class, she can go back and forth between the roles of teacher and student. This approach will work best, I feel, because students will see that their responses are valued and will openly participate in class discussions. Probst argues, "Having abandoned the authority of might—the threat of grades and tests—a teacher may retain the authority of reason. Rather than present the result of her thoughts, she joins in the process of thinking, giving the class the authority both to challenge her and to observe her" (54). And so, children will look at literature in a different light. Children may even begin to feel that it is okay to challenge a teacher's theories. At the same time, the teacher's responses and thoughts can be models for the class. Her responses are not necessarily the correct or best ones, but her responses will give the class members an idea about literary structures that they have not yet discovered.

Teachers also need to consider the range of responses that children can be expected to make. They need to remember that there will be a variety of responses to any piece of literature. Probst suggests five "rough" categories that can be used as a checklist to class discussions. Responses can be personal, topical, interpretative, or formal. Readers may also address broad literary concerns. While each type of response has its values, I feel it is important for the teacher to note the kinds of responses and to guide the class discussion towards personal evaluations.

Reader response teaching can be very demanding. Response papers take time to write, and they take time to read. Careful thought must be put into the teacher's responses to students. I would agree with Probst when he says, "To teach these patterns everyday, five periods a day, may well be too exhausting" (61). However, I do not think that asking a child to do a reader response once or twice a week is too demanding. And I believe that these responses on outside class readings will create meaningful class discussions. Children will have thought about what they read, and they will be able to respond to the text in a active way.

Actually, I used some of Probst's ideas with Georgia. After I read Georgia's journal, we discussed *The Wish Giver*. Georgia explained that she basically liked all of the characters. Since most of the characters were her age, she found them easy to identify with, and she enjoyed them more than the story's plot. It didn't really matter to Georgia that Adam received something good from his wish while Polly and Rowena did not. Apparently, the feminist perspective of stereotypic characterization does not concern her at this point. She also said it was easier for her to predict the outcome of the wishes after she read the first two episodes. I expect that Georgia will remember our conversation and that she will be able to predict stories about wishing more easily in the future.

I wanted to share some of the conventions in this book that Georgia did not seem to know about. However, I did not want Georgia to think that these ideas were better than hers. I wanted Georgia to look at me as her equal in our discussion. In order for her to do that, I had to phrase my discussion so that she would not feel threatened. Therefore, I said, "Some people believe that feminist criticism works well with this book because of the stereotypic roles of men and women," and "I've learned about a technique called irony where the author expects us to see how the character is choosing the wrong thing before the character does." Georgia did not feel threatened by my additional information. She did gain new knowledge that she can use when she is reading her next book.

Reader response criticism is a learning process—an experience in reading. It may seem long and hard at first, but I now feel that it is a method that children will understand and like. I believe that we must give children a chance to understand how literature works, that this process allows them to explore literature and express their ideas. Furthermore, it will help teachers understand how children's literature really works.

References

Bill Brittain. *The Wish Giver*. New York: Harper & Row, 1983.

Georgia Kollintzas. Schererville, IN. Personal interviews and reader response journal, October 25–November 12, 1991.

Robert E. Probst. *Response and Analysis: Teaching Literature in Junior and Senior High School*. Portsmouth, NH: Boynton/Cook Publishers, 1988.

9

Adults and Children Interpreting Children's Literature Together

Our conversations have come full circle. You have explored literary theory with me and have read about students in courses of children's literature who became critics in their own right. I hope you have read some of the books and articles listed in the bibliographies and have begun to search out the meaning of these children's books for yourself. As you close this book, you may wonder, "What now? How do I make this work for me in my day-to-day living?" There is no one answer to that question—everyone has different needs when they read. Most of us are more interested in our individual pursuit of children's literature than in sharing literature, but we will need to know what writing works for children and how adults are sharing literature with them.

If you are a children's librarian, you may use your newly acquired literary understanding when selecting new materials for the library's collection, planning literature programs for children, and creating book lists for adults who will share children's literature in their homes and schools. If you're in the arts, you may want to explore children's theater and its possibilities, look at picture-book illustration and format as an artistic endeavor, consider creating children's films, or become a storyteller. Your studies have just begun! You will want to pursue new journals, attend artistic events linked to children's literature, go to theater productions, attend storytelling workshops. If you're a parent, you may want to introduce your children to the ideas shared in this book. You will have the best opportunity to keep your communications open with your youngsters if you have shared experiences, and your literature explorations may help you to better understand each other as the years go by. If you are a teacher, you must consider how you can share literature and literary criticism with children. Most of this chapter will deal with how teachers share literature, an important issue for everyone since children's education affects all of us.

Reading for pleasure is largely an uncritical process—it does not demand analytical follow-up to work. It is a solitary act that is satisfying. When I read for pleasure, it does not matter whether I discuss the book with someone else or not. Once I enter into a community of readers, however, I demand more of myself and my literature. I can still enjoy the pleasures of plot and characterization, but usually I want to discuss other elements that seem to set the book apart from previously read stories and to discuss the books with people who share a common background. This means that I must know about other books in the field. When we want to compare experiences, we must be knowledgeable in the field. Part of that knowledge involves audience appeal. All of us must read, listen, and discuss literature together if we truly want to understand how reader's response works in children's literature.

Listening is one of the most difficult and rewarding challenges when teaching with and about literature. Listening to talk about children's literature means learning to pause and reflect with young readers, to trust their judgments, to honor their perceptions of how a story works or doesn't work. Listening implies respect, and it suggests that the listener understands where the speaker is coming from, what sorts of values are being espoused, when the listener should join in the discussion. A good share of critical activity happens when we are sharing our literary experiences.

Critical insights about earlier readings often evolve within oral discussions. Earlier perceptions about the author's style and meaning can be reevaluated by adults and children alike when they share literature. Aesthetics become pleasurable in different ways when a work's audience defines the beauties of a certain piece together and begins to suggest alternative ways of viewing a "commonplace scene." The personal discoveries of individuals become shared interpretations.

Some of the teachers I have had in classes are good role models for us to consider. This chapter includes teachers' papers discussing how teaching with and about literature changed when they considered critical theory, the children they were working with, and their school's curriculum. All the examples stress the need to practice good listening strategies.

Sometimes the books we share are ones other people give us. How do we evaluate those books? Where do we place them in the curriculum? Becky DeWitt teaches in a transitional kindergarten/grade one classroom in rural Indiana. While she was a student in my picture-book class, I gave her a book by Peter Parnall to share with her students. As she listened to the children's conversation, she realized that their understanding of the book was more sophisticated than her first perceptions. Becky stood back and began to consider her role when she shared a new book. In the end she wrote the following paper.

Exploring the Evaluation Process:
Quiet by Peter Parnall

BY BECKY DEWITT

When a teacher wants to share a book with her class, she often chooses one that has a good story. She may not consider the choice of good illustrations important. Teachers seldom take time out to look at the illustrations in a picture book when they are sharing a book. Maybe they feel that students will pay more attention to what is happening in the pictures than what is happening in the story itself. Teachers need to learn how to evaluate picture books.

One way teachers can learn more about picture books is to look for the book's artistic qualities and its intended audience. A teacher should be able to observe any picture book with an open mind. The book *Quiet* by Peter Parnall was given to me, and I explored the evaluation process as I shared the book.

When I first flipped through the pages of *Quiet,* I noticed the unusual angle of the illustrations. The reader is able to be a part of the illustrations. The boy in *Quiet* is lying on the ground "sharing with nature's creatures their silent bond." The animals cannot figure out what the boy is when he is lying on the grass, stretched out flat. The reader sees the scene as if she were one of the animals sitting off to the side and watching the boy and the other animals. I would say that the reader could be one of the chickadees in the scene.

Parnall has created a feeling of closeness between the animals and the boy. Although the boy lies flat, he is eager for the chickadees to fly down on his chest and taste the apple seeds lying there. Parnall has shown the boy's purposeful actions in his illustrations. On the dedication page Parnall captures the boy as he places the apple core and seeds on his chest. Parnall suggests that this could be based on someone real. *Quiet* is dedicated to Bryan; the boy in the two-page spread could be Bryan.

The illustrations reflect nature. The illustrations are mostly in blues, greens, and yellows. Parnall uses red as an emphasis, much like George Cruikshank and Edward Ardizzone. Of course, Parnall uses red on the apple core pieces placed on the boy's chest. Parnall lets his illustrations flow off both sides of his two-page-spreads. The illustrations flow off both sides of the page. For instance, on the page where the text reads, "Chipmunk comes when he sees me there, a quiet, wrinkled thing under a pile of seeds and apple cores" you can see the boy's chin all the way down to his waist where the illustration gradually washes off the page. On the next page Raven comes close to the boy, but the reader only sees Raven's wings. The rest of the bird is washed off the page.

Parnall puts very few words on a page. The two-page spreads are large, close-up illustrations with much detail. This is how he sets a mood for his illustrations. The viewer can tell that Parnall is fond of animals by viewing his illustrations. This reflects his life and attitudes; Parnall spent his childhood in the country and is still deeply interested in animals. Often he finds inspiration for his work when taking long walks to watch deer and other wild creatures (Commire 221). He once commented about the media he uses when he draws, saying, "I started by doing only wildlife illustrations by using only pen and ink, branched out into tempera, then combined black-and-white with color washes and found the sky was the limit when dealing with inks" (Kingman 156).

When I looked at the book, I decided that my favorite illustration is the one with the text, "As I wait, I hear Mouse rustle under leaves by my head" because I can sense the moment. On the left side of the page a few scattered yellow leaves conceal a mouse who is peeping out from beneath one leaf. At first glance I missed the boy's head lying in the leaves and grass because the boy's hair is blond and it blends in with the yellow leaves. On the right side of the two-page-spread evergreens are depicted at a distance with the round sun shining brightly. Parnall has added a touch of blue to the scene by including two small wildflowers in the grass and leaves.

Quiet could be shared with children ages five through eight. I shared it with my six- and seven-year-old students. They told me that their favorite character in the book was Raven. When I came to the page where Raven comes close enough to the boy "to mess my hair" one of my students said, "Wow!" I knew right then that the illustration had worked for him.

My students were confused by the illustration with the text, "From the sea where Vikings roamed near Maine and maybe met a bird on an outstretched hand . . .". This two-page-spread shows a man's bearded face. His hand is stretched out, and a chickadee is perched on it. The previous page's text discusses the wind whispering from the sea, so if the children had really been listening, they might have been able to understand the illustration. Still, the man doesn't seem to fit in the book's presentation. All of the other illustrations are to the point, and they reflect the text presented on that page.

I was surprised to learn how my students interpreted the illustrations and noticed points I had missed. For instance, they noticed that the sun is depicted on all of the pages. On the dedication page it appears to be rising. Since time is an obvious factor in the story, my students and I decided that the boy went out to the clearing during the morning. Parnall's use of perspective makes it difficult to view the skyline, and he is unable to place the sky overhead the boy. However, towards the end of the story the sun appears to be setting. My children watched the sun's position as we read the story. They pointed out that when the text reads, "Raven watches. He watches Chipmunk and me, and Chickadees" the sun is depicted behind the evergreen trees where Raven sits. Once the page was turned, the scene is turned around. Raven is in the forefront, and he is looking at the boy in the distance. Immediately, the children noticed that Parnall had moved the sky around, that it was now setting behind the boy. One of the children said, "Hey! He made a mistake." We stopped to look at the sun's position throughout the book again, and in the end we decided that Peter Parnall did make a mistake when he placed the sun in this last illustration. We talked about the importance of perspective in illustrations, and we all noticed how Parnall used angles in his illustrations. Then the children drew pictures using perspective in them.

I am pleased that my students are becoming more aware of the illustrations in picture books. They are naturally curious about pictures in books, and they enjoy discussing them with one another. After they look closely at the pictures, these children grow curious about the words placed on the pages with the illustrations. Our discussions bring the two together in meaningful ways, and the two help to extend the story's impact. In this way, we can explore a contextual meaning of the story.

References

Anne Commire, ed. *Something About the Author,* Vol. 16. Detroit: Gale Research, 1979.

Lee Kingman, Joanna Foster, and Ruth Giles Lontoft. *Illustrators of Children's Books, 1957–1966*. Boston: The Horn Book, Inc., 1968.
Peter Parnall. *Quiet*. New York: Morrow Junior Books, 1989.

Becky encourages her children to discuss the books they are sharing as they go along. She listens closely to their comments. When their discoveries add to the book's presentation, she either stops and follows up with immediate conversation or makes note of it mentally and begins a dialogue about overheard comments when the book is finished. Furthermore, Becky evaluates the literature for herself first; as she is discussing the book with the children she can tell them what her original thoughts were and they can discuss other perceptions of the same story. When Becky listens, she is learning about children and their ability to understand a story. She can take their comments into consideration, and she and the children can see the successes and failures of the authors/illustrators who create books for children.

Becky's approach is less judgmental than one that centers on student performances. She does not demand that the children retell the plot or identify the characters. Instead, she guides their conversations to considering what they liked, who appealed to them, why authors or illustrators might choose to create a story in a certain way. When she listens to the classroom discussion, she can tell whether the children understood the story or not. In addition, she can learn how the story works with its first and most important audience—children.

Becky will not give her students a comprehensive exam when she finishes this lesson and will not hand out a worksheet to fill out. Her evaluation has taken place as the students talked, and she is aware that some of the students' comments have led the class discussion in a particularly meaningful way. Probably she will jot down some comments in her teacher's journal about the discussion, noting who made specific comments that shaped the conversations, who joined in the conversation, and who seemed reticent to talk. As she looks at the class illustrations, she can add notes about good illustrations that demonstrate perceptions discussed. She can place those illustrations around the class and encourage her students to look at them. If she wants, she can follow up with a discussion of the difficulty of creating point of view through illustrations. These children have experienced and created visual attempts to suggest point of view, and they will probably enjoy the discussion. However, if they seem disinterested, Becky can wrap the conversation up quickly and consider the lesson done. Her students have been introduced to several significant ideas that she can later return to in discussions: sequencing, narrative and visual point of view, perspective in art, book format, and the relationship between text and art in picture books.

Learning to listen and learning to respond have been valid concerns of educators in English studies for some time. In 1966 forty-six educators gathered at Dartmouth College to consider how to make English more relevant and teachable. One of the Canadian members who attended the Dartmouth conference, Merron Chorny of the University of Calgary, established a series of summer institutes to further the conversations. In 1983 the University of Calgary sponsored an institute called "Teacher as Learner/Teacher as Researcher." Merron Chorny edited and published the keynote papers from that institute. These papers are useful reading for us all because they address several issues in education, including ways to create readers, how writing is best integrated into the school curriculum, and how teachers can develop school contexts for learning. All the papers stress a need for a "listening community," a place where mutual respect is stressed in day-to-day activities. James Britton was the keynote speaker at Calgary. He suggested that learning is best achieved when teachers stand back and listen to their students. Britton argued,

> . . . if education is seen as an effect of community it will be the teacher's concern to make the class a genuine community, where learning from each other and learning with each other can flourish. . . . To create and maintain community is a task that relies heavily on language, which means that as teachers of English and Language Arts we are at the core of the operation. "Community" and "communion" are close relations—communion in the sense of face to face talk . . . and the nature of the talk that goes on in the classroom is crucial to learning. (5)

When we listen to several groups of children discuss the same books we find that communal sharing does not create predictable outcomes. Different communities of readers will view the same story in very different ways. When he was writing about Rosenblatt and reader response theory, editor Joel Taxel asserted, "I have come to understand that aesthetic reading is shaped not only by the idiosyncratic likes, dislikes, interests, experiences and concerns that readers bring to the text, but also by the particular interpretative communities in which readers are socialized" (vii). Taxel further argues that a teacher's stance changes when she becomes interested in aesthetic readings, that these teachers become pupils who learn about literature, about children, and about learning as they share literature.

How do teachers establish a community that enjoys face-to-face talk? They can take time to consider what they have learned in their college classes and what they suspect children's literary responses will be based on what they have learned. They will want to listen to their students' comments about the books shared to see how children respond to the stories shared. They need to consider how conversation about literature encourages more interaction among students, how teachers best facilitate discussion for interpretation.

Sylvia Briscoe entered a graduate level children's literature course with a wealth of teaching experience. Recently, she had been a teacher of students in inner city Philadelphia. When she entered my class, she was beginning graduate studies and teaching in Lafayette, Indiana. This was her first experience in small town living. And it was her first entry into a predominantly white lower-middle-class setting. Most of Sylvia's students had never talked to an African-American woman. Now they had an articulate African-American teacher from the East Coast. It might have been difficult for them to become a community of listeners, but Sylvia's teaching style made it easy. She was a good listener. She reflected on classroom experiences. She thought of her students as individuals with personal ideas, talents, and needs. And she began to share children's literature about places that looked like her East Coast home. Finally, Sylvia sat down and wrote this short paper.

Picture Books: Lessons or Enjoyment?

BY SYLVIA BRISCOE

"The visual image is the most engaging of sensory messages, imprinting its outline upon the subconscious like an acid etch" (MacCann 183). So, the picture book can be very powerful to the reader. The author-illustrator has two powerful mediums: the word and the picture. Furthermore, MacCann has stated, "Pictures are the primary message vehicle, and text tends to be extremely minimal" (183). Will this hold true when books are examined?

MacCann's arguments hold true for *Dreams* by Ezra Jack Keats. The pictures really relate the story. There is a child hero, Roberto. Roberto takes a hero's journey. He leaves his apartment on a mental adventure and returns. During the night, Roberto save Archie's cat from a snarling dog. He saves the cat with a paper mouse that falls from the window sill. The pictures and story merge at this point to produce a wonderful experience. As the mouse falls, the reader watches the shadow grow larger and larger. Roberto saves the cat through a vicarious experience, goes to bed, and is dreaming when everyone else is getting up.

Stevie, by John Steptoe, also uses the power of image and text. Steptoe relies on both pictures and words to communicate to the reader. *Stevie* is a wonderful book about a boy who has another child come stay in his home. The book's main character is Robert, an only child. Stevie comes to stay with Robert and sends him on a journey that changes his life. Robert shares his toys and his room with Stevie. He suffers teasing from his friends and yelling from his father. He wishes Stevie were not around. But in the end, Robert changes and remembers the good times with Stevie:

> So then he left. The next mornin' I got up to watch cartoons and I fixed two bowls of corn flakes. Then I just remembered that Stevie wasn't here. Sometimes we had a lot of fun runnin' in and out of the house. Well, I guess my bed will stay clean from now on. But that wasn't so bad. He couldn't help it cause he was stupid. (14)

I read both books to my second grade class. The children liked the books equally, and they really enjoyed the pictures. When I asked them how the books were similar, they commented,

Andy: Both use paints.

Crystal: Both are colorful.

Steve: Steptoe's pictures are colorful.

Morgan: Keats' got the whole thing. He got the inside and the outside. Steptoe just got the inside.

Matt: I like Ezra Jack Keats because, see, like that's suppose to be a bedroom in there, and that's a sky in the different windows.

Justin: I like Ezra Jack Keats because Steve was right that he [Steptoe] has more colorful colors but I like that [Keats] because it has more detail and stuff.

Andy: What details?

Justin: If you draw a picture and it has windows.

Andy: Detail has more picturing in it.

When asked which book they liked best and why, the children responded,

Mike: I like *Dreams* because it has a lot of colors and I like how he draws the boy—his hair—and I like how he makes pictures in the window.

Matt: I like *Stevie*. I like the part about all the fluorescent colors on the skirt. I like the little boy.

Steve: I like the book *Stevie* because it's my name and the pictures were colorful. I like the boy named Stevie cause he was small just like me.

Kyle: I like *Dreams* because I like how the mouse gets bigger and bigger.

Chassidy: I like when the mouse scared the dog away.

Holly: I like *Stevie*. I liked how he outlined the pictures.

Jon: I like John Steptoe because it looked like he used chalk.

Crystal: I like how Ezra Jack Keats filled up the whole picture.

Justin: The rats were cool.

Matt: He [Robert] didn't like him [Stevie]. Now he does.

Elisabeth: In *Stevie* he [Roberto] misses him [Stevie].

Both books were written for the real reader's enjoyment, for children. There are no obvious lessons to be learned. There are no acceptable or unacceptable forms of behavior defined for the main characters in the books. *Dreams* takes the reader on an imaginative adventure. *Stevie* takes the reader through a common experience. These books are a source of pleasure for the real reader. This class enjoyed talking about the aspects of format that they enjoyed. As teachers, I believe it is important for us to remember that it's okay to simply enjoy the books we share.

References

Ezra Jack Keats. *Dreams*. New York: Macmillan Co., 1974.

Donnarae MacCann and Gloria Woodard, ed. *The Black American in Books for Children: Readings in Racism*. Metuchen, NJ: Scarecrow Press, 1985.

John Steptoe. *Stevie*. New York: Harper and Row, 1969.

Sylvia tape recorded her students' comments during their discussion so that she could transcribe their remarks and search for clues about class interpretations and individual reactions. If she wanted, she could continue to record discussion sessions when books were shared to see how children reacted to their literature, how their perceptions changed, the sorts of classroom dynamics that evolved in literature sharing. However, just reviewing this particular session shows us a good deal about Sylvia's teaching style and her children's responses to literature.

It is obvious that Sylvia listens to her students' responses and that they know she listens to their comments. Her respect has caused the children to respect each other and to listen to one another as they discuss their literature. They ask each other questions and use peer responses to build their own interpretations. They are willing to disagree without thinking that their opinion is the only right one. They explain why a book appeals to them in terms of visual art. All these skills are literary ones. These children are practicing discussion skills that are analytical and collaborative. All in all, Sylvia Briscoe's class is a model of teacher/student collaboration for meaning.

It is interesting to note that Sylvia did not use literature to teach values to her class, and she did not believe that the author/illustrators had purposefully set up a conflict in order to teach children how to act in similar situations. Although she could have used the books to teach about the inner city, she did not. Instead, she explored the books for their literary merits and asked the students to critique them for artistic style and to explain their individual choice of a favorite only after the children had completed their group discussion.

In 1987 the English Coalition Conference was held. This group contained professionals from eight major professional organizations—including the Modern Language Association and the National Council of Teachers of English—who remembered and read about the 1966 conference. Classroom teachers, elementary education faculty, and English professors worked side by side. In 1990, the Modern Language Association published Peter Elbow's qualitative summary of the Coalition. He explained that the participants did not always feel a need to agree with one another, but shared a desire to communicate and discover what English education meant for each of them. They did not strive to find a product of teaching techniques (or text-like method), but to find a process that could work for them. Elbow remarked,

> When people assume a consensus model, they assume there *is* an answer, and inevitably the goal becomes to settle the question of what it is. Thus people will fight for what's true, who's right, who gets to occupy or name the consensus. An emphasis on theory, in contrast . . . invites people to be more willing to accept differences—and be different. (60)

If we wish to teach a generation of children how to appreciate cultural diversity, we must learn to go beyond consensus, to look for ways to become implied readers and listeners. We must show children that reading implies listening, thinking, and returning to shared materials before we each decide what a particular piece of writing means for ourself. If we discuss literature together, children can see that when knowledge is shared, opinions become individual interpretations stretched through shared discussions.

Al Enlow, one of my graduate students who was teaching third grade when he took my evening children's literature class, wanted his students to go beyond first encounters with the texts they read and to consider how implied readers view what they read. He was interested in how second readings work and wanted to combine individual literature explorations with classroom collaboration in a unit on literary assessment. In addition, he decided to teach some basic literary patterns while using traditional language arts methods for group and individual exercises. Al kept a teacher's journal as he shared *Sarah, Plain and Tall* in his class, and he referred back to it as he wrote the following paper.

The Benefits of a Second Reading

BY AL ENLOW

For students to enjoy literature as implied readers, they must become familiar with the practice of re-reading. In order to understand the benefits students gain from a second reading of the same book, I chose to orally read *Sarah, Plain and Tall* to my third grade class. At the conclusion of a second reading, I wanted the individual students to have a better understanding of the setting, main characters' traits, and the major events in the story. I was also curious to see what influence a second reading would have on each child's opinion of the book.

To prepare the class for our experience with re-reading, we discussed the importance of re-reading and why we re-read at times. During our discussion, students remarked that re-reading is done "if you really liked the story" or "you forgot what you read the first time." I prompted them by asking them if they thought they could learn more about the characters from a second reading, and they agreed they could. Some of the students emphasized that sometimes the first reading was "just for fun." The group did not seem to agree about the influence that re-reading had on their opinion of a book. I also asked if anyone had partially or entirely read a book two or more times and found many had.

The students were aware that I would be reading *Sarah, Plain and Tall* to them twice. I surveyed the class to see who had already read *Sarah, Plain and Tall,* and I discovered that none of them had. This surprised me, and I showed them two different book jackets to ensure that they knew what book I was asking about. I determined that everyone would have both a real reader's and implied reader's experience in this class.

As our discussion about re-reading piqued, I told them that our first reading would begin the next day during our regular story time. We moved out of our seats, and we followed with a discussion about Patricia MacLachlan and her books. I wrote information about MacLachlan on chart paper and kept it posted next to me during our first reading so that the students might relate some of the events in the story to MacLachlan's own life. As we read along, they did incorporate information.

I began the next day by telling the students that as of November 1983, Mac-

Lachlan still lived in Massachusetts with her husband and three children. The students were interested in finding out if *Sarah* was a "true story" or not. I told them that there is a true story behind the story about Sarah. According to Mac-Lachlan, the true story began in 1910 on the Kansas prairie when a mail order bride came west from Maine. MacLachlan's mother met her as a small child (Courtney 883). The mail order bride married MacLachlan's great uncle. Due to the closeness of the family, this woman greatly influenced MacLachlan's life. Later, as I read and listened to the children, I realized that they accepted the 1910 Kansas prairies as the real setting for a true story. I realized that I should have emphasized the fact that the setting in the book is slightly different from the one in the true story.

We continued our first information session by reviewing what a novel is and how some adult critics viewed MacLachlan's *Sarah, Plain and Tall* as a mini-novel. I told them that one reviewer had called it a "near perfect mini-novel that fulfills the ideal of different levels of meaning for children and adults" (Hearne 1254). Hearne also emphasized that the plot, style, and characterization were deceptive. I told the children about this, and I suggested that there are themes in this story, even though MacLachlan may not have intended to write them into her story. Finally, the students asked if MacLachlan had written any other books, so I listed some of her books and noted some of the awards she had received. Then we discussed why the awards she had received were given to books. Sparked by questions about the other books, I told them briefly about each book and I mentioned that Sarah first appeared in *Arthur, for the Very First Time* (Hickman 883). The children seemed interested to learn that a character could appear in two stories with two different names. Finally, we looked at the book's format. We discovered if there were illustrations to accompany the story, what the copyright for the book was, and how the title page was set up. We also looked for a prologue and an epilogue. I asked what they wanted to know about the cover illustration and found that they wanted to know if the scene really happened in the story. I assured them that it did.

Since the discussion took a fairly long time, I only read the first three pages on the first morning. I could see that my students needed to move, that they had used up a lot of mental energy and physical patience. However, I was able to continue our reading during the afternoon.

As we first explored the story together, I could not tell if the children were interested in the book. They did not involve themselves in discussions. I would ask them about characters and events in a way that would force them to ask questions about the story or about each other's responses. Occasionally I would ask them to review MacLachlan's life and to see if it contained similar events.

After six days we concluded our reading. Then I had them do individual story webs. Their webs had to include five areas that I would later compare in a second web after our second reading. I asked that they include the title in the middle of the page as their starting point. The students were to include the major events or problems found in the story, their solutions, the setting, the main characters, and their own reader's responses to the story. I asked them to include as many details as they could.

After I looked at the first webs, I noticed that 75% of the children noticed that Sarah longed to be near the sea. They wrote sentences like, "Sarah missed the sea" and tied that to ideas like, "Caleb was afraid that Sarah was going to move back to Maine." These children had focused their webs around Sarah's homesickness. The children only mentioned Sarah's arrival, the proposed wedding, and the storm as important events. Furthermore, only two children placed the story in Kansas in

1910. The others simply said it "happened on a farm" or "in the country in winter." I noticed that the children could not determine how Sarah overcame her problems after this first reading. One student wrote, "Sarah learned to adjust," while three others wrote, "She drew the sea."

When I looked at what the children had written about the main characters, I was amazed. First of all, most of the children liked every character that they remembered. Secondly, they only wrote about the character traits of Sarah and Caleb.

Finally, I looked at their opinions of the book. Four students did not like the book. As a teacher who would spend a good deal of time re-reading the story, I was concerned about their reactions to a second reading. The rest of the opinions ranged from "good" to "great" and even to "rad," which I concluded must mean great. I decided to let some time elapse before we began our second reading.

The next week I read a Manus Pinkwater book that the class had been wanting to hear. Next we reviewed the information about Patricia MacLachlan, the role of main characters in fiction, and how to recognize the setting and events in a story. During this brief discussion most of the children who were contributing ideas cited examples from *Sarah, Plain and Tall*, which seemed interesting to me because most of the examples were not ones they had placed on their story webs.

The second reading of *Sarah, Plain and Tall* was very exciting. There were children's hands going up all of the time to interrupt my reading, and they made valuable points. The students were interested in knowing whether or not Mac-Lachlan lived on a farm. They also wanted to know if MacLachlan is like Sarah, and one child asked, "Why did Jacob let Sarah go to town even though he did not know why she wanted to go?" The students were enthusiastic about this second reading.

The second story webs proved to be much more interesting than the first ones. The number of events and problems written into the webs tripled. Most of the students mentioned Sarah's arrival, the scene where the family jumps on the straw dune, Sarah's trip into town, and Sarah's learning to drive a wagon. One student remembered the time when Sarah learned to ride a horse. Three children considered Mama's death a major event in the story even though Anna was telling about her memories of the day her mother died. As I read the webs, I noticed a personal tie to the story: one of the children who considered Mama's death a major event had an infant sister in the hospital with a brain tumor. And I believe that the children's ability to visualize scenes made an impact on their retellings. Some of the students wrote about the time Sarah convinced the children to go swimming in the cow pond.

The setting was much more vividly described. The children all continued to recognize the farm setting, but they also commented that the story started in the winter and progressed through every season. They seemed to agree that the story took place in the late 1800s or early 1900s. Some of the children still thought that the story took place in 1910.

The characters' traits were recognized much better after the second reading. Sarah, Anna, and Caleb were accurately described. Over half of the class noted that Sarah was "stubborn, a quick learner, caring, nice, kind, and independent." Anna was remembered as "the person who told the story" by many of the children and "a hard worker" and "serious" by some of the class. The number of main characters was greatly reduced—usually to four, Caleb, Sarah, Anna and Jacob—which I was glad to see. These children always remembered Caleb as "a worrier" and several said he was a constant nag. The children did not view his questioning as a good thing, perhaps a reflection of how their parents view their questioning. Jacob was labelled "loving" and "patient" based on the little information there was about him in the story.

While the other areas that I was comparing changed dramatically, the children's opinions of *Sarah, Plain and Tall* did not. Two children did move from "boring" to "good" and "OK" to "I liked it." Some of the children explained why they changed their rating. One boy wrote that it was better the second time, but one girl who still did not rate the story highly wrote, "It's too short." Another girl added "interesting characters" to her web, but she did not change her evaluation.

To make sure that the students had included everything they could, I interviewed each child. I explained why I wanted to talk with them and proceeded to remind them what they had previously written about the book. None of the children had anything substantial to add during the interview. Four children added more to the setting, saying that the story also had "summer and spring" in it.

I believe that the time spent on this project was worthwhile. The students and I enjoyed the re-reading and found that our discussion was more developed and full of examples during the second reading. Furthermore, the children are still using the experience in their literature experiences. They continue to refer to Caleb and Sarah when they discuss characterization. As I re-read the students' perceptions of characterization, setting, and plot I found they had improved.

I also believe that the students' previous experiences improved the re-reading. Most of these children were already readers when they entered my classroom. They have simply developed new skills at analysis without lessening their interest in reading. They have also learned that there is more to reading than answering questions. Recently they told me, "Reading is understanding what happens in a story and why." Re-reading *Sarah, Plain and Tall* gave each student the opportunity to enjoy the story and develop an appreciation for MacLachlan's writing. The students also had practice in developing an understanding of characterization, recognizing the setting, and determining the main events, problems, and solutions in a fiction book. Now I firmly believe that combining pleasure with acquired knowledge by re-reading is a valuable practice for every reader.

References

Anne Commire, ed. *Something About the Author,* Vol. 42. Detroit: Gale Research, 1986.

Ann Courtney. Review in *Language Arts.* Vol. 62:7 (1985).

Betsy Hearne. Review in *Booklist.* Vol. 81 (May, 1985).

Janet Hickman. Review in *Language Arts.* Vol. 62:8 (1985).

Charlotte S. Huck, Susan Hepler, and Janet Hickman. *Children's Literature in the Elementary School.* New York: Holt, Rinehart, & Winston, Inc., 1987.

Gerard Senick, ed. *Children's Literature Review,* Vol 14. Detroit: Gale Research, 1988.

At the end of the semester, Al argued for a school-wide planned program of literary studies, stating, "Children need exposure to various literary styles, cultures, dialects, genres, and well written literature." Al's ideal literature program would have to be flexible; it could not be based on certain texts, whether they would be created by a textbook company or by a school corporation because cultural and linguistic patterns change, and literature reflecting them changes at the same time. However, he does want children to appreciate "well-written literature." How would this happen? Al continued, "Due to the fact that there are tens of thousands of children's books available, our students need early exposure for a concentrated number of years to gain a better understanding of the values of good literature." Al explained that a good literary studies program would need "an ample selection of books, thorough teacher preparation, sound literary training of teachers in their undergraduate programs, and various avenues for students to respond to literature." He said that the program needed to contain teacher and student freedom and a positive atmosphere "free of threatening remarks or attitudes" so that children would feel comfortable expressing their own opinions and critiquing one another. Finally, Al argued against a set curriculum with imposed activities, saying, "My children have been able to adjust and to work at the activities they want to do. In the end, a lot of great discussions have come about as natural responses to our literature." Al did not mention any books that he felt needed to be shared.

When Charles Temple began to contemplate the book that he and Patrick Collins would edit for Christopher-Gordon Publishers, he asked if I would write a piece on the Children's Literature Association canon. I agreed. By the time Charles wrote back to me, he had something very specific in mind. Why not call it "Is there a canon in children's literature? And if there is, what is it?" I knew Charles, and I knew me. I couldn't write that piece because it seemed to assume that the answer was "Yes, and here it is." I knew that Charles wouldn't want me to write that if I didn't believe there is a set of books that everyone should know. So I wrote what I believe. In the end, I argued against a set of books that everyone shares in every school in the nation, but I felt uneasy about what I wrote because of teacher education in America.

Could school teachers ever become so flexible that they could give up a controlled curriculum with prescribed books, lessons, and skills, I wondered. I sensed that teachers found it hard to surrender old habits and venture into a new discipline—literary criticism—so that they could place it in their classrooms. American teachers are used to being given booklists, so when I studied the California literature plan, I was not surprised to find lists of books that could be described as a California canon. I talked to teachers across the United States who taught in schools where literature had taken over the language arts and reading programs and found that they usually discussed sharing children's literature to teach traditional language arts and reading skills such as decoding and predictability. I queried my friends who studied children's literature and discovered that many of them were unfamiliar with critical theory. Finally, I came back to my office and thought. The people whom I had seen as innovators and facilitators in the elementary schools were teachers who understood critical theory and included it in their explorations of children's literature with children. The schools where I had been invited to give teacher in-service programs were ones that held one of my former university students who remembered our classroom discussions and wanted a community of adult readers in their schools. They hoped to develop a schoolwide program like the one Al Enlow suggested. Yet I was not sure that many teachers were advocating literacy instruction that stressed critical analysis skills over the skills practiced in New Criticism. And I sensed an urgent call to "teach a canon of children's literature in the schools."

The following fall, I asked the graduate students in my upper division children's literature class to divide into small groups and consider the following question: Is there a canon in children's literature? There were five groups involved. When we reassembled as one group, the small groups each made a presentation. Our discussion did not lead to consensus. Two of the groups' summaries show how the canon question continues to cause divisiveness.

One of the groups included two former high school English teachers who had recently entered Purdue's graduate program, one elementary school classroom teacher, and one of my graduate students who had majored in elementary education and special education and who had taken three courses in children's literature as an undergraduate. Currently she was teaching a section of the undergraduate children's literature class. Since Beth Halterman had the strongest background in canon formation and in children's literature, she acted as the recorder.

Is There a Canon in Children's Literature?

Lots of discussion! Is there a canon in children's literature?

• We expect there to be . . .
• We look and search for it . . .

Essentially, all we find are bibliographies or lists of books chosen by various groups of critics, librarians, authors, and teachers, to name a few "authority groups" that suggest titles we should share. So, we concluded that there really is **not** a canon in children's literature. We would not hunt for one, but we would focus our teaching/awareness in the following areas:

• Genre studies (for example, fantasy, romance as patterns)
• Plug and chug books (books children enjoy)
• Current books along with "classics"
• Critical schools (for example, mythic criticism, structuralism, minority literature)
• Learning to develop a personal viewpoint and take a stand
• Becoming more aware of the role of the critic in the past, present, and future of book publications
• Looking deeper (past "real response") at society, trends, and issues in contemporary culture

The main purpose of a literature program, we agreed, is to encourage children to understand the components and concepts of different genres and apply them to individual works.

In the end, we decided that we would still have book reviews, lists, librarians, and other outside sources help us identify a variety of novels to use in our classes. Our group realized that we may miss or fail to include some of the "great" books along the way. But, by changing books, weeding out others, and retaining a few that children enjoy and openly discuss, we, as teachers working with children, will develop our own favorites that are "teachable." They may be similar to the books chosen by others, but they will be ones we know. Most important, our books will not be set in stone; change will be an integral part of our curriculum.

The second group had one returning high school teacher, one foreign student who taught English as a second language in her own country, a public school librarian, and an elementary classroom teacher. They did not identify their recorder.

Is There a Canon in Children's Literature?

There appears to be a canon in children's literature that is based on specific types of literature for particular age groups; however, there seem to be gaps in this canon.

It is assumed in our society that adults have been introduced to certain fairy tales and legends. Our exposure to this type of literature occurs during pre-school and beginning school year ages. There is a paradox in this "hidden canon" because the tales that constitute this part of the "cultural canon" are not necessarily taught in schools. Yet, almost everyone in America has knowledge of such tales as "Cinderella," "Snow White," "Little Red Riding Hood," "The Three Pigs," etc. Many of the United States legends in the cultural canon are included as part of the elementary school curriculum. Children usually encounter tales like *The Legend of Sleepy Hollow* and *Babe the Blue Ox* (of Paul Bunyan fame) in grades ranging from the second to the sixth. Most school curriculums incorporate simplified versions of the classic legends from the Greek myths. Therefore, although this canon is quite limited, it extends beyond our culture to universal literature.

Gaps appear in the early elementary grades concerning literature shared, especially at the third, fourth, and fifth grade levels. This may be due to the emphasis placed on teaching skills of reading and decoding rather than an absence of literature that is appropriate to draw from. The works studied during these years are more fluid, and teachers focus on contemporary writers and current cultural themes as well as literature that shows the transition from childhood to adolescence.

A defined canon reappears in the middle school or the high school. This canon incorporates many of the classics in drama, prose, and poetry: Shakespeare, the Romantic poets, writers of the Victorian, Romantic, and Modern eras. Titles such as *The Old Man and the Sea, Romeo and Juliet, Jane Eyre, The Return of the Native,* and *The Great Gadsby* are usually studied. Modern American writers such as Mark Twain, Aldous Huxley, and John Steinbeck are included. At this level, the canon is relatively large and it can never be completely covered in the grades 6–12. However, it is considered covered, and when adults enter the working world they are expected to be familiar with the works of the canon.

The class could not reach a consensus about the importance of such lists; some of us wanted to see particular titles taught in all schools while others of us felt this limited regional and individual classroom needs. However, we all agreed that there is a canon that is implied in cultural literacy, and we all agreed that while it corresponds with what is shared in the elementary school, more of the titles are shared in middle school and high school English programs.

When Peter Elbow wrote about the English Coalition Conference, he admitted that those in attendance did not discuss literary texts and cultural canons. Mostly, he said, there would have been disagreements about the books and authors that should be included, and the members sensed a more urgent need to argue against standardized texts and tests, to support an integrated curriculum that included reading/listening/writing. Finally he admitted, "By avoiding working out the literature question, we were avoiding potential violence . . . I am tempted to say we are a profession both polarized and paralyzed around literature" (101). Elbow is pointing at one of our largest problems. We do not want to single out particular texts as the best, but we know that society already has determined that everyone has (or should have) read certain stories.

Currently, canons and canon formation are not popular topics among English professors. Most of the recent research in all areas call for an end to the traditional canon. All advocate a more solid understanding of critical theory and cultural literacy. The Modern Language Association published two books that demonstrate the professional call for a change in attitudes about canonical literature. In 1990 the MLA released *Redefining American Literary History,* edited by A. LaVonne Brown Ruoff and Jerry W. Ward, Jr. In their Introduction they wrote about the need to reform the American historical canon and noted that many minority or divergent voices have been disregarded in the study of American literature. Ruoff and Ward concluded that we must "transform our habitual ways of thinking about history, culture, and literature" (4). Joseph Gibaldi edited *Introduction to Scholarship in Modern Languages and Literatures* (1992). This book addresses scholarship in linguistics, rhetoric, composition, literary studies, and cross-disciplinary and cultural studies. Intended for an academic audience, it ends with a cautionary epilogue from Gerald Graff. Graff suggests that recent scholarly research has more potential interest for those outside the academy, but argues that many scholars still write in ways that cannot easily be shared with nonprofessionals. Graff calls for a broader discourse on literary studies, and he says,

> The broadening of the concept of research makes it possible to foresee an end to the conflict between research and teaching. . . . Instead of trying to protect the interests of general education from those of research, it would be productive for academic institutions to take advantage of whatever in research is potentially of general interest to non-professionals. Instead of discouraging scholars from letting their research obtrude into

their undergraduate teaching, institutions would begin encouraging scholars to teach their research, as many scholars have in fact done successfully for some time, particularly in the fields influenced by new theories of culture and society. (355)

I would argue that even if we all taught the same pieces of literature in every grade, we would not give children the same experiences. Each of us will end up having a favorite school of critical theory about literature and will unconsciously prefer some interpretations over others. If we did not, we would not need to read books. We could just read someone else's opinion of any book and trust that it worked for us too. It isn't a particular story that is important, and it isn't one way of looking at the story that defines why different people like it. Reading has more to do with the reader's response and its place in critical interpretation than with naming books that we've all read and coming up with a common interpretation. The canon argument has two directives for me: There is no one set of books that is best and there is no one way to look at what we read.

If we remember that there is no one set of books that everyone agrees on as the "best literature for all children," we will see that the Newbery and Caldecott books represent one set of standards, as do the Hans Christian Andersen winners, the Coretta Scott King award winners, and the books on Children's Choices. We can agree that these lists are excellent bibliographies, but we need not choose all our literature from any one of these lists. We can continue to read reviews and new books and can learn to value children's discussions of their favorites when we select our titles. We must continually share and discuss books with our peers, remembering that readers choose to read books they feel reflect their ideals, needs, and understanding. We need to remember that all political and social opinions are the products of personal values, and we must consider how literature can expand our experiences. Then we should listen and appreciate someone else's interpretation of a material, even if it contradicts our own.

Perhaps we can then understand that children will grow up to be adults who will pick books that best fit their own needs—or they will grow up to be nonreaders. That choice will largely depend on how they perceive literature and its meaning. If they only read those stories everyone "must" know, they will not develop the pleasurable habit of looking for materials to read and share that contain new and interesting stories. Many children's books that readers enjoy do not win awards, make the best-seller list, or stay in print forever. They are, however, more widely read by contemporary readers than most of the classics found on the ChLA Touchstones list.

We need to become ruminating kinds of folks. We need to search for shared reading experiences by working through diverse texts and interpretations. We need to "practice what we teach" within the universities before we set out to impose our methods of inquiry on children. We need to pause and reflect as we read, to finish our shared discussions without seeking closure, to find out what others have written about the books, movies, and theories that puzzle us, and to return again to the same book or movie or critical article after we have thought on our own. We need to seek each other out, to listen to everyone's ideas, and to determine how we have come to value certain ideas or writing styles.

As teachers and explorers of children's literature, we need to collaborate—both inside the classroom and outside it—and to search for better ways to share children's literature with its real audience—children. We should take time to visit one another in elementary school classrooms, to listen to the discussions that are occurring, and to consider how children in different settings interpret their literature.

Peter Elbow's book looked at the activity at the English Coalition Conference and suggested how it fits with current theory. Richard Lloyd-Jones and Andrea A. Lunsford were selected to edit the group's resolutions. In their Introduction they explain that all participants advocated continual and varied reading, and felt that local social and institutional conditions would affect what books teachers hoped to share with students. The elementary strand's report stated,

> Children bring to the classroom their language proficiency, their curiosity, their own learning styles, their sense of themselves as learners and as people, and their own special authority and expertise. . . . In an environment of trust and respect, sharing and collaborating between children and among children and adults are the norm.
>
> Sometimes the roles that teacher and children play are shared ones. Both the teacher and the children are responsible for being contributing members of the classroom community. Both are evaluators of their progress, sometimes finding reason to celebrate, sometimes finding a need to reconsider and reengage any experience. Both are thinkers. Children think about the experiences they engage in and reflect on their learning. The teacher thinks about the teaching/learning interactions with the children and reflects on how and why. Within the classroom community, both teacher and children are active learners. (8)

Throughout this book I have asked you to consider how criticism works. I have suggested that once we consider how we read, what we read, and why we read, we must go beyond and consider who the author/artist created the story for, why the book was published, how it fits within literature. Children's literature, I have suggested, is different because it was not published for adults, but is analyzed and reviewed by adults. And most lists of the "best children's literature" are based on adult interpretations of children's literature. In the end, however, I have urged you to remember that the real audience for children's literature is children, and I have suggested that if we show children how critics look at books, and allow them to practice those skills together, they can do it too. After that, we must listen. As the primary readers of their texts, they can be the best critical interpreters of children's literature.

References

Chapter 1

Garth Boomer. "Introduction: A Recent History of Teaching English in Five Countries," in *English Teachers at Work: Ideas and Strategies from Five Countries*. Edited by Stephen N. Tchudi, et al. Upper Montclair, NJ: Boynton/Cook Publishers, 1986.

Trevor H. Cairney. "The Purpose of Basals: What Children Think," in *The Reading Teacher*, January 1988.

Northrop Frye. "Elementary Teaching and Elemental Scholarship," in *The Stubborn Structure: Essays on Criticism and Society*. Ithaca, NY: Cornell University Press, 1970.

Guidelines for the Preparation of Teachers of English Language Arts. Urbana, IL: National Council of Teachers of English, 1986.

Bruce Hammonds. "Helping Children Make Sense of Their World," in *English Teachers at Work: Ideas and Strategies from Five Countries*. Edited by Stephen Tchudi, et al. Upper Montclair, NJ: Boynton/Cook Publishers, 1986.

Rod McGillis. "Editor's Comments," in *The Children's Literature Association Quarterly*, Fall 1988.

Perry Nodelman, ed. *Touchstones: Reflections on the Best in Children's Literature*. Vol. One. West Lafayette, IN: ChLA Publications, 1985.

Roger Trigg. *Reality at Risk: A Defence of Realism in Philosophy and the Sciences*. New York: Barnes & Noble Books, 1980.

Chapter 2

Louisa May Alcott. *Little Women*. New York: Grosset & Dunlap, 1947.

Jane Bingham, ed. *Writers for Children: Critical Studies of the Major Authors Since the Seventeenth Century*. New York: Charles Scribner's Sons, 1988.

Maud Bodkin. *Archetypal Patterns in Poetry: psychological studies of imagination*. New York: Vintage Books, 1958.

Wayne Booth. *The Rhetoric of Fiction*. Chicago: The University of Chicago Press, 1961.

Children's Literature: Annual of the Modern Language Association on Children's Literature and The children's Literature Association. Vol. 4 (1975).

Patricia Dooley, comp. *The First Steps: Best of the Early ChLA Quarterly*. West Lafayette, IN: ChLA Publications, 1984.

Northrop Frye. *Anatomy of Criticism: Four Essays*. Princeton, NJ: Princeton University Press, 1957.

————.*The Educated Imagination*. Bloomington: Indiana University Press, 1964.

Kenneth Grahame. *The Wind in the Willows*. New York: Scribner, 1933.

Norman N. Holland. "Reading Readers Reading," in *Researching Response to Literature and the Teaching of Literature: Points of Departure*. Charles R. Cooper, ed. Norwood, NJ: Ablex Publishing Corporation, 1985.

Anne Devereaux Jordan. "Early Days and Sweet Dreams," in *Festschrift: A Ten Year Retrospective*. Perry Nodelman and Jill P. May, eds. West Lafayette, IN: ChLA Publications, 1983.

Frank Kermode. *The Sense of an Ending: Studies in the Theory of Fiction*. New York: Oxford University Press, 1967.

Joseph Krumgold. *And Now Miguel*. New York: Crowell, 1953.

————. *Onion John*. New York: Crowell, 1959.

Lawrence Lipking. "Teaching America," in *Profession 90*. New York: Modern Language Association of America, 1990.

Rebecca Lukens. *A Critical Handbook of Children's Literature*, 4th ed. Glenview, IL: Scott, Foresman/Little, Brown Higher Education, 1990.

Jill P. May, ed. *Children and Their Literature: A Readings Book*. West Lafayette, IN: ChLA Publications, 1983.

Samuel Pickering, Jr. "The Function of Criticism in Children's Literature, in *Children's Literature in Education*, Vol 13:1 (1982).

Alan Purves. "That Sunny Dome: Those Caves of Ice," in *Researching Response to Literature and the Teaching of Literature: Points of Departure*. Charles R. Cooper, ed. Norwood, NJ: Ablex Publishing Corporation, 1985.

Jon C. Stott. "Literary Criticism and Teaching Children," in *ChLA Quarterly*, Vol. 6: 1 (1981).

————. "The Presidential Address," in *Festschrift: A Ten Year Retrospective*. Perry Nodelman and Jill P. May, eds. West Lafayette, IN: ChLA Publications, 1983.

Booker T. Washington. *Up from Slavery: An Autobiography*. Garden City, NY: Doubleday, 1922.

Laura Ingalls Wilder. *The Little House in the Big Woods*. New York: Harper, 1953.

Chapter 3

Lloyd Alexander. *The Wizard in the Tree*. New York: Dutton, 1975.

Raymond Briggs. *The Snowman*. New York: Random House, 1978.

Margaret Wise Brown. *Goodnight Moon*. New York: Harper, 1947.

John Bunyan. *The Pilgrim's Progress*. New York: American Tract Society, 1830.

Barbara Cohen. *Molly's Pilgrim*. New York: Lothrop, Lee & Shepard, 1983.

Niki Daly. *Not So Fast Songologo.* New York: Puffin, 1985.

Ezra Jack Keats. *The Snowy Day.* New York: Viking, 1952.

C. S. Lewis. *The Lion, the Witch and the Wardrobe.* New York: Macmillan, 1951.

L. M. Montgomery. *Anne of Green Gables.* New York: Grosset & Dunlap, 1935.

Uri Shulevitz. *One Monday Morning.* New York: Scribner, 1967.

William Sleator. *House of Stairs.* New York: Scholastic Books, 1974.

Gertrude Warner. *The Boxcar Children.* Scott Foresman, 1942.

E. B. White. *Charlotte's Web.* New York: Harper, 1952.

Chapter 4

Terry Allen, ed. *The Whispering Wind: Poetry by Young American Indians.* Garden City, NY: Doubleday & Company, Inc., 1972.

John Bierhorst. *In the Trail of the Wind: Indian Poems and Ritural Orations.* New York: Farrar, Straus and Giroux, 1971.

Peter Collier. *When shall they rest? The Cherokees' Long Struggle with America.* New York: Holt, Rinehart and Winston, 1973.

Alice Dalgliesh. *The Courage of Sarah Noble.* Illustrated by Leonard Weisgard. New York: Charles Scribner's Sons, 1954.

James Daugherty. *Daniel Boone.* New York: The Viking Press, 1939.

A. Grove Day. *The Sky Clears: Poetry of the American Indians.* New York: Macmillan Company, 1951.

Walter D. Edmonds. *The Matchlock Gun.* New York: Dodd, 1941.

Paul Heins. "History Alive: Some Considerations," in *The Bulletin of the Children's Literature Assembly,* Vol. VIII: 1 (1982).

Jamake Highwater. *Anpao: An American Indian Odyssey.* Philadelphia: J. B. Lippincott Company, 1977.

Arnold Krupat. *The Voice in the Margin: Native American Literature and the Canon.* Berkeley: University of California Press, 1989.

Leonard S. Marcus. "Life Drawings: Some Notes on Children's Picture Book Biographies," in *The Lion & the Unicorn,* Vol. 4:1 (1980).

Milton Meltzer. "The Possibilities of Nonfiction," in *Children's Literature in Education,* Vol. 11:3 (1980).

———. "The Reader and the Writer," in *The Bulletin of the Children's Literature Assembly,* Vol. VIII: 1 (1982).

Olive Beaupre Miller, ed. *Up One Pair of Stairs of My Book House.* Chicago: The Book House for Children.

Roy Harvey Pearce. *Savagism and Civilization: A Study of the Indian and the American Mind.* Reprint of the 1967 book, *The Savages of America.* Los Angeles: University of California Press, 1988.

Joyce Rockwood. *To Spoil the Sun.* New York: Holt, Rinehart and Winston, 1976.

Zena Sutherland and May Hill Arbuthnot. *Children and Books.* 7th ed. Glenview, IL: Scott, Foresman and Company, 1986.

Irwin Unger. *These United States: The Questions of Our Past.* 4th ed. Englewood Cliffs, NJ: Prentice-Hall, 1989.

Jack Zipes. "Second Thoughts on Socialization through Literature for Children," in *The Lion & the Unicorn,* Vol. 5 (1981).

Chapter 5

Lloyd Alexander. "Future Conditional," in *The Children's Literature Association Quarterly,* Vol. 10:4 (1986).

Peter Alexander. "Grimm's Utopias: Motives and Justifications," in *Utopias.* Alexander and Roger Gill, eds. London: Gerald Duckworth & Co. Ltd., 1984.

Frances Bartkowski. *Feminist Utopias.* Lincoln: University of Nebraska Press, 1989.

Mary Ann Caws. *Reading Frames in Modern Fiction.* Princeton, NJ: Princeton University Press, 1985.

Northrop Frye. *The Educated Imagination.* Bloomington: University of Indiana Press, 1964.

The Brothers Grimm. *Household Stories, from the Collection of the Bros. Grimm.* Lucy Crane, translator. Walter Crane, illustrator. New York: Dover Publications, 1963.

———. *Snow White.* Paul Heins, translator. Trina Schart Hyman, illustrator. Boston: Little, Brown and Company, 1974.

Charlotte S. Huck, Susan Hepler, and Janet Hickman. *Children's Literature in the Elementary School,* 4th ed. New York: Holt, Rinehart and Winston, Inc., 1987.

Trina Schart Hyman, adaptor and illustrator. *Little Red Riding Hood.* New York: Holiday House, 1983.

———. *Self-Portrait: Trina Schart Hyman.* Reading, MA: Addison-Wesley, 1981.

U. C. Knoepflmacher. "Roads Half-Taken: Travel, Fantasy, and Growing Up," in *Proceedings of the Thirteenth Annual Conference of the Children's Literature Association,* University of Missouri (1986). ChLA Publications, 1988.

Madonna Koblenschlag. *Kiss Sleeping Beauty Good-Bye: Breaking the Spell of Feminine Myths and Models.* San Francisco: Harper & Row, 1988.

Donna E. Norton. *Through the Eyes of a Child: An Introduction to Children's Literature.* New York: Macmillan, 1991.

Jean Pfaelzer. *The Utopian Novel in America 1886–1896: The Politics of Form.* Pittsburgh: University of Pittsburgh Press, 1984.

Peter Ruppert. *Reader in a Strange Land: The Activity of Reading Literary Utopias.* Athens: The University of Georgia Press, 1986.

Robert Scholes and Robert Kellogg. *The Nature of Narrative.* New York: Oxford University Press, 1966.

Jack Zipes. "The Changing Function of the Fairy Tale," in *The Lion and the Unicorn,* Vol. 12:2 (1988).

Chapter 6

Avon Crismore. *Talking with Readers: Metadiscourse as Rhetorical Act.* New York: Peter Lang, 1989.

Everett Dick, "The Way West," in *The Social Fabric: American Life from 1697 to the Civil War,* 2nd ed. John H. Cary and Julius Weinberg, eds. Boston: Little, Brown and Company, 1978.

Joan M. Jensen and Darlis A. Miller. "The Gentle Tamers Revisited: New Approaches to the History of Women in the American West," in *Pacific Historical Review,* Vol. 49:2 (1980).

Barbara Johnstone. *Stories, Community and Place: Narratives from Middle America.* Bloomington: Indiana University Press, 1990.

George Levine. *The Realistic Imagination: English Fiction from Frankenstein to Lady Chatterley.* Chicago: The University of Chicago Press, 1981.

Perry Nodelman. "'I Think I'm Learning a Lot': How Typical Children Read Typical Books about Typical Children on Typical Subjects," in *Proceedings of the Seventh Annual Conference of The Children's Literature Association.* Priscilla Ord, ed. New Rochelle, NY: Children's Literature Association, 1982.

Billi Rosen. *Andi's War.* New York: Puffin Books, 1991.

Marjorie Filley Stover. *Trail Boss in Pigtails.* New York: Atheneum, 1972.

Ann Turner. *Dakota Dugout.* Illustrated by Ronald Himler. New York: Macmillan Publishing Company, 1985.

Jill Paton Walsh. "The Art of Realism," in *Celebrating Children's Books.* Betsy Hearne and Marilyn Kaye, eds. New York: Lothrop, Lee & Shepard Books, 1981.

———. *Fireweed.* New York: A Sunburst Book, 1988.

Chapter 7

William L. Andrews. "The Novelization of Voice in Early African-American Narrative," in *PMLA*, January 1990.

Maud Bodkin. *Archetypal Patterns in Poetry: pschological studies of imagination.* New York: Vintage Books, 1958.

Eduardo Galeano. "In Defense of the Word:Leaving Buenos Aires, June 1976," in *The Graywolf Annual Five: Multicultural Literacy.* Rick Simonson and Scott Walker, eds. Saint Paul: Graywolf Press, 1988.

Henry Louis Gates, Jr. "The African-American Writer and the South," in *The Southern Review and Modern Literature, 1935–1985.* Lewis P. Simpson, James Olney, and Jo Gulledge, eds. Baton Rouge: Louisiana State University Press, 1985.

———. *Figures in Black: Words, Signs and the "Racial" Self.* New York: Oxford University Press, 1987.

———. "Introduction: 'Tell Me, Sir, . . . What Is "Black" Literature?'" in *PMLA.* January 1990.

Patricia C. McKissack. *Mirandy and Brother Wind.* Illustrated by Jerry Pinkney. New York: Alfred A. Knopf, 1988.

Walter Dean Myers. *Fast Sam, Cool Clyde, and Stuff.* Copyright, Walter Dean Myers, 1975. New York: Puffin Books, 1988.

Valerie Smith. *Self-Discovery and Authority in Afro-American Narrative.* Cambridge: Harvard University Press, 1987.

Myron C. Tuman. *A Preface to Literary: An Inquiry into Pedagogy, Practice, and Progress.* Tuscaloosa: The University of Alabama, 1987.

Chapter 8

Patricia Dooley. "'First Books': From Schlock to Sophistication," in *Children's Literature Association Quarterly,* Vol. 7:1 (1982).

Nancy Huse. "My Book House as Bildung," in *Children's Literature Association Quarterly,* Vol. 13:3 (1988).

Sylvia Patterson Iskander. "Anne Frank's Reading," in *Children's Literature Association Quarterly*, Vol. 13:3 (1988).

Rod McGillis. "I'm On The Case Now," in *Children's Literature Association Quarterly*, Vol. 13:3 (1988).

Jill P. May. "Mass Marketing and the Toys Children Like," in *Children's Literature Association Quarterly*, Vol. 7:1 (1982).

———. "Two Children's Responses to Literature," in *Children's Literature Association Quarterly*, Vol. 13:3 (1988).

Perry Nodelman. "Introduction to Commercial Culture for Children: A Context for Children's Books," in *Children's Literature Association Quarterly*, Vol. 7:1 (1982).

———. "The Other: Orientalism, Colonialism, and Children's Literature," in *Children's Literature Association Quarterly*, Vol. 17:1 (1992).

George Shannon. "Once and Forever a Platypus: Child Reader to Writing Adult," in *Children's Literature Association Quarterly*, Vol. 13:3 (1988).

Peggy Whalen-Levitt, ed. "Literature and Child Readers," in *Children's Literature Association Quarterly*, Vol. 5:4 (1980).

Angelea E. Williamson and Norman J. Williamson. "Mamie Pickering's Reading, Part Two: Girlhood Literature, A Phenomenon of Nineteenth Century Children's Literature," in *Children's Literature Association Quarterly*, Vol. 9:2 (1984).

Norman J. Williamson and Angelea E. Williamson. "Mamie Pickering's Reading, Part One: The Role of Books in the Social Life of a Late Victorian Child," in *Children's Literature Association Quarterly*, Vol. 9:1 (1984).

Virginia L. Wolf. "Readers of Alice: My Children, Meg Murry, and Harriet M. Welsch," in *Children's Literature Association Quarterly*, Vol. 13:3 (1988).

Chapter 9

James Britton. "Teachers, Learners, and Learning," in *Teacher as Learner*. Merron Chorny, ed. Calgary, Alberta, Canada: Language in the Classroom Project, Department of Curriculum and Instruction, University of Calgary, 1985.

Peter Elbow. *What Is English?* New York: The Modern Language Association of America, 1990.

Joseph Gibaldi, ed. *Introduction to Scholarship in Modern Languages and Literature*, 2nd ed. New York: Modern Language Association, 1992.

Richard Lloyd-Jones and Andrea A. Lunsford, eds. *The English Coalition Conference: Democracy through Language*. Urbana, IL: National Council of Teachers of English, 1989.

A LaVonne Brown Ruoff and Jerry W. Ward, eds. *Redefining American Literary History*. New York: The Modern Language Association, 1990.

Joel Taxel. "Notes from the Editor," in *The New Advocate*, Vol. 4:2 (1991).

Charles Temple and Patrick Collins, eds. *Stories and Readers: New Perspectives on Literature in the Elementary Classroom*. Norwood, MA: Christopher-Gordon Publishers, Inc., 1992.

Glossary of Literary Terms

Aesthetic experience Reading that centers on a developing appreciation of the author's style, use of language, and construction of story is aesthetic. The reader enjoys the experience without looking for moral implications, without looking at the story's lessons.

Allegory In allegory, an idea is represented in a concrete image that reflects an interpretation of something in everyday life. Authors who use allegory in their stories use singular events, characters, and settings to suggest universal meanings or attitudes. Because the allegory depends on the reader's acceptance of the story at two levels, the symbols must reflect societal myths and symbols.

Arcadia Frye discusses this as a typical pattern in the romance novel. The name Arcadia stems from a mountainous region of ancient Greece that is famed in legend for its rustic lifestyle. There, people lived in contentment with nature. Frye discusses it as a place without strife, a place where women do not cause male heroes to alter their behavior, a place where man and nature live in harmony.

Archetype Carl Jung's theory that stories contain an historical, unconscious set of patterns that formulate their underlying meanings helped to develop a method of reading that depended on the "collective unconscious" strands in all stories. Archetypes hold these patterns. They are the remnants of earlier religious beliefs, cultural rituals, and personal desires.

Bildungsroman A story pattern that begins by depicting an adolescent or youthful hero who is facing a problem and follows that hero on a personal journey toward maturity. The plot concerns the hero's struggle to solve her or his conflict. Therefore, the journey is one of self-discovery, whether or not the hero leaves home.

Binaries in literature   Literature often depends upon the author's ability to build opposite ideas into the story through language. Basic binaries exist in several disciplines; these are incorporated into texts quite naturally. For instance, it is not unusual to see man pitted against the natural elements or good pitted against evil. However, literary scholars have discovered and discussed more subtle opposites that are built into an author's texts, such as security against freedom, independence against conformity, knowledge against goodness. These binary structures are often introduced through the author's structural use of language. They signal the author's attempt to recreate meaning within the already accepted realms of a cultural system. Binary structures break down old interpretations of reality and form a new reality of their own.

Bipolarism   Frye argued that texts contain tensions created by the differences between myth (or cultural assumptions about occurrences) and mimesis (or the realities of events). Stories display that polarism by introducing a conflict for the hero to confront and reaching a resolution that values one of the two over the other. Virginia Wolf argues that in much of children's literature mimesis is placed in a romantic mode and realities are tempered by evocative, highly emotional imagery. (*Children and Their Literature,* 65–70).

Caldecott Award   An annual award presented by the American Library Association's Children's Services Division to the illustrator of "the most distinguished picture book" published in the United States the preceding year. Unless also the illustrator, the author is not recognized. This is an award for illustrations, not for text. Named after the British illustrator Randolph Caldecott, it was sponsored by Frederic Melcher and was first presented in 1938 to *Animals of the Bible,* illustrated by Dorothy P. Lathrop. The entire list, including titles named as runners-up, should be available at your public library.

Canon   Generally, a canon is an accepted rule. In literary terms a canon is the established set of books that determine what is acceptable or exemplary in thinking and/or writing.

Comedy   True comedy entertains without becoming slapstick. It contains events that the reader recognizes as odd or illogical. These events lead to a change within the society depicted. Initial conflicts are resolved by placing everything into a new, orderly domain. Usually the happy ending has been effected through a change in society. Although comic heroes seem realistic, they are depicted in a lighthearted and amusing story that ends happily.

Deconstruction   Deconstructionist criticism gained prominence after America became involved in the Vietnam conflict. A group of young critics who were disenchanted with the American myth of a superior aesthetics based on Eurocentric values sought to look at literature as linguistic metaphors of reality. They argued that by examining the author's use of language, the critic could determine the text's meaning. Many argued that all ideas contained in literature were already in society, and that authors merely constructed texts containing what was "already there." Further, they insisted that since literary texts could be interpreted in different ways at different times or in different situations, they "deconstructed" themselves, or caused unreliable meanings to be accepted as authoritative interpretations. Deconstructionists, then, sought to affirm that language is a system of symbols and patterns that imply meaning by their structures and cultural interpretations. They did not privilege texts for their "great mimetic structures," but sought to deconstruct the language patterns in order to reveal the text's potential readings.

Didactic literature In literary criticism, didacticism has been used to describe writing designed to give guidance, particularly in a moral, religious, or ethical way, to the reader. The authors who write didactic literature have a definite audience in mind. They believe that they know what is right for that audience and want to influence their readers' values and practices through their stories. Authors who are considered didactic are said to write in order to teach their readers rather than to entertain them.

Dominant impression The most important and influential element in a story. This is what most influences the reader's interpretation and understanding of the plot and its relationship to the characterization. While authors strive to create a dominant impression through description, tone, and mood as they write, their readers may pick an element other than the one the author believes will dominate because of their own reading and life experiences. Thus, Jill Paton Walsh writes, "I think that though it is possible to learn from books of fiction, it is not possible to teach with them; though it is possible for a book to heal psychic wounds, it is not possible to use books for the practice of psychic medicine. And the reason for this is the quirky, various, and totally unpredictable nature of the individual reaction to a book" ("The Art of Realism" 40).

Epilogue Authors write epilogues to their stories when they want to give their readers a concluding statement about the characters, future actions, or problematic resolutions that do not fit with the story's mood or structure. Sometimes, as is in *Trail Boss in Pigtails,* the epilogue asserts that the story just related is true, that the people lived, and that their final actions can be recorded.

Fable Children's literature often refers to the stories in LaFontaine's and Aesop's fables as the fable. These short stories contain talking beasts and quickly told adventures that reveal a moral about human behavior. The story is often being told to explain and/or justify a cultural code for behavior. Although these stories hold the archetypal pattern of the fable, they are not the only kind of fable. A modern fable can be an allegory which suggests that the fictional situation in the story compares with a modern one and entails a way to react in similar situations.

Fantasy Fantasy literature contains events that can never happen in the world as we know it. The reader is expected to suspend disbelief and follow the adventures of those involved as if they were realistic. Fantasy is imaginative literature that often contains the same magical motifs and devices found in folklore. It is written by an author who wishes to explore the possibilities of mankind within a newly created world devoid of traditional cultural myths and traditions. Often, however, the fantasy world does not differ much from our own world. Characters act and talk in familiar ways, and solutions to problems seem to be logical according to contemporary society's practices.

Feminist criticism Women critics began during the 1930s to re-evaluate the literary canon and discuss the implications that traditional literary criticism had on women as writers and readers. Feminists look at texts to expose societal attitudes about the woman's role within society; to espouse prejudices about women and their intellectual capacities causing them to be excluded from the academy; to find and re-evaluate women writers from past centuries; and to discuss a feminine aesthetics. Although early feminist critics were linked to the feminist movement and to the growth of programs of Women's Studies, today feminist criticism in children's literature is practiced by men as well as women and generally is a literary rather than political exploration of literature.

Folklore   Folklore has been broadly defined as those stories, legends, and myths that evolve from the unrecorded patterns of a people. Many university scholars from diverse fields have studied folklore and have defined it in different ways. Priscilla Ord has called children's folklore "complex," and has suggested that it holds two major strands: folklore for children and folklore of children. She maintains that it has the following general traits: It is oral; it is traditional; it exists in different versions of the same tale; it is anonymously composed/written/told; it fits a form and is repetitive.

Foreshadowing   Foreshadowing is a conventional device used in writing to allow the reader to participate in the story and "guess" what might happen next. Authors place clues in their stories that will help the reader discover why things happen as they do, how characters will act in future scenes, what the final outcome of the adventure will be. When talking with a group of educators, Robert Cormier once said, "No author of any worth would place an object or a scene into his story if it did not have later relevance." He is suggesting that a reader should watch for clues about the story by paying attention to the details the author uses throughout the story. Then the reader becomes a detective, using the clues to predict what will follow. An author may emphasize a personality trait that will cause the reader to accept unusual happenings later on. If so, the reader understands the character and believes that things might happen as they do in the story. Whatever method authors or artists use, they choose to foreshadow events and their outcome so that the reader can view the action as realistic or predictable.

Framing   Critics can look at an author's or artist's interruption in the story's action to set up a particular character, scene, or icon and can determine why this element has been placed within the plot. An author or artist who pauses in the story and sets up a new element within the natural framework of the plot is causing the reader to look more carefully at that element, to re-value it in terms of the story's actions and outcome.

Genre   First used to define types or styles or modes of writing, such as comedy, tragedy, romance, and irony, today genre is used to describe groups of works containing formally recognized techniques in composition that are commonly discussed in criticism.

Herstory   Feminist critics who study historical retellings of history and common literary patterns taught in schools have suggested that literature and history retell events in male-dominant ways. For instance, historical representations of the past concentrate on names and dates of those involved in major political or social reforms. Most of the people who are favorably discussed in books are men. Those women who have been discussed in the past usually have fit into three categories: women who acted in supportive roles to male leaders; women who have chosen to live out of step with mainstream society as artists or social reformers; women in highly visible occupations, such as in the theater or sports. Literature, they have argued, also focuses the reader on an acceptance of the male perspective by concentrating on male reactions to female behavior instead of the female's struggles to find a place within a male-dominated society. History, they contend, is not her story, but is his story. These critics call for new interpretations of the past that look at events and change as they affect woman's place in society. They ask that history be complemented with herstory of the past.

Historical fiction A story that uses people, events, and/or places to reconstruct the past into a plausible series of events. In these stories, fictional characters must represent known attitudes and must be placed within the contexts of recorded events or conflicts. The historical novelist must create as accurate a picture of the past as she can, using people who are representative of known cultural attitudes.

Imagery Imagery in a broad literary analysis sense means those visual depictions and sensual interpretations that are placed within a text to create meaning to the scenes being depicted. A book may be said to have a strong sense of imagery if the author uses thematic images to reinforce the plot's underlying interpretation or point of view. Images cause the reader to react to scenes in a particular way. Carefully controlled and repeated images can sustain an single mood and theme. Clusters of diverse images can cause the reader to refocus on events and reinterpret the adventure. Critics look at imagery to see how the author consciously shapes her descriptive and illusory language in order to affect the reader's interpretation of the story. When discussing imagery from a rhetorical sense, the critic concentrates on the author's "image patterns" that shape the plot and suggest an implied meaning for the story.

Irony This works when there is an unstated understanding between the author and the reader that all is not as it seems. At the lowest level authors use figures of speech that express the opposite reality from what is happening or is believed to be true. In literature, irony causes a reader to become detached from the characters or events because he is forced to see that the story contains contradictions in actions, resolutions, or characterization. The reader can intellectualize about why the story has these incongruities and can see them in relation to reality as he knows it. Because the reader must be able to see that the author is playing with ideas, irony is a sophisticated literary form.

Literary fairy tale This tale resembles folk literature in its use of patterns and motifs. Some tales are simple recreations of older oral tales. However, if the author uses a well-known tale for the core of his retelling, the author is purposely recreating a folkloric pattern in order to extend, spoof, refocus, or change the original tale. Some tales appear to be original folk tales because they hold the symbolism and structure of well-known folk tales, but the characterizations, plots, and underlying messages are those of the tales' authors. Literary fairy tales can be traced to a writer who lives in a particular culture; oral folklore can be traced to a body of recorded tales that reflect the values of a culture.

Marxist criticism Marxist criticism is founded on the supposition that economic issues cause the formation of governments which generally support the rich leaders of a country and their values. As a result, the working classes join together and struggle against this privileged class, hoping to reform the government and establish a classless society. Since the 1930s, Marxist critics have sought to define the role that literature plays within a society's political arena. Specifically, they seek to establish an understanding of the relationships in literary evaluations to aesthetics and economics; to de-privilege the canon, showing how classical literature holds implied ideological messages; to recover or discover unheralded pieces of writing that come from the lower classes; and to determine how art and economics are connected in literary evaluations.

Metaphor   An author creates a metaphor when she uses language to identify one object with another and indirectly suggests that the two share characteristics. Metaphors suggest a second meaning for the story that is being told; they indirectly affect our understanding of an author's underlying reason for writing a particular tale.

Mimetic art   Critics look at stories as mimetic when they mimic reality. Thus, the description of a tree seems realistic, the actions of characters true to life, and the details of events valid to the scene. Mimetic art reflects the reality of the world as the reader knows it exists. It reproduces people, places, and events with lifelike visions.

Mimetic theory   A theory of reading that depends on Aristotle's idea that art imitates reality and becomes a reproduction of nature, of man, or of society itself. The emphasis in this theory is on the relationship of the imagery to reality.

Minority criticism   Most minority criticism seeks to establish an aesthetics for evaluating literature that is distinctly different from those established in New Criticism. Critics in minority criticism argue that ethnicity causes divergent cultures to form writing patterns dependent on religious, cultural, and social conditions distinct to a particular group of people. It looks at historical and political events and ideas that have caused writers within a particular ethnic group to construct stories and poems that reflect their experiences.

Mood   An author's mood is reflected in her expression of ideas. She may approach a subject many ways, but throughout a text the approach should be consistent. Authors of literary works use mood as a vehicle of communication between the author and the reader. Mood is strongly related to the author's choice of tone, but the mood reflects the author's response to a topic, while the author chooses to write in a particular tone to evoke the wanted reader's response to her text.

Mythic criticism   A school of criticism that looks at archetypes and mythic patterns to define a text's meaning. These critics see new literature as a reflection of earlier cultural and religious patterns, and they place stories in categories (or genres) based on the structural and metaphoric patterns embedded in the text. While this criticism does look at the past, it is more interested in social practices or rituals than history. Always looking backward for structural significance, the mythic critics develop formulas for interpreting. Yet they seek to practice a critical method that would not demythify the text, which would not rationalize its reading, causing the reader's initial response to be lost in a labeling practice instead of a method for exploring the stories shared. Because this school of criticism relies on rituals, legends, and stories from past cultures, it privileges certain myths over others. In turn, this helps to justify a canon of literature that all people need to share in order to understand contemporary writing.

Newbery Award   An award annually given by the Children's Services Division of the American Library Association to the author of "the most distinguished contribution to children's literature" published in the United States the preceding year. Named after John Newbery, the British publisher who first turned to children's literature as a market, the award was initially sponsored by Frederic Melcher. It has been awarded to an author since 1922 when Hendrik Willem Van Loon won for his book *The Story of Mankind*. A complete listing of the award winners and the runners-up should be available at your public library.

New Criticism   A school of criticism that evolved in America during the 1930s and is still practiced today by some scholars in literary studies. Though these critics do not adhere to one way of reading, they do concentrate on reading a piece of literature and studying it for its intrinsic values. They do not condone several interpretations of one selection; to New Critics each piece of literature has an ideal reading that comes from the ideal reader. New Criticism does not advocate author-ial or historical study as a means of interpretation. And it does not allow for reader response in interpretation.

Nonfiction   Writing based on factual information. An author who writes nonfic-tion cannot make up characters, events, or attitudes. He must carefully construct a sense of realism, using only what is known to be accurate. Milton Meltzer says that nonfiction involves the author's artistic construction of reality. He concludes, "Imagination, invention, selection, language, form—these are just as important to the making of a good book of biography, history, or science as to the making of a piece of fiction" ("Where Do All the Prizes Go?" 92).

Pastoralism   Books that contain a pastoral framework give homage to simplicity, serenity, and nature. The word itself comes from the Latin word pastor, meaning shepherd, and most authors who use this technique sustain positive rural imagery in their characterization, setting, and plot. The stories often contain country scenes complete with rolling hills, peaceful animals, and good weather. Man is seen to be best when in tune with his surroundings; pastoral heroes usually have little formal education.

Personification   In personification, authors take objects, animals, or ideas and give them human personalities. In this way, an author can introduce an abstraction into a story and convince the reader that the abstraction is a living, breathing reality.

Reader response theory   This is a theory about reading that did not come from one group of people who identified with one another and worked together. A broad movement in literary theory that came to prominence in the 1950s, reader response theorists argue that literary studies must focus on the reader's reactions to what is being read. According to these theorists, a text's meaning is discovered as one reads. Most reader response critics argue that readers bring their own experi-ence with them and use that experience to shape meaning from the text.

Realism   Realism is found in literature when authors depict, in a matter-of-fact way, life as it really exists. Often, realism deals with "ordinary people" facing typical societal problems. Many characters in adult realism are lower-class or poor people. Elizabeth Segal has defined realism within children's literature as "a form that would reflect more accurately the random and inconclusive nature of actual events and the complex individuality of actual people" (*The First Steps* 46). She has argued that the most striking element in children's literature is the development of psychologically complex characters who extend children's literature beyond the topical taboos—bad parents, poverty, war, death, and sex—that have affected writers of other genres in children's literature.

Realistic fiction   A story that places primary emphasis on honest representations of characters, places, and events. A story that is mimetic and holds realism.

Rhetoric   All authors use rhetoric to shape their writing. It is a way of organizing the material they present so that they can be convincing to their audience. The author's effective use of style and language can create a feeling that what is being reported is true or realistic. When we look at the author's use of rhetoric, we are often asking ourselves the questions suggested by Edward W. Said: What is it that maintains texts inside reality? What keeps some of them current while others disappear? How do authors imagine for themselves the "archive" of their time into which they propose to put their text? What are the centers of diffusion by which texts circulate? (*The World, the Text, and the Critic,* 152–153).

Rhetorical criticism   A critical study of a piece of writing for its implied messages that shape reader's responses to the text. A rhetorical critic looks at narrative patterns, persuasive language, and literary devices to determine the author's artistic use of persuasive narrative. Rhetorical criticism suggests that all literature, whether fiction or nonfiction, holds cultural and ethical messages within the text, that no author is neutral or completely objective when discussing a particular subject or describing a particular scene.

Romance   The earliest romance stories evolved from medieval romances where knights battled evil forces and saved kingdoms from destruction. Usually the stories were quest narratives whose protagonists set out to meet a particular challenge and return triumphant. The romance pattern ends happily ever after, with evil banished and heroism rewarded. Because the tales often involved the hero's marriage to a "fair maiden," the stories became identified as tales about love. Today's romance novels hold incidents and characters who are too good or too bad to be true to life. Romance settings are often picturesque and unrealistic. Events are highly dramatic and idealistically portrayed. In the end, wickedness is punished and bravery re-warded.

Science fiction   A subgenre in fantasy that allows the author to combine scientific knowledge within a fanciful plot. Authors project future existence into an imagin-ary world that is created using information about existing technology and its future implications. Margaret Esmonde called it a significant subgenre in children's litera-ture, and concluded, "It is particularly suited to fire the youthful imagination 'to boldly go where no man has gone before!'" (*The First Steps* 55).

Social criticism   Social criticism formally evolved after World War I and was first practiced by a group of intellectuals who were opposed to the premises of New Critics. These critics rejected close readings that privileged certain texts for their style. Instead, they advocated looking at texts for the social and moral messages which they contained. In the early days, many were also Marxist critics. Later, they came from divergent camps, such as feminist criticism, African-American, Latino, and Asian Aesthetics. Many of the social critics have suggested that literature must be studied for its psychological, political, economic, and historical implications.

Most social critics do not support the idea that there is one canon of literature that must be taught as the central body of literary studies.

Tone An author uses a tone to establish a relationship with his audience. He may write in a formal, informal, intimate, playful, ironic, serious, dramatic, or abstract way in order to affect his reader's responses to what she is reading. The author's tone establishes a mood for the text by choosing literary devices that will create a rhythmic pattern for his reader. When the author is successful, the tone seems natural, not contrived.

Tragic hero or heroine A person of high character who faces her or his fate with nobility and courage. A hero who is faced with societal conflicts that she or he is not able to overcome.

Tragedy The plot of tragedy is somber. It concerns a noble hero who is not in tune with the society he or she lives in, somber events that lead to the hero's downfall, and unhappy resolutions to the story's conflict. Because tragic heroes do not succeed in the worlds where they are placed, their lives meet unhappy ends. Often they break the taboos that have been set by their society and pit themselves against cultural or religious values. Because readers realize their transgressions, they do not anticipate a happy ending to the story. Thus, things work out as the reader expects, but not as the reader might wish. Tragic stories contain elements of realism, and they are mimetic in form.

Utopia Utopia comes from Greek roots, and derives its meaning from the words outopia, meaning "no place" and eutopia, meaning "a place where everything is right." In a sense, a utopian land in fiction becomes both a place that never quite existed as it is portrayed and a place where everything seems perfect. It is the imagined world of the writer that holds the best social, economic, political, and religious values. Whether the land is one strongly resembling the writer's own society or whether it is a fanciful world, it implies that certain values are better than others. Yet most utopian lands in fiction do have cultural conflicts. And they can only be viewed as utopian if the reader accepts the values placed in that world. A utopia, then, is the vision of perfection an author chooses to depict.

Validate In legal terms validation proves that something is founded on fact or evidence. In literature, validation most often is expected when an author writes realism or nonfiction. The author must prove that his portrayal of a group of people is based on real events, that it is carefully drawn to show how "things really were," and that the author has the "privileged background" to write the story. In the simplest sense, this means that the author must prove that research has been done and that the story told is an honest interpretation of real events, people, and issues. In a more complex sense, this can mean that the author needs to justify his right to write about a particular culture. He must assert that he is writing from "within" the culture rather than writing as an outsider.

Voice The author of any writing uses a set of verbs and pronouns that defines her writing style. If the author chooses the first person verbs of I, me, we, and us, she directly addresses her reader as if she were speaking to her. Authors who choose to use third-person narrative will use impersonal pronouns, such as "one," to discuss personal reflections. These distance the writer from the reader and cause the text to become less personal. Verb tense also causes the reader to respond in different ways. Present-tense verbs are selected to convince the reader that the subject is active and contemporary or pertinent to his world. Past-tense verbs can be used to suggest a reflective attitude or demonstrate that the events and ideas recorded come from the past.

APPENDIX B

Related Readings

Criticism

Books

Robert Bator. *Signposts to Criticism of Children's Literature*. Chicago: American Library Association, 1983.

Monroe Berger. *Real and Imagined Worlds: The Novel and Social Science*. Cambridge, MA: Harvard University Press, 1977.

Sacvon Berovitch, ed. *Reconstructing American Literary History*. Cambridge, MA: Harvard University Press, 1986.

Ralph Philip Boas and Katherine Burton. *Social Backgrounds of American Literature*. Boston: Little, Brown and Company, 1988.

Maud Bodkin. *Archetypal Patterns in Poetry: Psychological Studies of Imagination*. New York: Vintage Books, 1958.

Wayne C. Booth. *The Company We Keep: An Ethics of Fiction*. Berkeley: University of California Press, 1988.

———. *The Rhetoric of Fiction*. Chicago: University of Chicago Press, 1961.

Pierre Bourdieu. *Field of Cultural Production: Essays on Art and Criticism*. New York: Columbia University Press, 1993.

Michael Boyd. *The Reflexive Novel: Fiction as Critique*. Lewisburg, PA: Bucknell University Press, 1983.

Cleanth Brooks and Robert Penn Warren. *Understanding Poetry,* 3rd ed. New York: Holt, Rinehart and Winston, 1960.

Richard Harvey Brown. *Society as Text: Essays on Rhetoric, Reason, and Reality*. Chicago: University of Chicago Press, 1987.

Ross Chambers. *Story and Situation: Narrative Seduction and the Power of Fiction*. Minneapolis: University of Minnesota Press, 1984.

Seymour Chatman. *Story and Discourse: Narrative Structure in Fiction and Film.* Ithaca: Cornell University Press, 1978.

Joseph M. Conte. *Unending Design: The Forms of Postmodern Poetry.* Ithaca: Cornell University Press, 1991.

Philip A. Dennis and Wendell Aycock, eds. *Literature and Anthropology.* Lubbock: Texas Tech University Press, 1989.

John Elder. *Imagining the Earth: Poetry and the Vision of Nature.* Urbana: University of Illinois Press, 1985.

Andrew V. Ettin. *Literature and the Pastoral.* New Haven, CT: Yale University Press, 1984.

N. H. Freemun and M. V. Cox, eds. *Visual Order: The Nature and Development of Pictorial Representation.* Cambridge: Cambridge University Press, 1985.

Sigmund Freud. *The Future of an Illusion.* Translated by W. D. Robson-Scott. New York: Doubleday, 1957.

———. *On Creativity and the Unconscious: Papers on the Psychology of Art, Literature, Love, Religion.* Selected, with Introduction and Annotations by Benjamin Nelson. New York: Harper, 1958.

Northrop Frye. *Anatomy of Criticism: Four Essays.* Princeton: Princeton University Press, 1957.

———. *The Educated Imagination.* Bloomington: Indiana University Press, 1964.

Hans G. Furth. *The World of Grown-ups: Children's Conceptions of Society.* New York: Elsevior, 1980.

Catherine Garvey. *Children's Talk.* Cambridge: Harvard University Press, 1984.

Harry R. Garvin, ed. *Theories of Reading, Looking, and Listening.* Lewisburg, PA: Bucknell University Press, 1981.

John Griffith. *Charlotte's Web: A Pig's Salvation.* New York: Twayne Publishers, 1993.

Barbara Hardy. *Tellers and Listeners: The Narrative Imagination.* London: The University of London, The Athlone Press, 1975.

Geoffrey H. Hartman. *The Fate of Reading: and Other Essays.* Chicago: University of Chicago Press, 1975.

Mary Jane Hurst. *The Voice of the Child in American Literature: Linguistic Approaches to Fictional Child Languages.* Lexington: The University Press of Kentucky, 1990.

Hans Robert Jauss. *Toward an Aesthetic of Reception: Theory and History of Literature,* Vol. 2. Minneapolis: University of Minnesota, 1982.

Michael C. Jaye and Ann Chalmers Watts, eds. *Literature and the Urban Experience.* New Brunswick, NJ: Rutgers University Press, 1981.

Walter Kalaidjian. *Languages of Liberation: The Social Text in Contemporary American Poetry.* New York: Columbia University Press, 1989.

Frank Kermode. *The Art of Telling: Essays on Fiction.* Cambridge, MA: Harvard University Press, 1983.

Thomas M. Leitch. *What Stories Are: Narrative Theory and Interpretation.* University Park: The Pennsylvania University Press, 1986.

Vincent B. Leitch. *American Literary Criticism: From the Thirties to the Eighties.* New York: Columbia University Press, 1988.

Gareth B. Matthews. *Philosophy and the Young Child.* Cambridge: Harvard University Press, 1980.

———. *The Philosophy of Childhood.* Cambridge: Harvard University Press, 1994.

Perry Nodelman. *Words About Pictures: The Narrative Art of Children's Picture Books*. Athens: The University of Georgia Press, 1988.

Perry Nodelman, ed. *Touchstones: Reflections on the Best in Children's Literature*, Volumes I–III. West Lafayette, IN: ChLA Publishers, 1985, 1987, 1989.

Charlotte F. Otten and Gary D. Schmidt, eds. *The Voice of the Narrator in Children's Literature: Insights from Writers and Critics*. Wesport, CT: Greenwood Press, Inc., 1989.

Thomas G. Pavel. *Fictional Worlds*. Cambridge, MA: Harvard University Press, 1986.

James Phelan. *Reading People, Reading Plots: Character, Progression, and the Interpretation of Narrative*. Chicago: The University of Chicago Press, 1989.

I. A. Richards. *Practical Criticism*. New York: Harcourt Brace, 1959.

Thomas J. Roberts. *When Is Something Fiction?* Carbondale: Southern Illinois University Press, 1972.

Louise Rosenblatt. *The Reader, the Text, the Poem: The Transactional Theory of the Literary Work*. Carbondale: Southern Illinois University Press, 1978.

Edward W. Said. *The World, the Text, and the Critic*. Cambridge: Harvard University Press, 1983.

Roger Sale. *Fairy Tales and After: From Snow White to E. B. White*. Cambridge, MA: Harvard University Press, 1978.

Imre Salusinszky. *Criticism in Society*. New York: Methuen, 1987.

Fernando Savater. *Childhood Regained: The Art of the Storyteller*. New York: Columbia University Press, 1982.

Robert Scholes. *Protocols of Reading*. New Haven: Yale University Press, 1989.

Robert Scholes and Robert Kellogg. *The Nature of Narrative*. New York: Oxford University Press, 1966.

Patricia Meyer Spacks. *The Female Imagination*. New York: Alfred A. Knopf, 1975.

John Stephens. *Language and Ideology in Children's Literature*. New York: Longman, 1992.

Susan R. Suleiman and Inge Crosman. *The Reader in the Text: Essays on Audience and Interpretation*. Princeton, NJ: Princeton University Press, 1980.

Jane P. Tompkins, ed. *Reader-Response Criticism: From Formalism to Post-Structuralism*. Baltimore: The Johns Hopkins University Press, 1980.

Colin Wilson. *The Strength to Dream: Literature and the Imagination*. Westport, CT: Greenwood Press Reprint, 1975.

Articles

Phyllis Bixler. "Essay Review: 'Narrative Theory and Children's Literature,'" in *Children's Literature in Education*, Vol. 18:1 (1987).

Eleanor Cameron. "For Whom Does the Critic Write—and Why?" in *Children's Literature Association Quarterly*, Vol. 9:4 (1984–85).

John Cech. "Great Expectations: Children's Literature Criticism in The Year of the Child," in *The Lion and the Unicorn*, Vol. 5 (1981).

Patricia Demers. "Classic or Touchstone: Much of a Muchness?" in *Children's Literature Association Quarterly*, Vol. 10:3 (1985).

Duanne A. Grimme. "The Wonders of Language in the Picture Story Book," in *The CLA Bulletin*, Vol. 17:2 (1991).

Alethea Helbig. "Myra Cohn Livingston Offers a 'New Mythology' in *The Child as Poet*," in *Children's Literature Association Quarterly*, Vol. 11:3 (1986).

Pamela R. Howell. "Voice Is Voice Whether a Bat or a Poet: Randall Jarrell's The Bat-Poet," in *Proceedings of the Ninth Annual Conference of the Children's Literature Association,* March 1982. Priscilla Ord, ed. Boston: The Children's Literature Association.

Peter Hunt. "Narrative Theory and Children's Literature," in *ChLA Quarterly,* Vol. 9:4 (1984–85).

———. "Who Writes the Book? Writers, Parents, Society, and Children's Literature," in *The New Advocate,* Vol. 3:2 (1990).

Sylvia Patterson Isklander. "Readers, Realism, and Robert Cormier," in *Children's Literature,* Vol. 15 (1987).

Virginia Glasgow Koste. "Growing Hope: A Playwrights Dreams and Guesses About Young Audiences," in *Children's Literature Association Quarterly,* Vol. 12:4 (1987).

Millicent Lenz. "Landscape of Our Dreams: Ted Hughes's *Moon-Whales and Other Moon Poems,*" in *Children's Literature Association Quarterly,* Vol. 13:1 (1988).

Roderick McGillis. "Calling a voice out of silence: hearing what we read," in *Children's Literature in Education,* Vol. 15:1 (1984).

———. "Criticism in the Woods: Fairy Tales as Poetry," in *Children's Literature Association Quarterly,* Vol. 7:2 (1982).

———. "'The Delicatest Ear of the Mind,'" in *Children's Literature Association Quarterly,* Vol. 13:1 (1988).

———. "Literary Incompetence," in *Children's Literature Association Quarterly,* Vol. 10:3 (1985).

———. "Utopian Hopes: Criticism Beyond Itself," in *Children's Literature Association Quarterly,* Vol. 9:4 (1984–85).

Milton Meltzer. "The Reader and the Writer," in *The Bulletin of the Children's Literature Assembly,* Vol. 8:1 (1982).

———. "The Social Responsibility of the Writer," in *The New Advocate,* Vol. 2:3 (1989).

Anita Moss. "Varieties of Children's Metafiction," in *Studies in the Literary Imagination,* Vol. 18:2 (1985).

Geoff Moss. "Metafiction and the Poetics of Children's Literature," in *Children's Literature Association Quarterly,* Vol. 15:2 (1990).

Claudia Nelson. "Family Circle or Vicious Circle? Anti-Paternal Undercurrents in Louisa May Alcott," in *The Child and the Family: Selected Papers from the 1988 International Conference of the Children's Literature Association.* New York: Pace University, 1988.

Peter F. Neumeyer. "Randall Jarrell's *The Bat Poet:* An Introduction to the Craft," in *Children's Literature Association Quarterly,* Vol. 9:2 (1984).

Perry Nodelman. "The Art of the Children's Novel," in *Children's Literature Association Quarterly,* Vol. 11:1 (1986).

———. "The Case of Children's Fiction: or The Impossibility of Jacqueline Rose," in *Children's Literature Association Quarterly,* Vol. 10:3 (1985).

———. "Children's Literature as Women's Writing," in *Children's Literature Association Quarterly,* Vol. 13:1 (1988).

———. "The Eye and I: Identification and First-Person Narratives in Picture Books," in *Children's Literature,* Vol. 19 (1991).

———. "The Hidden Meaning and the Inner Tale: Deconstruction and the Interpretation of Fairy Tales," in *Children's Literature Association Quarterly,* Vol. 15:3 (1990).

———. "The Objectionable Other, or, Walter de la Mare Meets My Little Pony," in *Children's Literature Association Quarterly,* Vol. 12:2 (1987).

———. "Robert Cormier Does a Number," in *Children's Literature in Education,* Vol. 14:2 (1983).

Marilyn Solt. "Abigail, Elaine, and the Peasant on Route Seven: Kaye Starbird's Poems for Children," in *Children's Literature Association Quarterly,* Vol. 8:3 (1983).

John Stephens. "Language, Discourse, and Picture Books," in *Children's Literature Association Quarterly,* Vol. 14:3 (1989).

Sara J. Stohler. "The Mythic World of Childhood," in *Children's Literature Association Quarterly,* Vol. 12:1 (1987).

Jon C. Stott. "Architectural Structures and Social Values in the Non-fiction of David Macaulay," in *Children's Literature Association Quarterly,* Vol. 8:1 (1983).

———. "The Purposiveness of Evil: a Note on *Otto of the Silver Hand,*" in *Children's Literature Association Quarterly,* Vol. 8:2 (1983).

Robert D. Sutherland. "Hidden Persuaders: Political Idealogies in Literature for Children," in *Children's Literature in Education,* Vol. 16:3 (1985).

Virginia Walter. "Crossing the Pacific to America: The Uses of Narrative," in *Children's Literature Association Quarterly,* Vol. 16:2 (1991).

Jeanie Watson. "'Men Sell Not Such in Any Town': Christina Rossetti's Goblin Fruit of Fairy Tale," in *Children's Literature,* Vol. 12 (1984).

Laura Weaver. "'Plain' and 'Fancy' Laura: A Mennonite Reader," in *Children's Literature,* Vol. 16 (1988).

Nancy Willard. "When by Now and Tree by Leaf: Time and Timelessness in the Reading and Making of Children's Books," in *Children's Literature Association Quarterly,* Vol. 10:4 (1986).

Caroline Zilboorg. "Caddie Woodlawn: A Feminist Case Study," in *Children's Literature in Education,* Vol. 21:2 (1990).

Jack Zipes. "Taking Political Stock: New Theoretical and Critical Approaches to Anglo-American Children's Literature in the 1980s," in *The Lion and the Unicorn,* Vol. 14:1 (1990).

Education and Criticism

Books

Carolyn J. Bauer, ed. *The Best of The Bulletin of the Children's Literature Assembly of the National Council of Teachers of English.* Urbana, IL: National Council of Teachers of English, 1987.

Miriam Ben-Peretz. *The Teacher-Curriculum Encounter: Freeing Teachers from the Tyranny of Texts.* Albany: State University of New York Press, 1990.

Michael Benton and Geoff Fox. *Teaching Literature: Nine to Fourteen.* New York: Oxford University Press, 1985.

David Bloome, ed. *Classrooms and Literacy.* Norwood, NJ: Ablex Publishing Corporation, 1989.

Wayne C. Booth. *The Vocation of a Teacher: Rhetorical Occasions 1967–1988.* Chicago: University of Chicago Press, 1988.

Jerome S. Bruner. *Entry into Early Language: A Spiral Curriculum*. Swansea: University College of Swansea, 1975.

——. *On Knowing: Essays on the Left Hand*. Cambridge, MA: The Belknap Press of Harvard University Press, 1979.

William E. Cain. *The Crisis in Criticism: Theory, Literature, and Reform in English Studies*. Baltimore: The Johns Hopkins University Press, 1984.

G. Robert Carlson and Anne Sherrill. *Voices of Readers: How We Come to Love Books*. Urbana, IL: National Council of Teachers of English, 1988.

Carol Chomsky. *The Acquisition of Syntax in Children from 5 to 10*. Cambridge, MA: The MIT Press, 1969.

John Clifford, ed. *Experience of Reading: Louise Rosenblatt and Reader-Response Theory*. Portsmouth, NH: Boynton/Cook Publishers, 1991.

Marilyn Cochran-Smith. *The Making of a Reader*. Norwood, NJ: Ablex Publishing Corporation, 1984.

Robert Coles. *The Call of Stories: Teaching and the Moral Imagination*. Houghton Mifflin, 1989.

Charles R. Cooper, ed. *Researching Response to Literature and the Teaching of Literature: Points of Departure*. Norwood, NJ: Ablex Publishing Corporation, 1985.

Helen Cowie, ed. *The Development of Children's Imaginative Writing*. New York: St. Martin's Press, 1984.

Maureen and Hugh Crago. *Prelude to Literacy: A Preschool Child's Encounter with Picture and Story*. Carbondale: Southern Illinois University Press, 1983.

Avon Crismore. *Talking with Readers: Metadiscourse as Rhetorical Act*. New York: Peter Lang, 1989.

E. C. Cuff and G. C. F. Payne. *Crisis in the Curriculum*. London: Croom Helm, 1985.

Patricia Donahue and Ellen Quandahl, eds. *Reclaiming Pedagogy: The Rhetoric of the Classroom*. Carbondale: Southern Illinois University Press, 1989.

Eleanor Duckworth. *"The Having of Wonderful Ideas" & Other Essays on Teaching & Learning*. New York: Teachers College Press, 1987.

Kieran Egan and Dan Nadaner, eds. *Imagination and Education*. New York: Teachers College Press, 1988.

Janet Emig. *The Web of Meaning: Essays on Writing, Teaching, Learning and Thinking*. Portsmouth, NH: Boynton/Cook Publications, Inc., 1983.

Edmund J. Farrell and James R. Squire. *Transactions with Literature: A Fifty-Year Perspective*. Urbana, IL: National Council of Teachers of English, 1990.

Northrop Frye. *On Education*. Ann Arbor: The University of Michigan Press, 1988.

Henry A. Giroux. *Teachers as Intellectuals: Toward a Critical Pedagogy of Learning*. Granly, MA: Bergin & Garvey Publishers, Inc., 1988.

Henry A. Giroux, Roger I. Simon, and contributors, eds. *Popular Culture, Schooling, and Everday Life*. Granby, MA: Bergin & Garvey, Publishers, 1989.

William Glasser. *Schools Without Failure*. New York: Harper & Row, 1969.

Dixie Goswami and Peter R. Stillman, eds. *Reclaiming the Classroom: Teacher Research as an Agency for Change*. Upper Montclair, NJ: Boynton/Cook Publishers, Inc., 1987.

Gerald Graff. *Beyond the Culture Wars: How Teaching the Conflicts Can Revitalize American Education*. New York: W. W. Norton, 1992.

Geoffrey H. Hartman. *Criticism in the Wilderness: The Study of Literature Today.* New Haven: Yale University Press, 1980.

Susan Hynds and Donald L. Rubin, eds. *Perspectives on Talk and Learning.* Urbana, IL: National Council of Teachers of English, 1990.

Angela Jagger and M. Trika Smith-Burke, eds. *Observing the Language Learner.* Newark, DE: National Council of Teachers of English with the International Reading Association, 1985.

Terry D. Johnson and Daphne R. Louis. *Literacy through Literature.* Portsmouth, NH: Heinemann, 1987.

Nicholas J. Karolides. *Reader Response in the Classroom: Evoking and Interpreting Meaning in Literature.* New York: Longman, 1992.

Susan S. Lehr. *The Child's Developing Sense of Theme: Responses to Literature.* New York: Teachers College Press, 1991.

Andrew Levitt. *Storytelling Among Schoolchildren: A Folkloristic Interpretation.* University of Pennsylvania Ph.D. thesis, 1978.

Claudia Lewis. *A Big Bite of the World: Children's Creative Writing.* Englewood Cliffs, NJ: Prentice-Hall, Inc., 1979.

Alison Lurie. *Don't Tell the Grown-ups: Subversive Children's Literature.* Boston: Little, Brown and Company, 1990.

Robert J. Marzano. *Cultivating Thinking in English and the Language Arts.* Urbana, IL: National Council of Teachers of English, 1991.

Jill P. May, ed. *Children and Their Literature: A Readings Book.* West Lafayette, IN: ChLA Publications, 1983.

Anita Moss. *Exploring Literature in the Classroom: Content and Methods.* Norwood, MA: Christopher-Gordon Publishers, Inc., 1992.

Kostas Myrsiades, ed. *Margins in the Classroom: Teaching Literature.* Minneapolis, University of Minnesota Press, 1994.

Joseph O'Beirne Milner and Lucy Floyd Morcock Milner, eds. *Passages to Literature: Essays in Australia, Canada, England, the United States, and Wales.* Urbana, IL: National Council of Teachers of English, 1989.

Charles Moran and Elizabeth F. Penfield, eds. *Conversations: Contemporary Critical Theory and the Teaching of English.* Urbana, IL: National Council of Teachers of English, 1990.

Ben F. Nelms, ed. *Literature in the Classroom: Readers, Texts, and Contexts.* Urbana, IL: National Council of Teachers of English, 1988.

Mary Ann Paulin. *Creative Uses of Children's Literature.* Hamden, CT: Library Professional Publications, 1982.

Patricia Phelan, ed. *Talking to Learn.* Urbana, IL: National Council of Teachers of English, 1989.

———. *Literature and Life: Making Connections in the Classroom.* Urbana, IL: National Council of Teachers of English, 1990.

Alan Purves and Dianne L. Monson. *Experiencing Children's Literature.* Glenview, IL: Scott, Foresman, 1984.

Diane Ravitch. *The Schools We Deserve: Reflections on the Educational Crisis of Our Times.* New York: Basic Books, Inc., 1985.

Louise Rosenblatt. *Literature as Exploration.* New York: Modern Language Association, 1983.

Glenn Edward Sadler, ed. *Teaching Children's Literature: Issues, Pedagogy, Resources.* New York: Modern Language Association, 1992.

Robert Scholes. *Textual Power: Literary Theory and the Teaching of English.* New Haven: Yale University Press, 1985.

Jerome L. Singer. *The Child's World of Make-Believe.* New York: Academic Press, 1973.

Glenna Davis Sloan. *The Child as Critic: Teaching Literature in Elementary and Middle Schools.* Third edition. New York: Teachers College Press, 1991.

John Spink. *Children as Readers: A Study.* London: Clive Bingley, 1989.

Margaret B. Sutherland. *Everyday Imagining and Education.* London: Routledge & Kegan Paul, 1971.

Brian Sutton-Smith, ed. *Play and Learning.* Gardner Press, Inc., 1979.

Charles Temple and Patrick Collins, ed. *Stories and Readers: New Perspectives on Literature in the Elementary Classroom.* Norwood, MA: Christopher-Gordon, Publishers, Inc., 1992.

Nancy M. Theriot, ed. *The Child in Contemporary America.* Albuquerque, NM: New America, 1984.

Jack Thompson. *Understanding Teenagers' Reading: Reading Processes and the Teaching of Literature.* Australia: Methuen, 1987.

Barbara Tizard and Martin Hughes. *Young Children Learning.* Cambridge: Harvard University Press, 1984.

Myron C. Tuman. *A Preface to Literacy: An Inquiry into Pedagogy, Practice, and Progress.* Tuscaloosa: The University of Alabama Press, 1987.

Kay E. Vandergrift. *Child and Story: The Literary Connection.* New York: Neal-Schuman Publishers, 1980.

L. S. Vygotsky. *Thought and Language.* Edited and translated by Eugenia Hanfmann and Gertrude Vakar. Cambridge, MA: The MIT Press, 1962.

Shelby Anne Wolf and Shirley Brice Heath. *The Braid of Literature: Children's Worlds of Reading.* Cambridge: Harvard University Press, 1992.

Martha Wolfenstein. *Children's Humor: A Psychological Analysis.* Bloomington: Indiana University Press, 1978.

William Zinsser, ed. *Worlds of Childhood: The Art and Craft of Writing for Children.* Boston: Houghton Mifflin Company, 1990.

Articles

Gillian Adams. "Student Responses to *Alice in Wonderland* and *At the Back of the North Wind*," in *Children's Literature Association Quarterly,* Vol. 10:1 (1985).

Janice M. Alberghene. "Writing in *Charlotte's Web*," in *Children's Literature in Education,* Vol. 16:1 (1985).

Alida Allison. "What Would I Teach If I Had Only Six Months Left to Teach?" in *Children's Literature in Education,* Vol. 24:4 (1993).

Marilyn Apseloff. "Books for Babies: Learning Toys or Pre-literature?" in *Children's Literature Association Quarterly,* Vol. 12:2 (1987).

Tony Aylwin. "Using Myths and Legends in School," in *Children's Literature in Education,* Vol. 12:2 (1981).

Norma Bagnall. "It *Was Real* Exciting: Adults and Children Studying Children's Literature Together," in *ChLA Quarterly,* Vol. 12:3 (1987).

Diane Barone. "The Written Responses of Young Children: Beyond Comprehension to Story Understanding," in *The New Advocate,* Vol. 3:1 (1990).

Nina Bawden. "Returning to *The Secret Garden*," in *Children's Literature in Education*, Vol. 19:3 (1988).

Temma Berg. *"Anne of Green Gables:* A Girl's Reading," in *Children's Literature Association Quarterly*, Vol. 13:3 (1988).

Shauna Bigham, Darwin Henderson, JoAnn Martin, and Jill P. May. "It's All the Same But It's Really Different," in *Journal of Children's Literature*, Vol. 20:1 (1994).

Carol Billman. "The Child Reader as Sleuth," in *Children's Literature in Education*, Vol. 15:1 (1984).

Phyllis Bixler. *"I am the Cheese* and Reader-Response Criticism in the Adolescent Literature Classroom," in *Children's Literature Association Quarterly*, Vol. 10:1 (1985).

Hamida Bosmajian. "Tricks of the Text and Acts of Reading by Censors and Adolescents," in *Children's Literature in Education*, Vol. 18:2 (1987).

Marcia Burchby. "Literature and Whole Language," in *The New Advocate*, Vol. 1:2 (1988).

Bruce Chadwick. "A Theory of Writing for Young Children: Arguing for a Moffett-Vygotsky Reading of Beverly Cleary's *Dear Mr. Henshaw*," in *The Lion and the Unicorn*, Vol. 11:2 (1987).

Deborah A. Charren. "'They're Just 'Avageratting'' The Influence of Peers on Children's Oral Responses to Fiction Through Letter Writing," in *The CLA Bulletin*, Vol. 16:2 (1990).

Barbara Chatton. "Middle School Students Respond to Marc Talbert's Books," in *The CLA Bulletin*, Vol. 16:2 (1990).

Meredith Rogers Cherland. "Gendered Readings: Cultural Restraints Upon Response to Literature," in *The New Advocate*, Vol. 3:3 (1992).

Beverly Lynn Clark. "Fairy Godmothers or Wicked Stepmothers? The Uneasy Relationship of Feminist Theory and Children's Criticism," in *Children's Literature Association Quarterly*, Vol. 18:4 (1993–94).

Marilyn Cochran-Smith. "Looking for the Roots of the Reading Process: Some Directions for Study (Part I)," in *Children's Literature Association Quarterly*, Vol. 7:1 (1982).

———. "Looking for the Roots of the Reading Process (part II)" in *Children's Literature Association Quarterly*, Vol. 7:4 (1982/83).

———. "Reading Stories to Young Children," in *Children's Literature Association Quarterly*, Vol. 10:2 (1985).

Robert Coles. "The Child's Understanding of Tragedy," in *Children's Literature*, Vol. 15 (1987).

Christopher Collier. "Historical Novels in the Classroom: What They Can Do and How They Should Do It," in *The Bulletin of the Children's Literature Assembly*, Vol. 8:1 (1982).

Hugh Crago. "Why Readers Read What Writers Write," in *Children's Literature in Education*, Vol. 24:3 (1993).

———. "The Roots of Response," in *Children's Literature Association Quarterly*, Vol. 10:3 (1985).

Maureen Crago. "Creating and Comprehending the Fantastic: A Study of a Child from Twenty to Thirty-five Months," in *Children's Literature in Education*, Vol. 24: 3 (1993).

Boyd H. Davis. "Tangle in the Story Line," in *Children's Literature in Education*, Vol. 16:4 (1985).

Mary M. Dekker. "Books, Reading, and Response: A Teacher-Researcher Tells a Story," in *The New Advocate*, Vol. 4:1 (1991).

Aurelia Davila de Silva. "Prospective Elementary Teachers Respond to *Roll of Thunder, Hear My Cry*," in *The CLA Bulletin*, Vol. 17:3 (1991).

Anne Haas Dyson. "The Role of Stories in the Social Imagination of Childhood and Beyond," in *The New Advocate*, Vol. 3:3 (1990).

Barbara Edwards. "'Wouldn't Pa Be Amazed!' Connecting with Literature through Conversation," in *The New Advocate*, Vol. 4:4 (1991).

Maryann Eeds and Ralph Peterson. "Teachers as Readers: Learning to Talk About Literature," in *Journal of Children's Literature*, Vol. 20:1 (1994).

Elyse Eidman-Aadahl. "The Solitary Reader: Exploring How Lonely Reading Has to Be," in *The New Advocate*, Vol. 1:3 (1988).

Harriett H. Ennis. "Learning to Respond to Literature (Part 1): A Theoretical Framework for Investigation," in *Children's Literature Association Quarterly*, Vol. 11:2 (1986).

———. "Learning to Respond to Literature (Part II) : What counts in the classroom," in *Children's Literature Association Quarterly*, Vol. 12:2 (1987).

Virginia Burke Epstein. "Moral Reading: Children's Literature as Moral Education," in *Children's Literature Association Quarterly*, Vol. 11:2 (1986).

Kerry McNeil Evans. "Reading Aloud: A Bridge to Independence," in *The New Advocate*, Vol. 5:1 (1992).

Anne V. Farnsworth. "The Evaluation of Children's Responses to Fiction Through Letter Writing," in *The CLA Bulletin*, Vol. 16:2 (1990).

Cora Lee Five. "From Workbook to Workshop: Increasing Children's Involvement in the Classroom," in *The New Advocate*, Vol. 1:2 (1988).

Mary G. Flender. "Charting Book Discussions: A Method of Presenting Literature in the Elementary Grades," in *Children's Literature in Education*, Vol. 16:2 (1985).

Lorraine Foreman-Peck. "Evaluating Children's Talk about Literature: A Theoretical Perspective," in *Children's Literature in Education*, Vol. 16:4 (1985).

Lee Galda. "Readers, Texts, and Contexts: A Response-Based View of Literature in the Classroom," in *The New Advocate*, Vol. 1:2 (1988).

Charlene E. Gates. "Image, Imagination, and Initiation: Teaching as a Rite of Passage in the Novels of L. M. Montgomery and Laura Ingalls Wilder," in *Children's Literature in Education*, Vol. 20:3 (1989).

Carol Gay. "Reading, Writing, and the Community," in *Children's Literature in Education*, Vol. 16:2 (1985).

David Gooderham. "Still Catching Them Young? The Moral Dimension in Young People's Books," in *Children's Literature in Education*, Vol. 24:2 (1993).

John Gough. "Experiencing a Sequence of Poems: Ted Hughes's *Season Songs*," in *Children's Literature Association Quarterly*, Vol. 13:4 (1988).

———. "Poems in a Context: Breaking the Anthology Trap," in *Children's Literature in Education*, Vol. 15:4 (1984).

William and Betty Greenway. "Meeting the Muse: Teaching Contemporary Poetry by Teaching Poetry Writing," in *Children's Literature Association Quarterly*, Vol. 15:3 (1990).

Daniel D. Hade. "Being Literary in a Literature-Based Classroom," in *Children's Literature in Education*, Vol. 22:1 (1991).

———. "Children, Stories, and Narrative Transformations," in *Research in the Teaching of English*, Vol. 22 (1988).

Joyce Hanson. "Whose Story Is It?" in *The New Advocate*, Vol. 3:3 (1990).

Alethea Helbig. "Curriculum Planning in Literature for Children: Ways to Go," in *ChLA Quarterly*, Vol. 10:4 (1986).

Linnea Hendrickson. "Literary Criticism as a Source of Teaching Ideas," in *Children's Literature Association Quarterly*, Vol. 9:4 (1984–85).

Susan Hepler. "A Guide for the Teacher Guides: Doing It Yourself," in *The New Advocate*, Vol. 1:3 (1988).

———. "Reading Between the Guide Lines," in *Children's Literature in Education*, Vol. 19:1 (1988).

———. "Talking Our Way to Literacy in the Classroom Community," in *The New Advocate*, Vol. 4:3 (1991).

Sandra Josephs Hoffman. "Developing a Literary Orientation: A Parent Diary," in *ChLA Quarterly*, Vol. 8:3 (1983).

Kathleen Holland. "If We Use Children's Literature in Our Classroom, What's the Theory?" in *The CLA Bulletin*, Vol. 16:2 (1990).

Peter Hollindale. "The Critic and the Child," in *Signal*, No. 65 (May 1991).

Rachael Hungerford. "Creating Meaning: Preschoolers Responding to Literature," in *The CLA Bulletin*, Vol. 16:2 (1990).

Caroline Hunt. "Counterparts: Identity Exchange and the Young Adult Audience," in *ChLA Quarterly*, Vol. 11:3 (1986).

Nancy Huse. "*Sounder* and Its Readers: Learning to Observe," in *Children's Literature Association Quarterly*, Vol. 12:2 (1987).

Rosemary Oliphant Ingham and Barbara G. Samuels. "Using Literature to Connect Reading and Writing," in *The CLA Bulletin*, Vol. 14:1 (1988).

Kathleen T. Isaacs. "*Go Ask Alice:* What Middle Schoolers Choose to Read," in *The New Advocate*, Vol. 5:2 (1992).

David Jackson. "First Encounters: The Importance of Initial Responses to Literature," in *Children's Literature in Education*, Vol. 11:4 (1980).

Leland Jacobs. "Children and the Voices of Literature," in *The Advocate*, Vol. 3:1 (1983).

Paul B. Janeczko. "Confessions of a Collector," in *Children's Literature Association Quarterly*, Vol. 12:2 (1987).

Adrienne E. Kertzer. "Inventing the Child Reader: How We Read Children's Books," in *Children's Literature in Education*, Vol. 15:1 (1984).

Barbara Z. Kiefer. "The Child and the Picture Book: Creating Live Circuits," in *ChLA Quarterly*, Vol. 11:2 (1986).

Eric A. Kimmel. "Children's Literature Without Children," in *Children's Literature in Education*, Vol. 13:1 (1982).

Gillian Klein. "'Is Going Two Days Now the Pot Turn Down': Stories for All," in *Children's Literature in Education*, Vol. 17:1 (1986).

S. A. Koeller. "The Child's Voice: Literature Conversation," in *Children's Literature in Education*, Vol. 19:1 (1988).

Karla Kuskin. "Introducing Poetry and Children to Each Other," in *Proceedings of the Eighth Annual Conference of the Children's Literature Association*, March 1981. Priscilla Ord, ed.

Linda Leonard Lamme. "Same Book—Different Perspectives," in *The CLA Bulletin*, Vol. 16:2 (1990).

Sonia Landes. "Picture Books as Literature," in *Children's Literature Association Quarterly*, Vol. 10:2 (1985).

Nancy Larrick. "Give Us Books! . . . But *Also* . . . Give Us Wings!" in *The New Advocate*, Vol. 4:2 (1991).

Barbara A. Lehman. "Child Reader and Literary Work: Children's Literature Merges Two Perspectives," in *Children's Literature Association Quarterly*, Vol. 14:3 (1989).

Richard Lewis. "The Blossom Shaping: An Exploration of Chinese Poetry with Children," in *Children's Literature Association Quarterly*, Vol. 12:4 (1987).

———. "Huddling in a Corner: Children and Their Stories," in *Children's Literature in Education*, Vol. 14:4 (1983).

Myra Cohn Livingston. "Poetry: How? and Why?" *Proceedings of the Seventh Annual Conference of the Children's Literature Association*, March 1980.

Rebecca Lukens. "Why Children's Literature Should Be Taken Seriously," in *Children's Literature Association Quarterly*, Vol. 11:3 (1986).

Amy McClure. "Poetry: Six Current Anthologies," in *The CLA Bulletin*, Vol. 15:1 (1989).

Ruth MacDonald. "Children's Literature and Pre-Professional Students: The National Endowment for the Humanities," in *Children's Literature Association Quarterly*, Vol. 7:2 (1982).

Rod McGillis. "The Child Is Critic: Using Children's Responses in the University Classroom," in *Children's Literature Association Quarterly*, Vol. 10:1 (1985).

Margaret Mackey. "Many Spaces: Some Limitations of Single Readings," in *Children's Literature in Education*, Vol. 24:3 (1993).

———. "Ramona the Chronotope: The Young Reader and Social Theories of Narrative," in *Children's Literature in Education*, Vol. 22:2 (1991).

Jack Maguire. "Sounds and Sensibilities: Storytelling as an Educational Process," in *Children's Literature Association Quarterly*, Vol. 13:1 (1988).

Anthony L. Manna. "In Pursuit of the Crystal Image: Lee Bennett Hopkins' Poetry Anthologies," in *Children's Literature Association Quarterly*, Vol. 10:2 (1985).

Stuart Marriott. "'Me mum she says it's bigotry': Children's responses to *The Twelfth Day of July*," in *Children's Literature in Education*, Vol. 16:1 (1985).

Gareth Matthews. "Philosophy as Child's Play," in *Work and Play in Children's Literature: Selected Papers from the 1990 International Conference of the Children's Literature Association*, Susan R. Gannon and Ruth Anne Thompson, eds. New York: Pace University, 1990.

Jill P. May. "Creating a School Wide Literature Program: A Case Study," in *ChLA Quarterly*, Vol. 12:3 (1987).

———. "Exploring Book Illustration as a Work of Art," in *The CLA Bulletin*, Vol. 17:2 (1991).

———. "Judy Blume as Archie Bunker," in *Children's Literature Association Quarterly*, Vol. 9:1 (1984).

———. "On Becoming: Children and Poetry," in *The CLA Bulletin*, Vol. 16:1 (1990).

———. "Using Folklore in the Classroom," in *English Education*, Vol. 11 (1980).

———. "What Content Should Be Taught in Children's Literature," in *ChLA Quarterly*, Vol. 16:4 (1991).

Nina Mikkelsen. "Literature and the Storymaking Powers of Children," in *ChLA Quarterly*, Vol. 9:1 (1984).

Virginia Monseau. "The Adolescent as 'Mock Reader': Some Thoughts for the Teacher of Literature," in *ChLA Quarterly*, Vol. 12:3 (1987).

Argiro L. Morgan. "Reading Between the Lines of Dialogue in Children's Books: Using the Pragmatics of Language," in *Children's Literature in Education,* Vol. 20:4 (1989).

Elaine Moss. "Feeding the Artist [Literacy through Literature: Children's Books Make a Difference]," in *Signal,* Vol. 64 (1991).

Roni Natov. "Stories We Need to Hear, Or the Reader and the Tale," in *The Lion and the Unicorn,* Vol. 9 (1985).

Peter Neumeyer. "Children's Literature in the English Department," in *Children's Literature Association Quarterly,* Vol. 12:3 (1987).

W. Nikola-Lisa. "Letters, Twigs, Hats and Peter's Chair: Object Play in the Picture Books of Ezra Jack Keats," in *ChLA Quarterly,* Vol. 16:4 (1991).

———. "Read Aloud, Play a Lot: Children's Responses to Literature," in *The New Advocate,* Vol. 4:3 (1992).

Kimie Nix. "On Producing Brand-new Book Lovers," in *Children's Association Quarterly,* Vol. 12:3 (1987).

Billie Nodelman. "Science Books, Science Education, and the Religion of Science," in *Children's Literature Association Quarterly,* Vol. 12:4 (1987).

Perry Nodelman. "Talking About, and Teaching About, Pleasure," in *Children's Literature Association Quarterly,* Vol. 12:3 (1987).

———. "Teaching a Unit of Fairy Tales," in *ChLA Quarterly,* Vol. 7:2 (1982).

———. "Teaching Children, or Teaching Subjects," in *Children's Literature Association Quarterly,* Vol. 10:2 (1985).

———. "Teaching Children's Literature: An Intellectual Snob Confronts Generalizations," in *Children's Literature in Education,* Vol. 17:4 (1986).

Laura Apol Obbink. "The Book Needs You: Gary Paulsen's *The Winter Room* as a Writerly Text," in *The New Advocate,* Vol. 3:3 (1992).

Kathy L. O'Brien. "A Look at One Successful Literature Program," in *The New Advocate,* Vol. 4:2 (1991).

Michael O'Hara. "'Anything Goes' . . . Connecting Children to Literature-Based Classrooms," in *Children's Literature in Education,* Vol. 21:2 (1990).

Marilyn M. Ohlhausen and Mary Jepsen. "Lessons from Goldilocks: 'Somebody's Been Choosing My Books but I Can Make My Own Choices Now!'" in *The New Advocate,* Vol. 5:1 (1992).

Jack Ousbey. "'Little Factories of Understanding,'" in *Children's Literature in Education,* Vol. 11:4 (1980).

Roger Poole. "The Books Teachers Use," in *Children's Literature in Education,* Vol. 17:3 (1986).

David Pritchard. "'Daddy, Talk!': Thoughts on Reading Early Picture Books," in *The Lion and the Unicorn,* Vol. 7/8 (1983/84).

Robert Protherough. "How Children Judge Stories," in *Children's Literature in Education,* Vol. 14:1 (1983).

Victoria Purcell-Gates. "Fairy Tales in the Clinic: Children Seek Their Own Meanings," in *Children's Literature in Education,* Vol. 20:4 (1989).

S. Jeanne Reardon. "The Development of Critical Readers: A Look into the Classroom," in *The New Advocate,* Vol. 1:1 (1988).

Edward J. Rielly. "Reading and Writing Haiku in the Classroom," in *Children's Literature Association Quarterly,* Vol. 13:3 (1988).

Laura Robb. "Building Bridges: Eighth and Third Graders Read Together," in *The New Advocate,* Vol. 4:3 (1991).

———. "More Poetry, Please," in *The New Advocate,* Vol. 3:3 (1990).

Lucy W. Rollin. "Exploring Earthsea: A Sixth Grade Literature Project," in *Children's Literature in Education,* Vol. 16:4 (1985).

Judith B. Rosenfeld. "A Middle School Newbery Banquet," in *The CLA Bulletin,* Vol. 15:2 (1989).

Gary M. Salvner. "Readers as Performers: The Literature Game," in *ChLA Quarterly,* Vol. 12:3 (1987).

Charles Sarland. "Piaget, Blyton, and Story: Children's Play and the Reading Process," in *Children's Literature in Education,* Vol. 16:2 (1985).

Elizabeth Segel. "Collaborations: Putting Children's Literature Expertise to Work for Children at Risk," in *Where Rivers Meet: Confluence and Concurrents.* Susan R. Gannon and Ruth Anne Thompson, eds. New York: Pace University, 1989.

———. "Pushing Preschool Literacy: Equal Opportunity or Cultural Imperialism?" in *Children's Literature Association Quarterly,* Vol. 11:2 (1986).

———. "Side-by-Side Storybook Reading for Every Child: An Impossible Dream?" in *The New Advocate,* Vol. 3:2 (1990).

David Self. "A Lost Asset? The Historical Novel in the Classroom," in *Children's Literature in Education,* Vol. 22:1 (1991).

Patrick Shannon. "Unconscious Censorship of Social and Political Ideas in Children's Books," in *Children's Literature Association Quarterly,* Vol. 12:2 (1987).

Donna Fellows Skolnick. "Reading Relationships," in *The New Advocate,* Vol. 5:2 (1992).

Sarah Smedman. "Children, Literature, and ChLA: A Plea for a New Literate Age," in *Children's Literature Association Quarterly,* Vol. 18.4 (1993).

Marilou Sorenson and Kim Ruckman. "Joyful Noise: Poems for Two Voices— Some Teaching Suggestions," in *The CLA Bulletin,* Vol. 15:1 (1989).

Dorothy Stephens. "First Graders Taking the Lead: Building Bridges Between Literature and Writing," in *The New Advocate,* Vol. 2:4 (1989).

D. H. Stewart. "*Stalky* and the Language of Education," in *Children's Literature,* Vol. 20 (1992).

John Warren Stewig. "Participation Storytelling," in *The CLA Bulletin,* Vol. 16:1 (1990).

———. "Reading Pictures, Reading Text: Some Similarities," in *The New Advocate,* Vol. 5:1 (1992).

Jon C. Stott. "'It's not what you expect': Teaching Irony to Third Graders," in *Children's Literature in Education,* Vol. 13:4 (1982).

———. "The Spiralled Sequence Story Curriculum: A Structuralist Approach to Teaching Fiction in the Elementary Schools," in *Children's Literature in Education,* Vol. 18:3 (1987).

Sharon Stutzman and Susan Hepler. "The Three Bears Go to Kindergarten," in *The CLA Bulletin,* Vol. 16:1 (1990).

Jan Susina. "Editor's Note: The Dumbing Down of Children's Literature," in *The Lion and the Unicorn,* Vol. 17:1 (1993).

Mary-Agnes Taylor. "The Literary Transformation of a Sluggard," in *Children's Literature,* Vol. 12 (1984).

Charles Temple. "Seven Readings of a Folktale: Literary Theory in the Classroom," in *The New Advocate,* Vol. 4:1 (1991).

Jack Thomson. "Adolescents and Literary Responses: The Development of Readers," in *Children's Literature Association Quarterly,* Vol. 15:4 (1990).

Joan Russell Thron. "Children's Literature: Reading, Seeing, Watching," in *Children's Literature in Education*, Vol. 22:1 (1991).

Ann M. Trousdale. "Let the Children Tell Us: The Meanings of Fairy Tales for Children," in *The New Advocate*, Vol. 2:2 (1989).

Ann M. Trousdale and Violet J. Harris. "Missing Links in Literary Response," in *Children's Literature in Education*, Vol. 24:3 (1993).

Donna L. Waldron. "A 'Quiet' Response to Literature," in *The CLA Bulletin*, Vol. 16:2 (1990).

Liz Waterland. "Finding Their Levels While Losing Our Balance?" in *Signal*, Vol. 67 (1992).

Tony Watkins. "Mapping the Magnetic Field," in *Children's Literature Association Quarterly*, Vol. 12:1 (1987).

———. "Second Thoughts on Socialization through Literature for Children," in *The Lion and the Unicorn*, Vol. 5 (1981).

James Zarrillo. "Theory Becomes Practice: Aesthetic Teaching with Literature," in *The New Advocate*, Vol. 4:4 (1991).

Jack Zipes. "The Function of the Fairy Tale," in *The Lion and the Unicorn*, Vol. 12:2 (1988).

History

Books

Gillian Avery. *Nineteenth Century Children: Heroes and Heroines in English Children's Stories 1780–1900*. London: Hodder and Stoughton Limited, 1965.

Jane Bingham, ed. *Writers for Children*. New York: Scribner's, 1988.

Penny Brown. *The Captured World: The Child and Childhood in Nineteenth-Century Women's Writing in England*. New York: St. Martin's Press, 1993.

Francelia Butler and Richard Rotert, eds. *Reflections on Literature for Children*. Hamden, CT: Library Professional Publications, 1984.

John H. Cary and Julius Weinberg. *The Social Fabric: American Life from 1607 to the Civil War*. Second Edition. Boston: Little, Brown and Company, 1978.

George Dekker. *The American Historical Novel*. Cambridge, England: Cambridge University Press, 1987.

Simon Dentith. *A Rhetoric of the Real: Studies in Post-Englightenment Writing from 1790 to the Present*. Hemel Hempstead, Great Britain: Harvester Wheatsheaf, 1990.

Juliet Dusinberre. *Alice to the Lighthouse: Children's Books and Radical Experiments in Art*. New York: St Martin's Press, 1987.

Sarah Elbert. *A Hunger for Home: Louisa May Alcott and* Little Women. Philadelphia: Temple University Press, 1984.

Carol Fairbanks. *Prairie Women: Images in American and Canadian Fiction*. New Haven: Yale University Press, 1986.

Kate Flint. *Woman Reader, 1837–1914*. Pittsburgh: University of Pittsburgh Press, 1993.

James H. Fraser, ed. *Society & Children's Literature*. Boston: David R. Godine, Publishers, 1978.

Sandra Gilbert and Susan Gubar. *The Madwoman in the Attic: The Woman Writer and the Nineteenth-Century Literary Imagination*. New Haven: Yale University Press, 1979.

June Howard. *Form and History in American Literary Naturalism.* Chapil Hill: The University of North Carolina Press, 1985.

Alice M. Jordan. *Children's Classics.* Boston: The Horn Book, Inc., 1976.

Frank Kermode. *Poetry, Narrative, History.* Oxford, England: Basil Blackwell, Inc., 1990.

Elizabeth Lennox Keyser. *Whispers in the Dark: The Fiction of Louise May Alcott.* Knoxville: University of Tennessee Press, 1994.

Jerome Klinkowitz. *The Practice of Fiction in America: Writers from Hawthorne to the Present.* Ames: The Iowa State University Press, 1980.

Mary Llystad. *From Dr. Mather to Dr. Seuss: 200 Years of American Books for Children.* Cambridge: Schenkman Publishing Co., 1980.

Roderick McGillis, ed. *For the Childlike: George MacDonald's Fantasies for Children.* Metuchen, NJ: Scarecrow Press, 1992.

Anne MacLeod. *American Childhood: Essays on Children's Literature of the Nineteenth and Twentieth Centuries.* Athens: University of Georgia Press, 1994.

Eva Marie Metcalf. *Children in the Prime of Their Lives.* Hamden, CT: Garland Publishing, 1993.

Alison Millbank. *Daughters of the House: Modes of the Gothic in Victorian Fiction.* New York: St. Martin's Press, 1992.

Claudia Nelson. *Boys Will be Girls: The Feminine Ethic and British Children's Fiction, 1857–1917.* New Brunswick, NJ: Rutgers University Press, 1991.

Jeffrey Richards, ed. *Imperialism and Juvenile Literature.* Manchester, England: Manchester University Press, 1989.

Samuel F. Pickering. *Moral Instruction and Fiction for Children, 1749–1820.* Athens: University of Georgia Press, 1993.

Elaine Showalter, ed. *Alternative Alcott.* New Brunswick, NJ: Rutgers University Press, 1988.

Alan Sinfield. *Literature, Politics and Culture in Postwar Britain.* Berkeley: University of California Press, 1989.

Winifred Whitehead. *Old Lies Revisited: Young Readers and the Literture of War and Violence.* Pluto Press, 1991.

Articles

Joan Aiken. "Interpreting the Past," in *Children's Literature in Education,* Vol. 16:2 (1985).

Betty Baker. "History vs. The Writer," in *The Bulletin: Newsletter of the Children's Literature Assembly,* Vol. 10:1 (1984).

Joshua Brown. "Telling the History of *All* Americans: Milton Meltzer, Minorities, and the Restoration of the Past," in *The Lion and the Unicorn,* Vol. 11:1 (1987).

Marian E. Brown. "Three Versions of 'A Little Princess': How the Story Developed," in *Children's Literature in Education,* Vol. 19:4 (1988).

Robert DiYanni. "Kenneth Koch Revisited," in *Children's Literture Association Quarterly,* Vol. 9:1 (1984).

Susan Drain. "Community and the Individual in *Anne of Green Gables,*" *Children's Literature Association Quarterly,* Vol. 11:1 (1986).

Ann Hass Dyson. "The Role of Stories in the Social Imagination of Childhood and Beyond," in *The New Advocate,* Vol. 3:3 (1990).

Charles Frey. "Laura and Pa: Family and Landscape in *Little House on the Prairie*," in *Children's Literature Association Quarterly*, Vol. 12:3 (1987).

Susan Gannon. "The Illustrator as Interpreter: N. C. Wyeth's Illustrations for the Adventure Novels of Robert Louis Stevenson," in *Children's Literature*, Vol. 19 (1991).

Carol Gay. "'Kindred Spirits' All: Green Gables Revisited," in *Children's Literature Association Quarterly*, Vol. 11:1 (1986).

Joan Glazer. "Nuclear Holocaust in Contemporary Children's Fiction: A Surprising Amount of Agreement," in *Children's Literature Association Quarterly*, Vol. 11:2 (1986).

James Goldman. "Selling American History," in *The Lion and the Unicorn*, Vol. 6 (1982).

Erik Haugaard. "When Does the Past Become History?" in *The Child and Family: Selected Papers form the 1988 International Conference of the Children's Literature Association, College of Charleston*. New York: ChLA, 1988.

Paul Heins. "History Alive: Some Considerations," in *The Bulletin of the Children's Literature Assembly*, Vol. 8:1 (1982).

Alethea Helbig. "Presidential Address," in *Children's Literature Association Quarterly*, Vol. 9:4 (1984–85).

Janet Hickman. "The How and Why of Historical Literature," in *The Bulletin of the Children's Literature Assembly*, Vol. 8:1 (1982).

Sylvia Patterson Iskander. "Anne Frank's Autobiographical Style," in *Children's Literature Association Quarterly*, Vol. 16:2 (1991).

———. "Anne Frank's Changing Familial Relationships," in *The Child and the Family: Selected Papers from the 1988 International Conference of the Children's Literature Association*. New York: Pace University, 1988.

Winfred Kaminski. "War and Peace in Recent German Children's Literature," in *Children's Literature*, Vol. 15 (1987).

Diana Kelly-Bryne. "The 1984 Conference of The Children's Literature Association, Charlotte, North Carolina, May 24–27: A Participant's Response," in *Children's Literature Association Quarterly*, Vol. 9:4 (1984–85).

Beverly Klatt. "Abraham Lincoln: Deified Martyr, Flesh and Blood Hero, and a Man with Warts," in *Children's Literature in Education*, Vol. 23:3 (1992).

Katherine Lasky. "The Fiction of History: Or, What Did Miss Kitty Really Do?" in *The New Advocate*, Vol. 3:3 (1990).

Elizabeth Lennox Keyser. "Domesticity versus Identity: A Review of Alcott Research," in *Children's Literature in Education*, Vol. 16:3 (1985).

Millicent Lenz. "The Two-Handed Drinking Cup: Imagination in Four Historical Novels by Erik Christian Haugaard," in *Children's Literature Association Quarterly*, Vol. 15:1 (1990).

Robert Lipsyte. "Presenting the Past in Words," in *The Bulletin of the Children's Literature Assembly*, Vol. 8:1 (1982).

Ruth MacDonald. "The Progress of the Pilgrims in *Little Women*," in *Proceedings of the Seventh Annual Conference of the Children's Literature Association*, March 1980.

James Alan McPherson, "Going Up to Atlanta," in *A World Unsuspected: Portraits of Southern Childhood*, edited by Alex Harris. Chapel Hill: University of North Carolina Press, 1987.

Jill P. May. "Spirited Females of the Nineteenth Century: Liberated Moods in

Louisa M. Alcott's *Little Women,*" in *Children's Literature in Education,* Vol. 11 (1980).

Milton Meltzer. "Selective Forgetfulness: Christopher Columbus Remembered," in *The New Advocate,* Vol. 5:1 (1992).

Elisabeth-Christine Mulsch. "S.O.S. New York: German-Jewish Authors of Children's Literature in American Exile," in *The Lion and the Unicorn,* Vol. 14:1 (1990).

Jean Perrot. "War and Compulsion of Signs: Maurois's Rite of Initiation," in *Children's Literature,* Vol. 15 (1987).

Alan Richardson. "Reluctant Lords and Lame Princes: Engendering the Male Child in Nineteenth-Century Juvenile Fiction," in *Children's Literature,* Vol. 21 (1993).

Peter Roop. "Scott O'Dell: Using History to Tell His Story," in *Children's Literature Association Quarterly,* Vol. 12:4 (1987).

Masha Kabakow Rudman and Susan P. Rosenberg. "Confronting History: Holocaust Books for Children," in *The New Advocate,* Vol. 4:3 (1991).

Elizabeth Segal. "Realism and Children's Literature: Notes from a Historical Perspective," in *The First Steps: The Best of the Early ChLA Quarterly.* West Lafayette, IN: ChLA Publications, 1984.

Daniel Shealy. "'Families Are the Most Beautiful Things': The Myths and Facts of Louisa May Alcott's March Family in *Little Women,*" in *The Child and Family: Selected Papers from the 1988 International Conference of the Children's Literature Association.*

John Warren Stewig. "A Literary and Linguistic Analysis of Scott O'Dell's *The Captive,*" in *Children's Literature Association Quarterly,* Vol. 14:3 (1989).

Malcolm Usrey. "A Milestone of Historical Fiction for Children: *Otto of the Silver Hand,*" in *Children's Literature Association Quarterly,* Vol. 8:3 (1983).

Caroline Zilboorg. "*Caddie Woodlawn:* A Feminist Study," in *Children's Literature in Education,* Vol. 21:2 (1990).

Daniel L. Zins. "Nuclear Education in the Post-Cold War Era," in *Children's Literature in Education,* Vol. 18:3 (1993).

Deanna Zitterkopf. "Prairies and Privations: The Impact of Place in Great Plains Homestead Fiction for Children," in *Children's Literature Association Quarterly,* Vol. 9:4 (1984–85).

Literary Patterns

Books

Celia Catlett Anderson and Marilyn Apseloff. *Nonsense Literature for Children: Aesop to Seuss.* Hamden, CT: Library Professional Publications, 1989.

Nina Auerbach. *Communities of Women: An Idea in Fiction.* Cambridge, MA: Harvard University Press, 1978.

Betty Bacon, ed. *How Much Truth Do We Tell the Children? The Politics of Children's Literature.* Minneapolis: MEP Publications, 1988.

Barbara Bader. *American Picturebooks: From Noah's Ark to the Beast Within.* New York: Macmillan, 1975.

F. Anthony deJovine. *The Young Hero in American Fiction.* New York: Appleton-Century, 1971.

Gustavo Perez Firmat, ed. *Do the Americas Have a Common Literature?* Durham, NC: Duke University Press, 1990.

Rebecca Lukens. *A Critical Handbook of Children's Literature,* 4th ed. Glenview, IL: Scott, Foresman/Little, Brown Higher Education, 1990.

Lucinda Hardwick MacKethan. *The Dream of Arcady: Place and Time in Southern Literature.* Baton Rouge: Louisiana State University Press, 1980.

Susan Miller. *Rescuing the Subject: A Critical Introduction to Rhetoric and the Writer.* Carbondale: Southern Illinois University Press, 1989.

Jack Myers and David Wojahn, eds. *A Profile of American Poetry.* Carbondale: Southern Illinois University Press, 1991.

Robert Newsom. *A Likely Story: Probability and Play in Fiction.* New Brunswick, NJ: Rutgers University Press, 1988.

Perry Nodelman. *The Pleasures of Children's Literature.* New York: Longman, 1992.

Charlotte F. Otten and Gary D. Schmidt, eds. *The Voice of the Narrator in Children's Literature: Insights from Writers and Critics.* Wesport, CT: Greenwood Press, Inc., 1989.

Carol Pearson and Katherine Pope. *The Female Hero in American and British Literature.* New York: R. R. Bowker, 1981.

Lucy Rollin, ed. *The Antic Art: Enhancing Children's Literary Experiences through Film and Video.* Fort Atkinson, WI: Highsmith Press, 1993.

Paul Zweig. *The Adventurer.* New York: Basic Books, Inc., 1974.

Articles

Jane Agee. "Mothers and Daughters: Gender-Role Socialization in Two Newbery Award Books," in *Children's Literature in Education,* Vol. 24:3 (1993).

Celia Catlett Anderson. "Juvenile Editors on Style: A Survey Report," in *Children's Literarture Association Quarterly,* Vol. 10:3 (1985).

Arthur Arnold. "Big Bad Wolf," in *Children's Literature in Education,* Vol. 17:2 (1986).

Suzanne Barchers. "Beyond Disney: Reading and Writing Traditional and Alternative Fairy Tales," in *The Lion and the Unicorn,* Vol. 12:2 (1988).

Adam Berkin. "'I Woke Myself': *The Changeover* as a Modern Adaptation of 'Sleeping Beauty,'" in *Children's Literature in Education,* Vol. 21:4 (1990).

Hamida Bosmajian. "Conventions of Image and Form in Nuclear War Narratives for Young Readers," in *Papers on Language and Literature,* Vol. 26 (1990).

———. "Vastness and Contraction of Space in *Little House on the Prairie,*" in *Children's Literature,* Vol. 11 (1983).

Ruth B. Bottigheimer. "Iconographic Continuity in Illustrations of "The Goosegirl," in *Children's Literature,* Vol. 13 (1985).

Marianne Carus. "Translation and Internationalism in Children's Literature," in *Children's Literature in Education,* Vol. 11:4 (1980).

Christopher Clausen. "Home and Away in Children's Literature," in *Children's Literature,* Vol. 10 (1982).

Barbara Elleman. "The International Trends in Children's Literature," in *The CLA Bulletin,* Vol. 15:1 (1989).

William Epstein. "Inducing Biography," in *Children's Literature Association Quarterly,* Vol. 12:4 (1987).

Susan Gannon. "One More Time: Approaches to Repetition in Children's Literature," in *Children's Literature Association Quarterly*, Vol. 12:1 (1987).

Charlene E. Gates. "Image, Imagination, and Initiation: Teaching as a Rite of Passage in the Novels of L. M. Montgomery and Laura Ingalls Wilder," in *Children's Literature in Education*, Vol. 20:3 (1989).

John Gough. "Rivalry, Rejection, and Recovery: Variations of the Cinderella Story," in *Children's Literaure in Education*, Vol. 21:2 (1990).

Betty Greenway. "Island in the Stream: Island Literature for Children and Adults," in *The New Advocate*, Vol. 3:4 (1990).

Jerry Griswold. "There's No Place Like Home: *The Wizard of Oz*," in *The Antioch Review*, Vol. 45 (1987).

Diane Gunstra. "The Island Pattern," in *Children's Literature Association Quarterly*, Vol. 10:2 (1985).

John H. Hafner. "Southern Places in Adolescent Fiction," in *Children's Literature Association Quarterly*, Vol. 12:2 (1987).

Margaret Hamilton. "There's No Place Like Home," in *Children's Literature*, Vol. 10 (1982).

William Harmon. "Lear, Limericks, and Some Other Verse Forms," in *Children's Literature*, Vol. 10 (1982).

Michael Harrawood. "The Child on the Desert Isle: The Robinsonade and Family Formation," in *The Child and Family: Selected Papers from the 1988 International Conference of The Children's Literature Association*. New York: Pace University, 1988.

Barbara Harrison. "Howl Like the Wolves," in *Children's Literature*, Vol. 15 (1987).

Alethea K. Helbig. "The Forest as Setting and Symbol in Barbara Willard's Mantlemass Novels," in *Children's Literature Association Quarterly*, Vol. 7:1 (1982).

Ann Meinzen Hildebrand. "The Dreary Time: The Ethos of School in Award-Winning Fiction for Children," in *Children's Literature Association Quarterly*, Vol. 11:2 (1986).

Corinne Hirsch. "Perspectives on Literary Realism: A Review," in *The First Steps: The Best of the Early ChLA Quarterly*. West Lafayette, In: ChLA Publications, 1984.

Nancy Huse. "Journeys of the Mother in the World of Green Gables," in *Proceedings of the Thirteenth Annual Conference of the Children's Literature Association*, May 1986.

U. C. Knoepfflmacher. "Female Power and Male Self-Assertion: Kipling and the Maternal," in *Children's Literature*, Vol. 20 (1992).

Lois Kuznets. "Fiction, Faction, and Formula in the Regional Novels of Lois Lenski," in *Proceedings of the Ninth Annual Conference of the Children's Literature Association*. Gainesville: University of Florida, 1982.

———. "Permutations of Frame in Mary Norton's 'Borrowers' Series," in *Studies in the Literary Imagination*, Vol. 18:2 (1985).

Lois Kuznets and Eve Zarin. "Sweet Dreams for Sleeping Beauties: Pre-Teen Romances," in *Children's Literature Association Quarterly*, Vol. 7:1 (1982).

Millicent Lenz. "Through Blight to Bliss: Thematic Motifs in Jill Paton Walsh's *Unleaving*," in *Children's Literature Association Quarterly*, Vol. 13:4 (1988).

Roderick McGillis. "'Secrets' and 'Sequence' in Children's Stories," in *Studies in the Literary Imagination*, Vol. 18:2 (1985).

Kathy Piehl Mankato. "Changing the Human Landscape in Picture Books," in *The New Advocate*, Vol. 4:4 (1991).

Jill P. May. "Dr. Seuss and *The 500 Hats of Bartholomew Cubbins*," in *The Bulletin: The Children's Literature Assembly*, Vol. 11:3 (1985).

———. "Illustration as Interpretation: Trina Hyman's Folk Tales," in *Children's Literature Association Quarterly*, Vol. 10:3 (1985).

Milton Meltzer. The possibilities of nonfiction: a writer's view," in *Children's Literature in Education*, Vol. 11:3 (1980).

John David Moore. "Pottering About in the Garden: Kenneth Grahame's Version of Pastoral in *The Wind in the Willows*," in *The Journal of Midwest Modern Language Association*, Vol. 23:1 (1990).

Anita Moss. "The Spear and the Piccolo: Heroic and Pastoral Dimensions of William Steig's *Dominic* and *Abel's Island*," in *Children's Literature*, Vol. 10 (1982).

Roni Natov. "The Truth of Ordinary Lives: Autobiographical Fiction for Children," in *Children's Literature in Education*, Vol. 17:2 (1986).

Peter Neumeyer. "How Picture Books Mean: The Case of Chris Van Allsburg," in *Children's Literature Association Quarterly*, Vol. 15:1 (1990).

Anne Royall Newman. "Images of the Bear in Children's Literature," in *Children's Literature in Education*, Vol. 18:3 (1987).

Ouida Nikola-Lisa. "Pirates, Pirates Over the Salt, Salt Sea," in *Children's Literature in Education*, Vol. 24:2 (1993).

———. "Scribbles, Scrawls, and Scratches: Graphic Play as Subtext in the Pictures of Ezra Jack Keats," in *Work and Play in Children's Literature: Selected Papers from the 1990 International Conference of the Children's Literature Association*. Susan R. Gannon and Ruth Anne Thompson, eds. New York: Pace University, 1990.

Perry Nodelman. "Non-fiction for Children: Does It Really Exist?" in *Children's Literature Association Quarterly*, Vol. 12:4 (1987).

———. "Text as Teacher: The Beginning of *Charlotte's Web*," in *Children's Literature*, Vol. 13 (1985).

Lucy Rollin. "The Reproduction of Mothering in *Charlotte's Web*," in *Children's Literature*, Vol. 18 (1990).

George Shannon. "Writing the Empty Cup: Rhythm and Sound as Content," in *Children's Literature*, Vol. 19 (1991).

Marilyn Solt. "The Uses of Setting in *Anne of Green Gables*," in *Children's Literature Association Quarterly*, Vol. 9:4 (1984–85).

J. D. Stahl. "Satire and the Evolution of Perspective in Children's Literature: Mark Twain, E. B. White, and Louise Fitzhugh," in *Children's Literature Association Quarterly*, Vol. 15:3 (1990).

Jon C. Stott. "From Here to Eternity: Aspects of Pastoral in the Green Knowe Series," in *Children's Literature*, Vol. 11 (1983).

Jon C. Stott and Christine Doyle Francis. "'Home' and 'Not Home' in Children's Stories: Getting There—and Being Worth It," in *Children's Literature in Education*, Vol. 24:3 (1993).

Joyce Thomas. "'There Was an Old Man . . .': The Sense of Nonsense Verse," in *Children's Literature Association Quarterly*, Vol. 10:3 (1985).

———. "Woods and Castles, Towers and Huts: Aspects of Setting in the Fairy Tale," in *Children's Literature in Edcuation*, Vol. 17.2 (1986).

Toby Jane Tetenbaum and Judith Pearson. "The Voices in Children's Literature: The Impact of Gender on the Moral Decisions of Storybook Characters," in *Sex Roles,* Vol. 20 (1989).

David Topper. "On Some Burdens Carried by Pictures," in *Children's Literature Association Quarterly,* Vol. 9:1 (1984).

Malcolm Usrey. "The Child Persona in *Taxis and Toadstools,*" in *Children's Literature Association Quarterly,* Vol. 7:2 (1982).

Lucy E. Waddey. "Home in Children's Fiction: Three Patterns," in *Children's Literature Assocation Quarterly,* Vol. 8:1 (1983).

Janet Weiss-Town. "Sexism Down on the Farm? *Anne of Green Gables,*" in *Children's Literature Association Quarterly,* Vol. 11:1 (1986).

Virginia Wolf. "The Linear Image: The Road and the River," in *Proceedings of the Thirteenth Annual Conference of the Children's Literature Association.* New York: Pace University, 1988.

———. "Paradise Lost? The Displacement of Myth in Children's Novels," in *Studies in the Literary Imagination,* Vol. 18:2 (1985).

Jane Yolen. "Magic Mirrors: Society Reflected in the Glass of Fantasy," in *Children's Literature Association Quarterly,* Vol. 11:2 (1986).

Minority Literature and Criticism

Books

Paula Gunn Allen. *The Sacred Hoop: Recovering the Feminine in American Indian Traditions.* Boston: Beacon Press, 1986.

Houston A. Baker, Jr. *The Journey Back: Issues in Black Literature and Criticism.* Chicago: University of Chicago Press, 1980.

Houston A. Baker, Jr., ed. *Three American Literatures: Essays in Chicano, Native American, and Asian-American Literature for Teachers of American Literature.* New York: The Modern Language Association of America, 1982.

Patricia Bell-Scott, ed. *Double Stitch: Black Women Write about Mothers and Daughters.* Boston: Beacon Press, 1991.

Sacvon Berovitch, ed. *Reconstructing American Literary History.* Cambridge, Mass: Harvard University Press, 1986.

Barbara Christian. *Black Women Novelists: The Development of a Tradition, 1892–1976.* Westport, CT: Greenwood Press, 1980.

Harvey A. Daniels, ed. *Not English Only: Affirming America's Multilingual Heritage.* Urbana, IL: The National Council of Teachers of English, 1990.

Melvin Dixon. *Ride Out the Wilderness: Geography and Identity in Afro-American Literature.* Urbana: University of Illinois Press, 1987.

Henry Louis Gates, Jr. *Figures in Black: Words, Signs, and the "Racial" Self.* New York: Oxford University Press, 1987.

Esther Mik Yung Ghymn. *Shapes and Styles of Asian-American Prose Fiction.* New York: Lang, 1992.

Dianne Johnson-Feelings. *Telling Tales: The Pedagogy and Promise of African-American Literature for Youth.* New York: Greenwood Press, 1990.

Albert Keiser. *The Indian in American Literature.* New York: Octagon—Farrar, Straus and Giroux, 1970.

Christa Kamenetsky. *Children's Literature in Hitler's Germany: The Cultural Policy of National Socialism.* Athens: Ohio University Press, 1984.

Albert Keiser. *The Indian in American Literature.* New York: Octagon—Farrar, Straus and Giroux, 1970.

Merri V. Lindgren, ed. *The Multicultured Mirror: Cultural Substance in Literature for Children and Young Adults.* Fort Atkinson, WI: Highsmith Press, 1991.

Donnarae MacCann and Gloria Woodard, eds. *The Black American in Books for Children: Readings in Racism.* Second Edition. Metchen, NJ: The Scarecrow Press, Inc., 1985.

Toni Morrison. *Playing in the Dark: Whiteness and the Literary Imagination.* Cambridge: Harvard University Press, 1992.

Oyekan Owomoyela. *Visions and Revisions: Essays on African Literatures and Criticism.* New York: Peter Lang Publishing, 1991.

Jerome Rothenberg. *Technicians of the Sacred: A Range of Poetics from Africa, America, Asia, & Oceania.* Garden City, NY: Doubleday, 1968.

A. LaVonne Brown Ruoff and Jerry W. Ward, Jr., eds. *Redefining American Literary History.* New York: The Modern Language Association of America, 1990.

Louis D. Rubin, Jr. *The Edge of the Swamp: A Study in the Literature and Society of the Old South.* Baton Rouge: Louisiana State University Press, 1989.

Rudine Sime. *Shadow and Substance: Afro-American Experience in Contemporary Children's Fiction.* Urbana, IL: National Council of Teachers of English, 1982.

Anna Lee Stensland. *Literature by and about the American Indian: An Annotated Bibliography.* Second Edition. Urbana, IL: The National Council of Teachers of English, 1979.

Arnulfo D. Trejo, ed. *The Chicanos: As We See Ourselves.* Tucson: The University of Arizona Press, 1980.

Susan Willis. *Specifying: Black Women Writing the American Experience.* Madison: The University of Wisconsin Press, 1987.

Articles

Marilyn Apseloff. "A Conversation with Virginia Hamilton," in *Children's Literature in Education,* Vol. 14:4 (1983).

———. "Creative Geography in the Ohio Novels of Virginia Hamilton," in *Children's Literature Association Quarterly,* Vol. 8:1 (1983).

Darcey H. Bradley. "John Steptoe: Retrospective of an Imagemaker," in *The New Advocate,* Vol. 4:1 (1991).

Carol Henderson Carpenter. "Native Folklore for Canadian Children," in *Proceedings of the Annual Conference of the Children's Literature Association, Harvard University.* Villanova, PA: ChLA, 1979.

John Cech. "Princess Redwing: Keeper of the Past," in *Children's Literature,* Vol. 10 (1982).

Marilyn Mei-Yang Chi. "Asserting Asian-American Children's Self and Cultural Identity through Asian-American Children's Literature," in *Social Studies Review,* Vol. 32 (1993).

Kirby Farrell. "Virginia Hamilton's *Sweet Whispers, Brother Rush* and the Case for a Radical Existential Criticism," in *Contemporary Literature,* Vol. 31 (1990).

Frances Smith Foster. "Literature for Children by Afro-American Writers: 1876–1986," in *Children's Literature Association Quarterly,* Vol. 13:1 (1988).

———. "What Matters the Color of the Tiger's Stripes?: The Significance of Bibliographies by Ethnic Identification," in *Children's Literature Association Quarterly*, Vol. 13:1 (1988).

Sandra Y. Govan. "Alice Childress's *Rainbow Jordon:* The Black Aesthetic in Adolescent Fiction," in *Children's Literature Association Quarterly*, Vol. 13:1 (1988).

Lucille H. Gregory. "The Puerto Rican 'Rainbow': Distortions vs. Complexities," in *Children's Literature Association Quarterly*, Vol. 18:1 (1993).

Virginia Hamilton. "The Known, the Remembered, and the Imagined: Celebrating Afro-American Folktales," in *Children's Literature in Education*, Vol. 18:2 (1987).

———. "On Being a Black Writer in America," in *The Lion and the Unicorn*, Vol. 9 (1986).

Mary Turner Harper. "Merger and Metamorphosis in the Fiction of Mildred D. Taylor," in *Children's Literature Association Quarterly*, Vol. 13:1 (1988).

Violet J. Harris. "No Invitations Required to Share Multicultural Literature," in *Journal of Children's Literature*, Vol. 20:1 (1994).

———. "Race Consciousness, Refinement, and Radicalism: Socialization in *The Brownies' Book*," in *Children's Literature Association Quarterly*, Vol. 14:4 (1989).

Darwin L. Henderson and Arlene Harris Mitchell. "Sharon Bell Mathis: Features of a Culture," in *Children's Literature Association Quarterly*, Vol. 13:1 (1988).

Craig Howes. "Hawaii Through Western Eyes: Orientalism and Historical Fiction for Children," in *The Lion and the Unicorn*, Vol. 11:1 (1987).

Karen Nelson Hoyle. "Resources for Study of Black Children's Literature at the University of Minnesota," in *Children's Literature Association Quarterly*, Vol. 13:1, (1988).

Guo Jian. "The Victorious Monkey: Favorite Figure in Chinese Literature for Children," in *Triumphs of the Spirit in Children's Literature*. Francelia Butler and Richard Rotert, eds. Hamden, CT: Library Professional Publications, 1986.

Dianne Johnson. "Brotherhood, Place and Identity: The Heating of the Rivers in Lucille Clifton's *All Us Come Cross the Water*," in *Where Rivers Meet: Confluence and Concurrents*. New York: Pace University, 1989.

———. "The Chronicling of an African-American Life and Consciousness: Lucille Clifton's Everett Anderson Series," in *Children's Literature Association Quarterly*, Vol. 14:4 (1989).

———. "'I See Me in the Book:' Visual Literacy, and African-American Children's Literature," in *Children's Literature Association Quarterly*, Vol. 15:1 (1990).

Raymond E. Jones. "The Plains Truth: Indians and Metis in Recent Fiction, in *Children's Literature Association Quarterly*, Vol. 12:1 (1987).

Meena Khorana. "The Ethnic Family and Identity Formation in Adolescents," in *The Child and Family: Selected Papers from the 1988 International Conference of the Children's Literature Association, College of Charlestin*. New York: ChLA, 1988.

Esther Latham. "Group Response to an Afro-American Book," in *The CLA Bulletin*, Vol. 16:2 (1990).

Julius Lester. "The Storyteller's Voice: Reflections on the Rewriting of Uncle Remus," in *The New Advocate*, Vol. 1:3 (1988).

Norma J. Livo. "Tales from Wigwams, Tipis, and Pueblos: Evaluating Native American Literature," in *The Bulletin: Newsletter of The Children's Literature Assembly*, Vol. 11:2 (1985).

Suzanne Lo and Ginny Lee. "Asian Images in Children's Books: What Stories Do We Tell Our Children?" in *Emergency Librarian*, Vol. 20:5 (1993).

Mawuena Logan. "Henty and the Ashantis," in *Children's Literature Association Quarterly*, Vol. 16:2 (1991).

Donnarae MacCann. "Effie Lee Newsome: African American Poet of the 1920s," in *Children's Literature Association Quarterly*, Vol. 13:1 (1988).

Robin McGrath. "Words Melt Away Like Hills in the Fog: Putting Inuit Legends into Print," in *Children's Literature Association Quarterly*, Vol. 13:1 (1988).

Susan Naramore Maher. "Encountering Others in Scott O'Dell's *Island of the Blue Dolphins* and *Sing Down the Moon*," in *Children's Literature in Education*, Vol. 23:4 (1992).

Anthony L. Manna. "Reading Jerry Pinkney Reading," in *ChLA Quarterly*, Vol. 16:4 (1991).

Jill P. May. "Modern Interpretations of Native American Legend," in *Southwest Folklore*, Vol. 3:4 (1980).

Nina Mikkelsen. "Censorship and the Black Child: Can the Real Story Ever Be Told?" in *Proceedings of the Ninth Annual Conference of the Children's Literature Association, March 1982*. Priscilla Ord, ed. Boston: The Children's Literature Association.

Barbara Mirel. "Lost Worlds of Tradition: Shtetl Stories for Suburban Children," in *Children's Literature Association Quarterly*, Vol. 9:1 (1984).

Opal Moore and Donnarae MacCann. "The Ignoble Savage: Amerind Images in the Mainstream Mind," in *Children's Literature Association Quarterly*, Vol. 13:1 (1988).

———. "On Canon Expansion and the Artistry of Joyce Hanson," in *Children's Literature Association Quarterly*, Vol. 15:1 (1990).

———. "Pateralism and Assimilation in Books About Hispanics," in *Children's Literature Association Quarterly*, Vol. 12:2 and Vol. 12:3 (1987).

———. "The Uncle Remus Travesty," in *Children's Literature Association Quarterly*, Vol. 11:2 (1986).

Alice Morrison Mordoh. "Folklife in the Work of Mitsumasa Anno," in *Children's Literature Association Quarterly*, Vol. 10:3 (1985).

Anita Moss. "Mythical Narrative: Virginia Hamilton's *The Magical Adventures of Pretty Pearl*," in *The Lion & the Unicorn*, Vol. 19 (1985).

Roni Natov. "Living in Two Cultures: Bette Boa Lord's Stories of Chinese-American Experience," in *The Lion and the Unicorn*, Vol. 11:1 (1987).

Gloria Naylor. "The Afro-American Writer and the South, A Panel Discussion," in *The Southern Literary Review and Modern Literature, 1935–1985*, Lewis P. Simpson, James Olney and Jo Gulledge, eds. Baton Rouge: Louisiana State University Press, 1985.

Noriko Shimoda Netley. "The Difficulty of Translation: Decoding Cultural Signs in Other Languages," in *Children's Literature in Education*, Vol. 23:4 (1992).

Peter Neumeyer. "Spanish Kids Got No Books?" in *Children's Literature Association Quarterly*, Vol. 8:2 (1983).

Perry Nodelman. "Eliminating the Evidence," *Children's Literature Association Quarterly*, Vol. 11:3 (1986).

Abiola Odejide. "The Journey as Training Ground in Nigerian Children's Fiction," in *Proceedings of the Thirteenth Annual Conference of the Children's Literature Association*, 1986. Susan Gannon and Ruth Anne Thompson, eds. New York: Pace University, 1988.

Priscilla Ord. "Recent Literature for Children By and About Native Americans," in *Children's Literature*, Vol. 3 (1978).

Valerie Ooka Pang. "Beyond Chopsticks and Dragons: Selecting Asian-American Literature for Children," in *Reading Teacher*, Vol. 46:3 (1992).

Suzanne Rahn. "Early Images of American Minorities: Rediscovering Florence Crannell Means," in *The Lion and the Unicorn*, Vol. 11:1 (1987).

Patrick Shannon. "I Am The Canon: Finding Ourselves in Multiculturalism," in *The Journal of Children's Literature*, Vol. 20:1 (1994).

Rudine Sims. "A Question of Perspective," in *The Advocate*, Vol. 3:3 (1984).

Jon C. Stott. "Joseph Campbell on the Second Mesa: Structure and Meaning in *Arrow to the Sun*," in *Children's Literature Association Quarterly*, Vol. 11:3 (1986).

———. "Narrative Expectations and Textual Misreadings: Jamake Highwater's *Anpao* Analyzed and Reanalyzed," in *Studies in the Literary Imagination*, Vol. 18:2 (1985).

———. "Native Tales and Traditions in Books for Children," in *The American Indian Quarterly*, Vol. 16 (1992).

———. "Otherness and Ourness: A Multicultural Approach to Children's Literature," in *The CLA Bulletin*, Vol. 17:3 (1991).

Jan Susina. "'Tell Him About Vietnam': Vietnamese-Americans in Contemporary American Children's Literature," in *Children's Literature Association Quarterly*, Vol. 16:2 (1991).

Clifford E. Trafzer. "'The Word Is Sacred to a Child': American Indians and Children's Literature," in *The American Indian Quarterly*, Vol. 16 (1992).

Ellen Tremper. "Black English in Children's Literature," in *The Lion and The Unicorn*, Vol. 3:1 (1979–80).

Malcolm Usrey. "A Response to Frances Smith Foster: Ethnicity or Humanity: The Test of True Literature," in *Children's Literature Association Quarterly*, Vol. 14:1 (1989).

Courtney Vaugh-Roberson. "'The Brownies' Book' and 'Ebony Jr.!': Literature as a Mirror of the Afro-American Experience," in *Journal of Negro History*, Vol. 58:4 (1989).

Norman Williamson. "The 'Indian Tales': Are They Fish or Fowl?" in *Children's Literature Association Quarterly*, Vol. 12:2 (1987).

Thomas A. Zaniello. "'Flowers in Bloom': The Varieties of Chinese Children's Literature," in *Children's Literature*, Vol. 7 (1978).

Meifang Zhang. "The Changing Role of Imagination in Chinese Children's Books," in *Reading Teacher*, Vol. 42:6 (1989).

Myth, Folklore, Fantasy, and Science Fiction

Books

Brian Attebery. *The Fantasy Tradition in American Literature: From Irving to Le Guin*. Bloomington: Indiana University Press, 1980.

Bruno Bettelheim. *The Uses of Enchantment.* New York: Alfred A. Knopf, 1976.

Margaret Blount. *Animal Land: The Creatures of Children's Fiction.* New York: Avon Books, 1977.

Robert H. Boyer and Kenneth J. Zahorski. *Fantasists on Fantasy: A Collection of Critical Reflections by Eighteen Masters of the Art.* New York: Avon Books, 1984.

Joseph Campbell. *The Hero with a Thousand Faces.* New York: Bollingen Foundation, 1949.

L. Sprague de Camp. *Literary Swordsmen and Sorcerers: The Makers of Heroic Fantasy.* Sauk City, WI: Arkharn House, 1976.

Sheila Egoff, G. T. Stubbs, and L. E. Ashley, ed. *Only Connect: Readings on Children's Literature,* 2nd edition. Toronto: Oxford University Press, 1980.

John M. Ellis. *One Fairy Tale Too Many: The Brothers Grimm and Their Tales.* Chicago: University of Chicago Press, 1983.

Sigmund Freud and D. E. Oppenheim. *Dreams in Folklore.* New York: International Universities Press, Inc., 1958.

Betsy Hearne. *Beauty and the Beast: Visions and Revisions of an Old Tale.* Chicago: University of Chicago Press, 1989.

Walter Hooper. *Past Watchful Dragons: The Narnian Chronicles of C. S. Lewis.* New York: Collier Books, 1979.

Kathryn Hume. *Fantasy and Mimesis: Responses to Reality in Western Literature.* New York: Methuen, 1984.

Rosemary Jackson. *Fantasy: The Literature of Subversion.* London: Methuen, 1981.

Christa Kamenetsky. *The Brothers Grimm & Their Critics: Folktales and the Quest for Meaning.* Athens: Ohio University Press, 1992.

Marion Lochhead. *Renaissance of Wonder: The Fantasy Worlds of C. S. Lewis, J. R. R. Tolkien, George MacDonald, E. Nesbit and Others.* San Francisco: Harper & Row, 1977.

Joseph O'Beirne and Lucy Floyd Morcock Milner, eds. *Webs and Wardrobes: Humanist and Religious World Views in Children's Literature.* Landham, MD: University Press of America, 1987.

George Slusser and Eric S. Rabkin. *Intersections: Fantasy and Science Fiction.* Carbondale: Southern Illinois University Press, 1987.

Charles William Sullivan III. *Welsh Celtic Myth in Modern Fantasy.* New York: Greenwood Press, 1989.

Ann Swinfen. *In Defence of Fantasy: A Study of the Genre in English American Literature Since 1945.* London: Routledge & Kegan Paul, 1984.

Maria Tatar. *Off With Their Heads! Fairy Tales and the Culture of Childhood.* Princeton: Princeton University Press, 1992.

John H. Timmerman. *Other Worlds: The Fantasy Genre.* Bowling Green, OH: Bowling Green University Popular Press, 1983.

Arland Ussher and Carl von Metzradt. *Enter These Enchanted Woods: An Interpretation of Grimm's Fairy Tales.* Dublin: The Dolmen Press, 1955.

Jennifer Waelti-Walters. *Fairy Tales and the Female Imagination.* Montreal: Eden Press, 1982.

Mark West, ed. *A Wonderous Menagerie: Animal Fantasy Stories from American Children's Literature.* Hamden, CT: Archon Books, 1993.

Jane Yolen. *Touch Magic: Fantasy, Faerie and Folklore in the Literature of Childhood.* New York: Philomel Books, 1981.

Jack Zipes. *Breaking the Magic Spell: Radical Theories of Folk and Fairy Tales.* Austin: University of Texas, 1979.

Articles

John Alego. "Oz and Kansas: A Theosophical Quest," in *Proceedings of The Thirteenth Annual Conference of the Children's Literature Association.* New York: Pace University, 1988.

Lloyd Alexander. "Fantasy and the Human Condition," in *The New Advocate,* Vol. 1:2 (1988).

Elizabeth A. Cripps. "Kenneth Grahame: Children's Author?" in *Children's Literature in Education,* Vol. 12:1 (1981).

Peter Dickinson. "Fantasy: The Need for Realism," in *Children's Literature in Education,* Vol. 17:1 (1986).

Barbara Elleman. "Fantasy: International Trends and Issues," in *The CLA Bulletin,* Vol. 16:3 (1990).

Leona W. Fisher. "Mystical Fantasy for Children: Silence and Community," in *The Lion and the Unicorn,* Vol. 14:2 (1990).

Richard Flynn. "Randall Jarrell's Mermaid: "The Animal Family" and "Semi-feminine" Poetics," in *Children's Literature in Education,* Vol. 23:3 (1992).

Barbara Carman Garner. "Lost and Found in Time: Canadian Timeslip Fantasies for Children," in *Children's Literature Association Quarterly,* Vol. 15:4 (1990).

James H. Gellert. "Once Upon a Time in a Paris Salon: Journeys and the Fairy Tales of Charles Perrault," in *Proceedings of the the Thirteenth Annual Children's Literature Association Conference,* May 1986.

Sarah Gilead. "The Undoing of Idyll in *The Wind in the Willows,*" in *Children's Literature,* Vol. 16 (1988).

Richard Gillin. "Romantic Echoes in the Willows," in *Children's Literature,* Vol. 16 (1988).

John Gilliver. "Religious Values and Children's Fiction," in *Children's Literature in Education,*" Vol. 17:4 (1986).

Ellen Greene. "Literary Uses of Traditional Themes: From *Cinderella* to *The Girl Who Sat by the Ashes and The Glass Slipper,*" in *Children's Literature Association Quarterly,* Vol. 11:3 (1986).

John Griffith. "*Charlotte's Web:* A Lonely Fantasy of Love," in *Children's Literature,* Vol. 8 (1980).

Carole and D. T. Hanks Jr. "Perrault's 'Little Red Riding Hood': Victim of Revision," in *Children's Literature,* Vol. 7 (1978).

Betsy Hearne. "Beauty and the Beast—Visions and Revisions of an Old Tale: 1950–1985," in *The Lion and the Unicorn,* Vol. 12:2 (1988).

———. "Booking the Brothers Grimm: Art, Adaptation, and Economics," in *Book Research Quarterly* (January 1987).

Caroline Hunt. "Form as Fantasy—Fantasy as Form," in *Children's Literature Association Quarterly,* Vol. 12:1 (1987).

Peter Hunt. "Landscapes and Journeys, Metaphors and Maps: The Distinctive Feature of English Fantasy," in *Children's Literature Association Quarterly,* Vol. 12:1 (1987).

Nancy Huse. "Tove Jansson and Her Readers: No One Excluded," in *Children's Literature,* Vol. 19 (1991).

Barbara Kiefer. "Image Maker, Magic Maker: Trina Schart Hyman," in *The Bulletin: The Children's Literature Assembly,* Vol. 11:2 (1985).

———. "The Roots of Fantasy in Wales," in *The Bulletin of The Children's Literature Assembly,* Vol. 10:1 (1984).

Norton D. Kinghorn. "The Real Miracle of *Charlotte's Web,*" in *Children's Literature Association Quarterly,* Vol. 11:1 (1986).

Paula Kiska. "Slavic Wonder Tales: An Overview," in *Children's Literature Association Quarterly,* Vol. 11:3 (1986).

Valerie Krips. "Mistaken Identity: Russell Hoban's Mouse and His Child," in *Children's Literature,* Vol. 21 (1993).

Lois Kuznets. "Toad Hall Revisited," in *Children's Literature,* Vol. 7 (1978).

Madeleine L'Engle. "Childlike Wonder and the Truths of Science Fiction," in *Children's Literature,* Vol. 10 (1982).

Anne Lundin. "On the Shores of Lethe: C. S. Lewis and the Romantics," in *Children's Literature in Education,* Vol. 21:1 (1990).

Joanne Lynn. "Hyacinths and Biscuits in the Village of Liver and Onions," in *Children's Literature,* Vol. 8 (1980).

Ruth MacDonald. "The Tale Retold: Feminist Fairy Tales," in *Children's Literature Association Quarterly,* Vol. 7:2 (1982).

———. "Why This Is Still 1893: *The Tale of Peter Rabbit* and Beatrix Potter's Manipulations of Time into Timelessness," in *Children's Literature Association Quarterly,* Vol. 10:4 (1986).

Rod McGillis. "Fantasy as Adventure: Nineteenth Century Children's Fiction," in *Children's Literature Association Quarterly,* Vol. 8:3 (1983).

Tony L. Manna. "The Americanization of the Brothers Grimm, or Tom Davenport's Film Adaptations of German Folktales," in *Children's Literature Association Quarterly,* Vol. 13:3 (1988).

———. "'Borrowing' C. S. Lewis: Aurand Harris's Dramatization of *The Magician's Nephew,*" in *ChLA Quarterly,* Vol. 11:3 (1986).

Leonard S. Marcus. "Picture Book Animals: How Natural a History?" in *The Lion and the Unicorn,* Vol. 7/8 (1983–84).

Gareth Matthews. "Bravery and Philosophy in the Adventures of Frog and Toad," in *Triumphs of the Spirit in Children's Literature.* Hamden, CT: Library Professional Publications, 1986.

Jill P. May. "Tom Davenport's Film Versions of Grimms' Folk Tales," in *Proceedings of the Seventh Annual Conference of the Children's Literature Association,* March 1980.

Eva-Marie Metcalf. "Astrid Lindgren's *The Robber's Daughter: A Twentieth-Century Fairy Tale,*" in *The Lion and the Unicorn,* Vol. 12:2 (1988).

Ann Moseley. "The Journey through the SPACE IN THE TEXT to WHERE THE WILD THINGS ARE," in *Children's Literature in Education,* Vol. 19:2 (1988).

Claudia Nelson. "The Beast Within: 'Winnie-the-Pooh Reassessed," in *Children's Literature in Education,* Vol. 21:1 (1990).

Perry Nodelman. "Little Red Riding Hood Rides Again—And Again and Again and Again," in *Proceedings of the Fifth Annual Conference of the Children's Literature Association,* March 1978.

———. "Some Presumptuous Generalizations About Fantasy," in *The First Steps:*

Best of the Early ChLA Quarterly. West Lafayette, IN: ChLA Publications, 1984.

Pat Pflieger. "Fables into Picture Books," in *Children's Literature Association Quarterly,* Vol. 9:2 (1984).

R. L. Platzner. "Child's Play: Games and Fantasy in Carroll, Stevenson, and Grahame," in *Proceedings of the Fifth Annual Conference of the Children's Literature Association* (Harvard University, 1978). Villanova, PA: Villanova University, 1979.

Frank P. Riga. "Mortals Call Their History Fable: Narnia and the Use of Fairy Tale," in *Children's Literature Association Quarterly,* Vol. 14:1 (1989).

Sally Rigsbee. "Fantasy Places and Imaginative Belief: *The Lion, the Witch, and the Wardrobe* and *The Princess and the Goblin,*" in *Children's Literature Association Quarterly,* Vol. 8:1 (1983).

David L. Russell. "*The Gammage Cup* as Utopian Literature for Children," in *Children's Literature in Education,* Vol. 24:4 (1993).

Elizabeth Segal. "Picture Books and Princesses: The Feminist Contribution," in *Proceedings of the Eighth Annual Conference of the Children's Literature Association, University of Minnesota, March 1981.* New Rochelle, NY: Iona College, 1982.

Janet Spaeth. "The Grimms' Housekeepers: Women in Transition Tales," in *Children's Literature Association Quarterly,* Vol. 7:2 (1982).

Kay F. Stone. "Re-awakening the Sleeping Beauty: P. L. Travers' Literary Folktale," in *Proceedings of the Eighth Annual Conference of The Children's Literature Association, University of Minnesota, March 1981.* New Rochelle, NY: Iona College, 1982.

Catherine Storr. "Folk and Fairy Tales," *Children's Literature in Education,* Vol. 17:1 (1986).

Jon C. Stott. "Midsummer Night's Dreams: Fantasy and Self-Realization in Children's Fiction," in *The Lion and the Unicorn,* Vol. 1:2 (1977).

———. "Of Time and the Prairie: Canadian Fantasies and the Search for Self-Worth," in *The CLA Bulletin,* Vol. 16:3 (1990).

C. W. Sullivan III. "Narrative Expectations: The Folklore Connection," in *Children's Literature Association Quarterly,* Vol. 15:2 (1990).

———. "Nancy Bond and Welsh Traditions," in *ChLA Quarterly,* Vol. 11:1 (1986).

———. "Traditional Welsh Materials in Modern Fantasy," in *Extrapolation,* Vol. 28:1 (1987).

Maria Tatar. "Tests, Tasks, and Trials in the Grimms' Fairy Tales," in *Children's Literature,* Vol. 13 (1985).

William Touponce. "The Journey as Cosmic Reverie: A Reading of Maurice Sendak's *In the Night Kitchen,*" in *Proceedings of The Thirteenth Annual Conference of the Children's Literature Association.* New York: Pace University, 1988.

Ann Trousdale. "The True Bride: Perceptions of Beauty and Feminine Virtue in Folktales," in *The New Advocate,* Vol. 2:4 (1989).

Michael O. Tunnell. "An Interview with Lloyd Alexander," in *The New Advocate,* Vol. 2:2 (1989).

Michael O. Tunnell and James S. Jacobs. "Fantasy at Its Best: Alexander's Chronicles of Prydain," in *Children's Literature in Education,* Vol. 21:4 (1990).

Kay E. Vandergrift. "Meaning-Making and the Dragons of Pern," in *Children's Literature Association Quarterly,* Vol. 15:1 (1990).

Jeanne Murray Walker. *"The Lion, the Witch, and the Wardrobe* as Rite of Passage," in *Children's Literature in Education,* Vol. 16:3 (1985).

Tony Watkins. "'Making a Break for the Real England': The River-Bankers Revisited," in *Children's Literature Association Quarterly,* Vol. 9:1 (1984).

Lesley Willis. "'A Sadder and a Wiser Rat/He Rose the Morrow Morn:' Echoes of the Romantics in Kenneth Grahame's *The Wind in the Willows,"* in *Children's Literature Association Quarterly,* Vol. 13:3 (1988).

Arlene Wilner. "'Unlocked by Love': William Steig's Tales of Transformation and Magic," in *Children's Literature,* Vol. 18 (1990).

Jeanne Morgan Zarucchi. "Audiences and Messages in Perrault's Tales," in *Children's Literature Association Quarterly,* Vol. 12:4 (1987).

Jack Zipes. "The Age of Commodified Fantasticism: Reflections of Children's Literature and the Fantastic," in *Children's Literature Association Quarterly,* Vol. 9:4 (1984–85).

———. "A Second Gaze at Little Red Riding Hood's Trials and Tribulations," in *The Lion and the Unicorn,* Vol. 7/8 (1984/84).

———. "Towards a Social History of the Literary Fairy Tale for Children," in *Children's Literature Association Quarterly,* Vol. 7:2 (1982).

———. "Who's Afraid of the Brothers Grimm?: Socialization and Politization through Fairy Tales," in *The Lion and the Unicorn,* Vol. 3:2 (1979–80).

Index